ANALYSING TEXTS

General Editor: Nicholas Marsh

Published

Chaucer: The Canterbury Tales   *Gail Ashton*
Aphra Behn: The Comedies   *Kate Aughterson*
Webster: The Tragedies   *Kate Aughterson*
John Keats: The Poems   *John Blades*
Shakespeare: The Sonnets   *John Blades*
Wordsworth and Coleridge: Lyrical Ballads   *John Blades*
Shakespeare: The Comedies   *R. P. Draper*
Charlotte Brontë: The Novels   *Mike Edwards*
George Eliot: The Novels   *Mike Edwards*
E. M. Forster: The Novels   *Mike Edwards*
Jane Austen: The Novels   *Nicholas Marsh*
William Blake: The Poems   *Nicholas Marsh*
Emily Brontë: Wuthering Heights   *Nicholas Marsh*
Philip Larkin: The Poems   *Nicholas Marsh*
D. H. Lawrence: The Novels   *Nicholas Marsh*
Shakespeare: The Tragedies   *Nicholas Marsh*
Mary Shelley: Frankenstein   *Nicholas Marsh*
Virginia Woolf: The Novels   *Nicholas Marsh*
John Donne: The Poems   *Joe Nutt*
Thomas Hardy: The Novels   *Norman Page*
Marlowe: The Plays   *Stevie Simkin*

Analysing Texts
Series Standing Order ISBN 0–333–73260–X
(*outside North America only*)

You can receive future titles in this series as they are published by placing a standing order. Please contact your bookseller or, in the case of difficulty, write to us at the address below with your name and address, the title of the series and the ISBN quoted above.

Customer Services Department, Palgrave Ltd
Houndmills, Basingstoke, Hampshire RG21 6XS, England

Mary Shelley: Frankenstein

NICHOLAS MARSH

palgrave
macmillan

First published 2009 by
PALGRAVE MACMILLAN

Palgrave Macmillan in the UK is an imprint of Macmillan Publishers Limited, registered in England, company number 785998, of Houndmills, Basingstoke, Hampshire RG21 6XS.

Palgrave Macmillan in the US is a division of St Martin's Press LLC, 175 Fifth Avenue, New York, NY 10010.

Palgrave Macmillan is the global academic imprint of the above companies and has companies and representatives throughout the world.

Palgrave® and Macmillan® are registered trademarks in the United States, the United Kingdom, Europe and other countries.

ISBN-13: 978–0–230–20097–5 hardback
ISBN-10: 0–230–20097–4 hardback
ISBN-13: 978–0–230–20098–2 paperback
ISBN-10: 0–230–20098–2 paperback

This book is printed on paper suitable for recycling and made from fully managed and sustained forest sources. Logging, pulping and manufacturing processes are expected to conform to the environmental regulations of the country of origin.

A catalogue record for this book is available from the British Library.

A catalog record for this book is available from the Library of Congress.

10   9   8   7   6   5   4   3   2   1
18 17 16 15 14 13 12 11 10 09

Printed and bound in the UK by The Lavenham Press Ltd, Suffolk.

For Doctors Barthelemy, Caillard, Perret
and Bahnini, in recognition of their services
to English Literature

Contents

General Editor's Preface   x

A Note on Editions   xi

Introduction   1

Part I   ANALYSING *FRANKENSTEIN*

1   The Narrative Frame   7
   Analysis: Walton's Narrative, pp. 15–17   8
   Analysis: Frankenstein's Narrative, pp. 33–35   17
   Analysis: The Daemon's Narrative, pp. 102–104   27
   Concluding Discussion   36
      A Journey to Revelation, or to the 'Centre'   36
      Conclusions to Chapter 1   41
   Methods of Analysis   44
   Suggested Work   45

2   Characterization   46
   Analysis: Walton, pp. 215–218   46
   Analysis: Frankenstein, pp. 170–171   55
   Analysis: The Daemon, pp. 136–137   65
   Analysis: Clerval, Elizabeth and Alphonse Frankenstein   69
   Concluding Discussion   80
      Walton and Victor Frankenstein   80
      The Daemon   81
      Clerval, Elizabeth and the Elder Frankenstein   81
      'Composite' Characterization   82
      Conclusions to Chapter 2   84

Methods of Analysis	85
Suggested Work	87

3 Nature, Society and Science — **88**

Nature, Natural Surroundings	88
Analysis, p. 38, pp. 97–98, p. 99	88
Nature, Human Nature	93
Analysis, p. 222	97
Society	101
Analysis, pp. 122–123	101
Science	109
Analysis, pp. 48–49	110
Analysis, p. 55	115
Conclusions	119
Methods of Analysis	125
Suggested Work	126

4 Symbol and Myth — **128**

Symbol	128
What is a Symbol?	128
Symbolism and Frankenstein	129
Frankenstein's Dream	129
The Daemon	132
The Moon, Water, Mountains and Storms	136
Sight and Hearing	144
Conclusions Regarding Symbolism	147
Myth	148
Frankenstein *and Earlier Myths*	148
The Modern Myth of Frankenstein	162
Concluding Discussion	169

5 Themes, and Conclusions to Part 1 — **171**

Masculine/Feminine	172
Nature and Knowledge	174
Society: Class and Injustice	176
Nature and Nurture (i.e. Romanticism vs. Determinism)	178
Conclusion	179

Part II   The Context and the Critics

6   Mary Shelley's Life and Works   **183**
The life of Mary Shelley   183
Mary Shelley's Works   197

7   The Historical and Literary Context   **203**
Some Historical Remarks   203
The Literary Context   206
   The Birth of Frankenstein   206
   Gothic Fiction   207
   Paradise Lost, *and the Faustus Story*   212
   The Influence of Frankenstein   214

8   A Sample of Critical Views   **220**
The Critical Reception   220
Muriel Spark   222
Sandra M. Gilbert and Susan Gubar   224
Anne K. Mellor   229
Mary Lowe-Evans   233
Joseph Kestner   235
Concluding Discussion   238

Notes   241

Further Reading   246

Index   253

General Editor's Preface

This series is dedicated to one clear belief: that we can all enjoy, understand and analyse literature for ourselves, provided we know how to do it. How can we build on close understanding of a short passage, and develop our insight into the whole work? What features do we expect to find in a text? Why do we study style in so much detail? In demystifying the study of literature, these are only some of the questions the *Analysing Texts* series addresses and answers.

The books in this series will not do all the work for you, but will provide you with the tools, and show you how to use them. Here, you will find samples of close, detailed analysis, with an explanation of the analytical techniques utilised.

At the end of each chapter there are useful suggestions for further work you can do to practise, develop and hone the skills demonstrated and build confidence in your own analytical ability.

An author's individuality shows in the way they write: every work they produce bears the hallmark of that writer's personal 'style'. In the main part of each book we concentrate therefore on analysing the particular flavour and concerns of one author's work, and explain the features of their writing in connection with major themes. In Part II, there are chapters about the author's life and work, assessing their contribution to developments in literature; and a sample of critics' views are summarised and discussed in comparison with each other.

Some suggestions for further reading provide a bridge towards further critical research.

Analysing Texts is designed to stimulate and encourage your critical and analytic faculty, to develop your personal insight into the author's work and individual style, and to provide you with the skills and techniques to enjoy at first hand the excitement of discovering the richness of the text.

A Note on Editions

Frankenstein was published in 1818 with a short preface written by Percy Bysshe Shelley. In 1831, Mary Shelley revised the novel for Colburn and Bentley's 'standard novels' series. The author carried out some extensive re-writing, particularly in the early chapters dealing with Frankenstein's childhood and upbringing; and she added her 'Introduction' explaining how the idea for *Frankenstein* came to her.

Critics and teachers differ as to which text they prefer, and there are a large number of editions available. In this book we have chosen to refer to the 1831 text, and all our references are to the Penguin Classics edition (ed. Maurice Hindle) revised in 2003. The advantage of this edition is that Appendix I gives a 'Select Collation of the Texts of 1831 and 1818', enabling readers to check the differences between the two texts. Readers can then judge for themselves both what Mary Shelley changed and which version they prefer.

Introduction

It is difficult to approach *Frankenstein* without preconceptions: the name 'Frankenstein' alone makes such an ubiquitous figure in popular culture that we cannot hear or read it without picturing an image from a film, and without activating our own particular reaction to 'horror' films or literature. In her 1831 Preface, Mary Shelley claims that she sought a story to 'speak to the mysterious fears of our nature and awaken thrilling horror – one to make the reader dread to look round, to curdle the blood, and quicken the beatings of the heart'.[1] So *Frankenstein* comes to the modern reader, billed as a 'chiller' and surrounded by unreliable assumptions about its content, derived from film or hearsay. We start by acknowledging all this baggage, in the hopes we can then set it aside, and approach the text itself in a spirit of open-minded inquiry.

Partly because of its celebrated position in popular culture, and partly because of the extraordinary circumstances in which it was born, *Frankenstein* has also attracted a particular kind of criticism. There exists a plethora of theories and interpretations, psychoanalytical, feminist, anthropological, historicist and so on. For example, Margaret Homans suggests that 'the novel concerns a woman writer's anxieties about bearing children, about generating bodies that would have the power to displace or kill the parent',[2] and develops the view that Mary Shelley criticizes 'interference' in childbirth by 'a masculine economy', but does so involuntarily because it is 'a criticism written in her own blood'.[3] Joseph Kestner comments on the scene in which Frankenstein corrects and augments Walton's notes: 'the men thus share the pen/penis, and the act of writing, like the act of narrating through the

1

mise en abyme, becomes a narcissistic and onanistic gesture'.[4] Other theories connect Mary Shelley's creation with her father, William Godwin; or as a veiled critique of her husband, Percy Shelley; or as a reaction to the death of her mother, Mary Wollstonecraft; or as an embodiment of Kant's *Critique of Judgment*, a comment on the Industrial Revolution, or a reaction to the French Revolution. The two examples quoted suffice to show that *Frankenstein* critics are often engaged in an effort to explain. Implicitly, there seems to be a vein of disbelief behind many criticisms: a disbelief that can be expressed by the question Mary Shelley herself asks in her 1831 'Introduction': 'How I, then a young girl, came to think of and to dilate upon so very hideous an idea?' (*F* 5). Attempting to answer this question, critics tend to explain the book in ways that move the focus away from the text itself. Are we reading about *Frankenstein*, or psychoanalysis of Frankenstein the character, or psychoanalysis of Frankenstein the real person he would have been had he not been a character, or Mary Shelley's biography, or psychoanalysis of Mary Shelley, or even psychoanalysis of Percy Shelley?

This is not to denigrate the criticism that has been written – far from it. As we will find in Chapter 8, the wide variety of theories *Frankenstein* has attracted make the criticism particularly rich, and provide an equally wide variety of illuminating insights. However, the aim of this book is different. In *Part 1*, Analysing *Frankenstein*, we intend to focus on how the text works: how the story is told, why it is so gripping and so exceptionally rich in implication; and, why it is such an intense and apparently unified reading experience. We will choose short extracts for detailed analysis, beginning with a close focus on the style and narrative framework. As our knowledge of the text grows, we will increasingly be able to discuss the significance of *Frankenstein*, building our own ideas on firm foundations. The final chapter in *Part 1* sets out the conclusions our study has produced. It is in the hope of approaching our study in *Part 1* with an open mind, that we have acknowledged the pervasive images of popular culture, and the varieties of critical opinion, in advance.

The three chapters of *Part 2*, The Context and the Critics, provide the background information students of *Frankenstein* will need. There is an account of Mary Shelley's life and works, and discussion of relevant features of the historical and cultural context, as well as an assessment of *Frankenstein*'s place in the development of the English novel. Additionally, a selection of critics' views are summarized and compared, and there are suggestions for Further Reading, in order to provide a bridge to the academic critical controversies *Frankenstein* has so plentifully spawned.

PART I
ANALYSING *FRANKENSTEIN*

1

The Narrative Frame

Frankenstein is in the form of a series of letters from St. Petersburgh, Archangel, and the Arctic Ocean, written by an arctic explorer called Robert Walton to his married sister Mrs Margaret Saville, in England. Mrs Saville only receives these letters – there is nothing from her in reply. So, the story of *Frankenstein* is told by Walton to his sister; he reports, apparently verbatim, the story Victor Frankenstein tells to him aboard his ship in the Arctic Ocean; and Victor Frankenstein purportedly reports verbatim the story the daemon tells to him when they meet on the 'mer de glace' in the Alps. In other words, *Frankenstein* is a story that comes to us via an elaborate series of frames. Such narrative framing devices are usually adopted to provide opportunities for the author to manipulate certain effects.

First, the story arrives to us mediated through the character of the narrator, and we are aware of him even when he is reporting another's speech verbatim. This means that the story is subjected to two points of view before it even reaches us, which should enable the author to exploit irony. Secondly, each 'frame' inserts a distance between story and reader, and this distance can have a variety of effects. Thirdly, the narrators of *Frankenstein* all use first-person narrative. Consequently, we expect self-revelation, but we are never in the company of an omniscient narrator.

In the case of *Frankenstein*, the framed structure of the narrative raises a further issue for modern readers, because most of us believe that we know the story before we start reading: after all, we are familiar with the mad scientist and his monster. We are therefore likely to be surprised when we begin to read about an explorer's arctic voyage. I have seen students glance back at the cover, to make sure that they have not picked up the wrong book by mistake.

We will start our study of *Frankenstein*, then, by looking at the three main narrators, in the order in which they appear: Walton, Victor, and the daemon. We take a passage for close analysis and comparison, from the beginning of each of their narratives.

Analysis: Walton's Narrative, pp. 15–17

Here are the opening paragraphs of Walton's first letter:

St. Petersburgh, Dec. 11th, 17

> You will rejoice to hear that no disaster has accompanied the com-
> mencement of an enterprise which you have regarded with such evil
> forebodings. I arrived here yesterday; and my first task is to assure my
> dear sister of my welfare, and increasing confidence in the success of my
> undertaking.
>
> I am already far north of London; and as I walk the streets of Peters-
> burgh, I feel a cold northern breeze play upon my cheeks, which braces
> my nerves, and fills me with delight. Do you understand this feeling?
> This breeze, which has traveled from the regions towards which I am
> advancing, gives me a foretaste of those icy climes. Inspirited by this
> wind of promise, my day dreams become more fervent and vivid. I try
> in vain to be persuaded that the pole is the seat of frost and desolation;
> it ever presents itself to my imagination as the region of beauty and
> delight. There, Margaret, the sun is for ever visible, its broad disk just
> skirting the horizon, and diffusing a perpetual splendour. There – for
> with your leave, my sister, I will put some trust in preceding navigators –
> there snow and frost are banished; and, sailing over a calm sea, we may
> be wafted to a land surpassing in wonders and in beauty every region
> hitherto discovered on the habitable globe. Its productions and features
> may be without example, as the phenomena of the heavenly bodies
> undoubtedly are in those undiscovered solitudes. What may not be
> expected in a country of eternal light? I may there discover the wondrous

power which attracts the needle; and may regulate a thousand celestial observations, that require only this voyage to render their seeming eccentricities consistent for ever. I shall satiate my ardent curiosity with the sight of a part of the world never before visited, and may tread a land never before imprinted by the foot of man. These are my enticements, and they are sufficient to conquer all fear of danger or death, and to induce me to commence this laborious voyage with the joy a child feels when he embarks in a little boat, with his holiday mates, on an expedition of discovery up his native river. But, supposing all these conjectures to be false, you cannot contest the inestimable benefit which I shall confer on all mankind to the last generation, by discovering a passage near the pole to those countries, to reach which at present so many months are requisite; or by ascertaining the secret of the magnet, which, if at all possible, can only be effected by an undertaking such as mine.

These reflections have dispelled the agitation with which I began my letter, and I feel my heart glow with an enthusiasm which elevates me to heaven; for nothing contributes so much to tranquillize the mind as a steady purpose – a point on which the soul may fix its intellectual eye. This expedition has been the favourite dream of my early years. I have read with ardour the accounts of the various voyages which have been made in the prospect of arriving at the North Pacific Ocean through the seas which surround the pole. You may remember that a history of all the voyages made for purposes of discovery composed the whole of our good uncle Thomas's library. My education was neglected, yet I was passionately fond of reading. These volumes were my study day and night, and my familiarity with them increased that regret which I had felt, as a child, on learning that my father's dying injunction had forbidden my uncle to allow me to embark in a seafaring life.

These visions faded when I perused, for the first time, those poets whose effusions, entranced my soul, and lifted it to heaven. I also became a poet, and for one year lived in a Paradise of my own creation; I imagined that I also might obtain a niche in the temple where the names of Homer and Shakespeare are consecrated. You are well acquainted with my failure, and how heavily I bore the disappointment. But just at that time I inherited the fortune of my cousin, and my thoughts were turned into the channel of their earlier bent.

Six years have passed since I resolved on my present undertaking. I can, even now, remember the hour from which I dedicated myself to this great enterprise. I commenced by inuring my body to hardship. I accompanied the whale-fishers on several expeditions to the North Sea; I voluntarily endured cold, famine, thirst, and want of sleep; I often worked harder than the common sailors during the day, and devoted my nights to the study of mathematics, the theory of medicine, and those branches of physical science from which a naval adventure might derive the greatest practical advantage. Twice I actually hired myself as an under-mate in a Greenland whaler, and acquitted myself to admiration. I must own I felt a little proud, when my captain offered me the second dignity in the vessel and intreated me to remain with the greatest earnestness so valuable did he consider my services.

And now, dear Margaret, do I not deserve to accomplish some great purpose? My life might have been passed in ease and luxury; but I preferred glory to every enticement that wealth placed in my path. Oh, that some encouraging voice would answer in the affirmative! My courage and my resolution is firm; but my hopes fluctuate, and my spirits are often depressed. I am about to proceed on a long and difficult voyage, the emergencies of which will demand all my fortitude: I am required not only to raise the spirits of others, but sometimes to sustain my own, when theirs are failing.   (*F* 15–17)

This extract contains a considerable amount of information about Walton. We have remarked how confused modern readers may be, but it is just as important that the original readers of *Frankenstein* were equally misdirected: contemporary readers expected a tale of marine exploration, just as modern readers worry that they have picked up the wrong book. Before we consider the overall effect of the Walton 'frame', however, let us study the passage.

First, we should look at the way this narrative is structured. Our extract consists of six paragraphs. We can summarize the subject-matter of these units as follows:

1. I have arrived in St. Petersburgh, and I am well.
2. I am driven by dreaming of wonderful and beautiful discoveries and by the hope of bringing benefits to humanity.
3. I am filled with enthusiasm, and I have dreamed of this undertaking since I was a child.

4. When I first read the poets, dreams of poetic fame displaced my dreams of exploration for a year, but as a poet, I failed.
5. Then I inherited money, and returned to this enthusiasm. I trained hard for this expedition for six years.
6. I therefore deserve to succeed; but my feelings are changeable, I am sometimes depressed. I wish someone would encourage me.

It is always helpful to make a brief summary like this. Not only does it reveal how clearly the paragraphs are organized into separate statements, but also it helps to bring out the bare bones of the narrator's utterance, by removing much complicating detail. Three points may strike us. First, notice that each paragraph has a purpose, to express one clear part of Walton's narrative: paragraph 1 is an announcement and greeting; paragraphs 2 and 6 are reflection; paragraphs 3, 4, and 5 give a narrative of Walton's upbringing. The transition from reflection to narrative is smoothed by the start of paragraph 3, from 'These reflections' to 'This expedition has been the favourite dream ...'. The transition back from narrative to reflection, between paragraphs 5 and 6, however, is bald and sudden: 'And now, dear Margaret ...', not graced by any stylish link. So, our summary reveals that this opening is organized into paragraphs which develop the narrator's character in stages of reflection and narrative.

Secondly, the summary shows that Walton is constructing an argument. Each paragraph supports his opinion that he is right to undertake his voyage (i.e. to bring delight to himself and benefits to humanity; because it has been a 'steady purpose' throughout his life; because he has trained hard; because he has turned his back on a life of luxury). We will say more about the quality of Walton's argument later; for now, we need only remark that it is natural for him to justify himself: we know, from her regarding the enterprise with 'evil forebodings', that Margaret disagrees with her brother.

Thirdly, re-read our summary, and you are struck by Walton's self-absorption. He predicts his sister's feelings ('You will rejoice') and bosses her opinion ('you cannot contest ...'), but does not ask after her: all his interest is in his own concerns, and the summary reads as 'I' feel this; 'I' seek glory; and 'I' deserve, with an admixture of 'poor me'. Keeping in mind the points that have arisen so far, we can now turn our attention to sentences.

There are many kinds of sentences, and our extract from Walton's letter shows a variety. The one beginning 'Inspirited by this wind of promise ...' in the second paragraph is a periodic sentence because the main clause ('my day dreams ... vivid.') comes at the end; whereas the one beginning 'There, Margaret, the sun is forever visible' is a loose sentence, its main clause coming at the start. There are several double sentences, such as 'My education was neglected, yet I was passionately fond of reading' from paragraph 3. We also find three questions: the first a plea for understanding; the other two plainly rhetorical; and an exclamation ('Oh, that some encouraging voice would answer in the affirmative!'); while some sentences are short to the point of abruptness, such as the eight-word 'I commenced by inuring my body to hardship' in paragraph 5, and others are very long (see, e.g., 'I accompanied the whale-fishers ... practical advantage' in paragraph 5–63 words; or 'But, supposing ... an undertaking such as mine' in paragraph 2–68 words). We can tell from this analysis that Walton's style is varied, with quick changes from statement to elaboration to questions and exclamations and back again suited to his argumentative purpose.

Our impression of Walton's self-absorption is confirmed by the number of phrases in which he is the main actor: 'I arrived', 'I am already', 'I feel', 'I am advancing' start an avalanche of 'I' phrases running throughout the extract to 'do I not deserve', 'I preferred glory', 'I am about to' and 'I am required' in the sixth paragraph. This insistent assertion of self also gives an impression of energy: 'I also became a poet', 'I dedicated myself', 'I commenced', 'I accompanied', 'I voluntarily endured', 'I often worked harder', 'I actually hired myself'. Many of these statements are boasts, including the false modesty of 'I must own I felt a little proud'. Our impression of a self-absorbed, self-justifying man arguing his point is enhanced.

However, there is something in this extract that irritates us: something about the way Walton connects his ideas is suspect. Notice the opening sentence, which begins 'You will rejoice' and ends with 'evil forebodings'. Does this happen again? It can be enlightening to compare the beginnings and the ends of sentences, to see how Walton's thoughts lead him from topic to topic or from mood to mood. For example, the second paragraph begins 'I am already far north of London', and the sentence ends with the word 'delight'. It is as if Walton means to give a prosaic account, but 'delight' bursts in on his narrative. Is this movement from negative emotion, to ecstasy, found again? Yes: Walton tries to think of the pole as 'the seat of frost and desolation', but ends this sentence also with 'delight'. The next paragraph begins by referring to 'the agitation with which I began my letter', but leads to 'a point on which the soul may fix its intellectual eye'. So, just as doubts yield to 'delight', 'agitation' yields to fixed permanence. This seems to be a recurrent motif, and shows how Walton shores up his spirits, irrespective of where his reflections begin. There is one startling example of the opposite movement, however; in paragraph 6 Walton appears close to outright contradiction, so suddenly does he fall from confidence into doubt: 'My courage and my resolution is firm; but my hopes fluctuate, and my spirits are often depressed.'

From the moment that the word 'delight' bursts into the text, Walton's diction is enthusiastic, and his emotion is grandiose. His daydreams are 'fervent and vivid' and he seeks a 'region of beauty and delight', the 'country of eternal light' lit by 'perpetual splendour'. His curiosity is 'ardent' and he will start his voyage with 'joy'; his 'enthusiasm ... elevates [him] to heaven', he read with 'ardour' and 'passionately'; poetry 'entranced' his soul and 'lifted it to heaven', then he 'dedicated' and 'devoted' himself to his undertaking. Clearly, Walton is a man of strong passions. Walton's diction is also rich in absolutes, superlatives and intensifying adjectives, so that every element of his reflections is heightened. So, for example, at the pole the sun is 'for ever' visible and 'perpetual'; and that region may surpass 'every' region hitherto discovered, its features 'without example' and its light 'eternal'. Magnetic power is 'wondrous', and his discoveries will last 'for ever', bringing 'inestimable' benefits to 'all' mankind to 'the last generation' so that his enthusiasm conquers 'all' fears. These superlatives and intensifiers build Walton's aims into that 'steady purpose' he admires, which he describes as 'a point on which the soul may fix its intellectual eye'. The language of enthusiasm and absolutism is already so marked that the reader is provoked to question Walton's wisdom, even on the second page. The mixed metaphors of a 'point' where the 'intellectual eye' of a 'soul' may 'fix' its regard strike a note of absurdity. Probably, such a 'fixed' and absolute ideal is a mistake, as it goes against nature. The near-comic mixing of metaphors adds to our doubts.

Another element of Walton's vocabulary fosters the reader's critical attitude. Notice that even the six paragraphs of our extract contain significant repetition. We have already remarked that the personal pronouns 'I', 'me', 'myself', 'my' and 'mine' occur frequently (e.g., 20 times in paragraph 5 alone), and that there are many superlatives such as 'ever', 'never', 'all' and 'only'. Walton also appears to have a repetitive vocabulary for describing his emotions: 'delight' appears twice, and he is both 'ardent' and feels 'ardour'. However, the two most revealing repetitions occur where the contexts differ. The first of these is the word 'heaven': Walton feels that his heart 'glows with an enthusiasm which elevates me to heaven', when talking of his voyage to the pole; then, he says that poetry 'lifted [his soul] ... to heaven' and continues the idea by remarking that poetry enabled him to live in a 'Paradise of my own creation'. The conjunction of 'elevated ... to heaven' and 'lifted ... to heaven', the one for an ideal he asserts is right, and the other for an ideal he admits was a mistake, suggests that he has learned nothing from his poetic failure; the further idea of a 'Paradise of my own creation' suggests that his present enthusiasm is as unrealistic as was the last.

The second revealing repetition is of the word 'enticements'. First, Walton describes his hopes from discovering the pole, and says that these are the 'enticements' that lead him on; then, he congratulates himself on rejecting 'every enticement that wealth placed in my path'. This repetition undermines his claim of self-denial. In voyaging to the pole, Walton is responding to 'enticements', and therefore doing what he wants to do. He prefers 'glory' to ease and luxury, further emphasizing the selfishness of his motive. Walton's dreams of glory are further confirmed when he explains his supposed altruism: he will be able to 'confer' benefits on all mankind. 'Confer' conveys a superior and patronizing position; Walton hopes to bask in fame and the gratitude of humanity. Notice that Walton has never been shy when dreaming of fame: as a poet, he hoped to equal 'Homer and Shakespeare', and used quasi-religious diction ('niche in the temple', 'consecrated') to imply the quasi-divine status to which he aspired. Walton is not a humble man, then! So, the repetitions of 'heaven' and 'enticements', added to the other features we have noticed, render us thoroughly suspicious of Walton and critical of his ideals, even within his first six paragraphs.

It remains for us to ask, what kind of an opening is this, for the novel? And, what kind of a narrator is Walton? We have learned that Walton is a self-justifying man who rationalizes his enthusiasms; and at the very beginning of the novel, he energetically argues his case against both his sister's 'evil forebodings' and his own latent doubts. We are bombarded by his self-absorption and his hyperbole: it is as if he must use absolute language, in order to silence any voice of contradiction. Walton's repetitions already convey the uneasy impression that his language has nowhere to go: having begun with 'fervent', 'ardent' and 'delight', 'for ever', 'never' and 'all', 'heaven' and 'Paradise', Walton's language allows him no space to grow over the succeeding 200 pages. The repetitions of 'heaven' and 'enticements' underline the serious doubts we already harbour about Walton's reasoning, which seems to be full of holes. Finally, there are strong hints of an over-demanding ego and vainglory: his motive may partly be to benefit humanity, but most of his drive seems to come from dreams of achieving a quasi-divine 'glory'.

At the same time, there are strong hints that Walton is insecure. The very vehemence of his arguments suggests that he wishes to silence his own doubts, and the story of his poetic failure casts doubt on his choice of object. This is a man who will be recklessly ambitious about something, and it hardly matters what.

For the reader, this must be a profoundly unsettling opening to the novel. First, it is in the nature of a framing device that there is a 'narratee' as well as a narrator. Walton's letter is addressed to his sister, so the first page of the novel pulls us into an intimate family relationship; and as we begin reading, we naturally compare our role with that of Mrs Saville, who does not write a word but only receives and reads. It would be wrong to regard Mrs Saville as entirely passive, however. Although she is not the author of a single word of *Frankenstein*, Mrs Saville is the outermost 'frame', and we must be alert to three aspects of her that are immediately apparent, even as we slot into our position alongside her. First, she is married and is in England: in other words, she is in a civilized life surrounded by family and domestic security, in contrast to Walton who writes from the borders of human habitation, about to venture into unexplored wastes. Secondly, Mrs Saville is female: so, there is an implicit gender conflict, as soon as Walton begins to argue his case. Thirdly, we are immediately informed that Mrs Saville is sceptical about his plans, for she harboured 'evil forebodings'. So, this outermost 'frame' encourages us to adopt a sceptical and implicitly feminine attitude; and highlights the contrast between our own civilized security and the perilous isolation of the adventurer.

The second point to notice about the opening is that it is a blatant mis-direction. Everything until Letter IV leads us to believe that the novel will be about polar exploration; then, as we meet Frankenstein and embark upon his narrative, we may well feel deceived: if Walton's voyage is irrelevant, why do we have to read about it? For a modern reader, familiar with the daemon and his creator from numerous films and popular culture, this irritation will arise sooner than was the case for the original readers, but the effect is the same: it is likely to foster both annoyance and surprise in the reader. If there is a moral to be drawn from this aspect of the outer 'frame', it may be that this novel's universe is unpredictable; for when you set out on a voyage of exploration, you cannot know what you will find. Like Walton himself, we set off on a voyage North, only to discover a horror that was born far to the South, at Ingolstadt.

We will return to these two matters later. For now, it will be enough to notice how our extract introduces the themes of *Frankenstein*, despite being a cul-de-sac in the story. By revealing a self-absorbed, ambitious but insecure idealist, Walton's opening paragraphs announce a major theme. First, there is ambition which seeks personal glory, combined with an idealistic philanthropy. Then, the character is isolated – either in conflict with or facing discouragement from his family; and his romantic dreams are likened to those of a romantic poet. Finally, he is unmistakably male, and engaged in a gender-argument against feminine scepticism. We have also noted signs of misplaced energy in these opening paragraphs: the heightened diction of absolutes, the bullying tone ('you cannot contest', 'do I not deserve ...?'), and some suggestive metaphors and terms initiate an exploration of the male idealist's psychology that will be a persistent concern of the novel. Critics have pointed to the sexual innuendo in Walton's desire to 'discover the wondrous power which attracts the needle'; and we could add that his 'fervent' dreams, anticipation of 'delight', and sensations of being 'elevated' and 'lifted' to 'heaven', all contribute to the idea that male idealism is being driven by a misdirected sexual energy.

Analysis: Frankenstein's Narrative, pp. 33–35

We will return to these issues later. Now let us turn to Victor Frankenstein's narrative. As with Walton, we will analyse the opening paragraphs of his story:

> I am by birth a Genevese, and my family is one of the most distinguished of that republic. My ancestors had been for many years counsellors and syndics; and my father had filled several public situations with honour and reputation. He was respected by all who knew him, for his integrity and indefatigable attention to public business. He passed his younger days perpetually occupied by the affairs of his country; a variety of circumstances had prevented his marrying early, nor was it until the decline of life that he became a husband and the father of a family.
>
> As the circumstances of his marriage illustrate his character, I cannot refrain from relating them. One of his most intimate friends was a merchant who, from a flourishing state, fell, through numerous mischances, into poverty. This man, whose name was Beaufort, was of a proud and unbending disposition and could not bear to live in poverty and oblivion in the same country where he had formerly been distinguished for his rank and magnificence. Having paid his debts, therefore, in the most honourable manner, he retreated with his daughter to the town of Lucerne, where he lived unknown and in wretchedness. My father loved Beaufort with the truest friendship, and was deeply grieved by his retreat in these unfortunate circumstances. He bitterly deplored the false pride which led his friend to a conduct so little worthy of the affection that united them. He lost no time in endeavouring to seek him out, with the hope of persuading him to begin the world again through his credit and assistance.

Beaufort had taken effectual measures to conceal himself; and it was ten months before my father discovered his abode. Overjoyed at this discovery, he hastened to the house, which was situated in a mean street near the Reuss. But when he entered, misery and despair alone welcomed him. Beaufort had saved but a very small sum of money from the wreck of his fortunes, but it was sufficient to provide him with sustenance for some months, and in the mean time he hoped to procure some respectable employment in a merchant's house. The interval was, consequently, spent in inaction; his grief only became more deep and rankling, when he had leisure for reflection; and at length it took so fast hold of his mind, that at the end of three months he lay on a bed of sickness, incapable of any exertion.

His daughter attended him with the greatest tenderness; but she saw with despair that their little fund was rapidly decreasing, and that there was no other prospect of support. But Caroline Beaufort possessed a mind of an uncommon mould, and her courage rose to support her in her adversity. She procured plain work; she plaited straw; and by various means contrived to earn a pittance scarcely sufficient to support life.

Several months passed in this manner. Her father grew worse; her time was more entirely occupied in attending him; her means of subsistence decreased; and in the tenth month her father died in her arms, leaving her an orphan and a beggar. This last blow overcame her, and she knelt by Beaufort's coffin, weeping bitterly, when my father entered the chamber. He came like a protecting spirit to the poor girl, who committed herself to his care; and after the interment of his friend he conducted her to Geneva, and placed her under the protection of a relation. Two years after this event Caroline became his wife.

There was a considerable difference between the ages of my parents, but this circumstance seemed to unite them only closer in bonds of devoted affection. There was a sense of justice in my father's upright mind, which rendered it necessary that he should approve highly to love strongly. Perhaps during former years he had suffered from the late-discovered unworthiness of one beloved, and so was disposed to set a greater value on tried worth. There was a show of gratitude and worship in his attachment to my mother, differing wholly from the doating fondness of age, for it was inspired by reverence for her virtues and a desire to be the means of, in some degree, recompensing her for the sorrows she had endured, but which gave inexpressible grace to his behaviour to her. Every thing was made to yield to her wishes and her convenience. He strove to shelter her, as a fair exotic is sheltered by the gardener, from every rougher wind, and to surround her with all that could tend to excite pleasurable emotion in her soft and benevolent mind. Her health, and even the tranquillity of her hitherto constant spirit, had been shaken by what she had gone through. During the two years that had elapsed previous to their marriage my father had gradually relinquished all his public functions; and immediately after their union they sought the pleasant climate of Italy, and the change of scene and interest attendant on a tour through that land of wonders, as a restorative for her weakened frame.

From Italy they visited Germany and France. I, their eldest child, was born at Naples, and as an infant accompanied them in their rambles. I remained for several years their only child. Much as they were attached to each other, they seemed to draw inexhaustible stores of affection from a very mine of love to bestow them upon me. My mother's tender caresses and my father's smile of benevolent pleasure while regarding me, are my first recollections. I was their plaything and their idol, and something better – their child, the innocent and helpless creature bestowed upon them by Heaven, whom to bring up to good, and whose future lot it was in their hands to direct to happiness or misery, according as they fulfilled their duties towards me. With this deep consciousness of what they owed towards the being to which they had given life, added to the active spirit of tenderness that animated both, it may be imagined that while during every hour of my infant life I received a lesson of patience, of charity, and of self-control, I was so guided by a silken cord that all seemed but one train of enjoyment to me.   (*F* 33–35)

At first reading Victor Frankenstein sounds quite distinct from Walton. Victor narrates in statements, without the rhetorical questions and argumentative features of Walton's letter; and Victor does not address his listener using the second person, whereas Walton addresses his sister as 'You' with his first word, and addresses her directly at regular intervals. Another difference we are likely to notice immediately is that Victor does not pepper his narrative with the personal pronoun. Indeed, it is remarkable that the only information he gives about himself is that he is a 'Genevese', before he digresses to tell us about his parents' marriage. Our first impression, then, is that Walton's agonized self-obsession and his self-justifying tone are absent from this narrative.

Let us begin, as before, by looking at how the extract is structured. Here is a summary of Victor's seven paragraphs:

1. I am from Geneva. I am from a first-class family and my father was a very important man who did not marry young.
2. I want you to understand my father's character, so I will tell you about his marriage. His rich friend Beaufort lost all his money and, with his daughter, hid himself in Lucerne. My father tried to find him to help him.
3. It took ten months, and misery was all he found at Beaufort's secret dwelling. When he moved there, Beaufort had had enough money to survive for a few months, and intended to find a job; but he became depressed and ill during the first three months.
4. His daughter nursed him, and took in plain work to earn a little money and keep them from starvation.
5. In the tenth month Beaufort died, and my father found the daughter destitute and weeping by the coffin. My father looked after her, and two years later they were married.
6. My father and mother loved each other strongly despite the disparity of age. My father gave up his public duties, and they went to Italy as soon as they were married.
7. Then they went to Germany and France. I was born at Naples. My parents loved me, and taught me good principles which I hardly noticed.

On re-reading this summary, we may be surprised: it does not support the idea of a calm, well-organized narrative. There are several jumps between different subjects, such as the first and most obvious 'I am by birth a Genevese, and my family ...', which leads to the assumption, by the second paragraph, that the narrative subject is Victor's father, not himself. Also, the narrative does not treat time chronologically: the story of Beaufort's illness and death is a flashback sandwiched between two accounts of Victor's father's arrival; and, most surprisingly, Victor continues his account of his parents' travels to mention Germany and France, then has to backtrack to mention his own birth at Naples.

The more we look at our summary, the more peculiar the arrangement of the narrative seems to be. Victor appears to begin in a settled style, but what he actually says is,

> *I will tell you about myself. My father . . .*
> *I will tell you about my father. His friend Beaufort . . .*
> *My father arrived. Ten months earlier . . .*
> *They went to Germany and France. Before that, at Naples . . .*

Our analysis shows that the story is already disorganized and rambling in the opening six paragraphs, even before Victor makes the astonishing mistake of rushing past his own birth, which he has to patch in, retrospectively, as it were. At this point a reader may remember the opening words, 'I am by birth a Genevese . . .'. Clearly, what Victor means by 'birth' is 'family', the high social position into which he was born, not the physical event of birth, which happened at Naples. The very disorganization of this narrative, then, raises questions. In particular, why does this narrator seem so reluctant to tell about himself? And, why is he so intent on skirting, rushing past, or suppressing the physical event of his own birth? This narrator is clearly not what he purports to be – that is, calm and clear. Despite the even surface of his style, his ideas are agitated. Even these opening paragraphs induce us to read him sceptically.

Victor's sentences have much to do with our initial impression of calmness and clarity. Most of them have the main clause at or near the beginning, and most of the main clauses are plain narrative statements. For example, we read, 'His daughter attended him . . .'; 'There was a considerable difference . . .'; 'There was a sense of justice . . .'; 'There was a show of gratitude . . .'. Where Victor uses double sentences, there is a clear causative link between the two statements (as in 'This last blow overcame her, and she knelt by Beaufort's coffin, weeping bitterly . . .'); or the sentence is structured as a zeugma ('He strove to shelter her . . . and to surround her . . .'). There are some sentences having the main clause at the end, but with one exception they are too short for their structure to be a noticeable feature (e.g., 'Two years after this event Caroline became his wife.').

The exception is the final sentence of our extract, which describes his parents' sense of their duty, then their tenderness, and then adopts a roundabout construction ('it may be imagined that while . . .'), then mentions the good principles his parents taught him, before finally making the equivocal statement, 'I was so guided by a silken cord that all seemed one train of enjoyment to me.' This sentence, then, stands out from the rest of our extract as the only periodic sentence of substantial length. Its content also stands out, for it is Victor's first potential comment on his own character; and we have been waiting for it, for some time.

We use the phrase 'potential comment' because this sentence, although provoking us to question, think, and perhaps judge, still falls short of making any comment itself. The question is, *was Victor spoiled?* The sentence gives us most, but not all, of an answer: his parents were conscious of their duty, and they loved him; so, they taught him, but so lovingly that he experienced no hardship. The implication comes in the contrast between the listed virtues – 'patience . . . charity . . . self-control' – and the easy phrase 'one train of enjoyment'. So we are left with the possible conclusion that Victor did not learn self-control because he never had to control himself. But the sentence does not comment, and we are therefore thrown back upon our beliefs. How do children learn? Do we learn from words or by example, as Victor was taught 'every hour'; or, do we only learn from experience? Victor's failure to comment therefore raises the fundamental question: how is character formed? Are we born with innate character, or are we shaped by our experiences? If the latter, then Victor was spoiled. This sentence is both unusual and characteristic of Victor: we will frequently find that he assembles all the facts that would normally lead to a judgement, but refrains from judgement himself.

At this point, we have considered structure and sentences, raising several questions both about Victor and about the content. Now let us look at the language.

Remembering what we found in Walton's diction, we will already have noticed that here, again, there is noticeable repetition. In particular, there are some abstract nouns and terms describing emotion, that are repeated: 'affection' and its variants, 'tenderness', 'honour', 'distinguished' and 'benevolent'. Added to this, Victor, like Walton, makes liberal use of intensifying adjectives, although he is not quite as insistently absolute as Walton. In the first two paragraphs, we find 'indefatigable', 'perpetually', 'most', 'truest', 'deeply' and 'bitterly'. It is no surprise, then, to read of Beaufort's daughter nursing him with the 'greatest' tenderness, or of Victor's parents and their 'devoted' affection, the 'inexpressible' grace of his father's behaviour or their 'inexhaustible' affection for Victor. Clearly, this narrator – like Walton – uses a heightened language suggesting dramatic events and emotions. It is also possible that Victor has a limited vocabulary of ethical and emotional terms, and consequently repeats them; although we cannot be sure of this yet, on the basis of one extract.

Victor also provides us with clusters of words and phrases, in a manner reminiscent of Walton, who listed his efforts when training for the polar expedition. In Victor's opening paragraphs, there are two noticeable clusters: first, Victor treats his father to 'honour', 'reputation', 'respected', 'integrity' and 'indefatigable attention' within three lines; and these terms of high approval are set against a background beat of 'public situations', 'public business' and 'affairs of his country'. Thereafter, the strong impression created by these praises needs only to be touched in. So, in paragraph 6, there is brief reference to the 'sense of justice' in 'my father's upright mind'. The cluster of terms with which the elder Frankenstein is introduced, then, prepares us for a motif of uprightness and duty that is repeatedly connected to his character. The second cluster describes the relationship between Victor's parents. Here we find 'bonds of devoted affection', 'gratitude and worship', 'attachment', 'reverence', 'virtues', 'desire', 'inexpressible grace', 'excite pleasurable emotion' and 'soft and benevolent'. Heightening the effect of this closely grouped set of terms is the metaphor of Victor's father as a gardener 'sheltering' his wife, a 'fair exotic', from 'every rougher wind'. Leaving the issue of gender stereotyping aside for the present, this cluster presents an uneasy grouping of terms. For example, 'worship', 'reverence' and 'grace' suggest a religious metaphor for Victor's father's love; then, 'means' and 'recompensing' suggest a mercantile way of thinking; these sit uneasily with 'desire' and 'excite pleasurable emotion', as well as the simile of a gardener sheltering a 'fair exotic'. Victor seems to be struggling to dismiss the age difference between his parents, to distinguish between his father's marriage and 'the doating fondness of age', but he is not wholly successful, as 'Every thing was made to yield to her wishes and her convenience.' Remarkably, this cluster of descriptive efforts only draws attention to the failure of Victor's attempt to explain his parents' love.

Victor's narrative contains more imagery than Walton's. We have remarked on the simile of the gardener and the religious diction surrounding his father's love. In this extract there are also four other significant images. First, the elder Frankenstein arrives at Beaufort's dwelling 'like a protecting spirit'; secondly, Victor's parents 'seemed to draw inexhaustible stores of affection from a very mine of love' to lavish upon him; thirdly, as an infant, Victor was their 'plaything and their idol'; and finally, he was brought up 'guided by a silken cord'.

The first of these images elevates the ideas already gathering around Victor's father (duty, respect, uprightness, etc.), and we briefly glimpse this pillar of virtue in a supernatural, all-powerful light. The metaphor of a 'mine of love' not only effectively conveys the affection lavished upon Victor, but also raises questions because it is set within a surprisingly apologetic context. He could simply have said that his parents loved him, but instead he makes another effort to explain what does not need explanation: that they loved each other, but still had lots of love left over (in the 'store', in the 'mine'), as it were, to spend on him. The image-idea treats love as a commodity, something that might run out. We sense insecurity in the man who has to explain that his parents had enough love to spare for him; we should also notice that this is Victor's second unsuccessful explanation. The third image – of the infant Victor as his parents' 'plaything and ... idol' – is also double-edged: he intends to convey a favoured childhood, but the choice of metaphors is questionable as both are objects. He was a toy, or a graven image for pagan worship: neither of these metaphors fits a human baby. Finally, and at the end of the exceptional sentence on which we have already remarked, Victor describes his upbringing as being 'guided by a silken cord', where 'silken' carries overtones of expense and luxury. This strengthens our suspicion that he was spoiled, and learned none of life's lessons as a result.

In short, all five of the images in this extract raise disturbing questions. The faultless, and then supernatural, father; the 'fair exotic' mother; Victor's insecurity about how much love there is to go around; his depiction of himself as an inanimate object; and his guiding 'cord' of luxury: all these provide fruitful areas for psychoanalytical speculations. If we add to these hints, the evasiveness of the narrative's organization, the burying of his own birth, and the disproportionate effort Victor puts into unsuccessful explanations, we realize that these opening paragraphs have – despite their evasiveness and delay – told us much about Victor Frankenstein that he never intended to reveal. The narrative presents an idealized picture of Victor's father, his parents' love, and his own early childhood. Victor's language, heavy with a limited range of positive terms such as 'tenderness' and 'devoted affection', with an admixture of neo-religious diction, and rich in intensifying adjectives, insists on this idealized picture. For the present, we are interested in Victor as one of the novel's narrators, and it is enough to say that the reader does not buy the story he tries to sell: we read sceptically, suspiciously, and treat him as an unreliable narrator.

In Walton's letter, we noticed that the 'misdirection' of its subject-matter belied the relevance of its theme: *Frankenstein* will not be about polar exploration, but it will be about male idealism and hubris. The present extract is similarly deceptive. Apparently telling a background story and saying little about Victor, the extract nonetheless announces three themes that will be central to the novel: social class and privilege; the father–child relationship; and the gender-stereotyping of women.

Social class is an apparent topic from the opening sentence, and is present in the 'silken cord' at the end of the extract. Victor's snobbery is even more glaringly revealed in the remainder of Chapter I, when Elizabeth is described as coming from a 'distinct species' with angelic connotations, different from her foster-siblings who were mere 'hardy little vagrants'. This theme, then, is prominently announced in Victor's opening chapter and will be central to the daemon's account of his life as an outcast, and his observations of human society.

The father–child relationship will also be a central topic of *Frankenstein*. It is the crux of the novel's determining event – the night when Victor animates and deserts his creation – and is debated at length between the daemon and Victor both on the 'mer de glace' and on Orkney. In this extract Victor emphasizes parental responsibility: his parents' duty was to bring him up to 'good', and his 'future lot it was in their hands to direct to happiness or misery, according as they fulfilled their duties towards me'. His parents had a 'deep conscious-ness of what they owed towards the being to which they had given life'. These statements are unequivocal, and will resonate through Victor's story as the daemon repeatedly challenges him to fulfil his parental duty. Notice, also, that Victor's statements are overwhelmingly deter-minist: life's ultimate 'misery' or 'happiness' will be determined by upbringing – by how one's parents 'fulfilled their duties'. We are aware of the irony. Walton has already told us that Victor is 'broken by mis-ery' and 'destroyed by misery': how can this be, if he was loved by parents with a 'deep consciousness' of their duty?

The stereotyping of women is a constant element of this extract, and is at its most obvious in the simile of the gardener sheltering Victor's mother, a 'fair exotic', because her 'soft' mind may not stand up to 'rough' winds. However, Caroline Beaufort's devotion to, and dependence on, first her father and then her husband, is elaborated throughout the extract. We should notice, for example, that Victor's father needs to 'approve highly', and know her 'tried worth' before lov-ing her; that she is no ordinary woman because she has 'courage'; and that she then becomes the recipient of her husband's 'worship', is 'shel-tered' by him, and all 'her wishes and her convenience' are indulged. As with the theme of social class, Victor's gender-stereotyping of women becomes even more obvious and extreme with the description of Elizabeth Lavenza's adoption, before the end of Chapter I (according to his mother, Elizabeth is 'a pretty present for my Victor'), and an exploration of masculine and feminine stereotypes remains a central concern of the novel throughout.

One further comment on this passage will serve for the present. The opening paragraphs of this, the second 'frame' narrative of the novel, appear to alter almost everything: the gender of the 'narratee' changes, the novel's setting moves several thousands of miles, and we – like Mrs Saville – become anonymous, second-hand witnesses as a completely new story re-starts. On the other hand, numerous features of this new narrative are surprisingly consistent with Walton's, and the themes announced in both are central to each other, and to the novel.

Analysis: The Daemon's Narrative, pp. 102–104

We now turn to the daemon's story: the account he gives to Victor when they meet on the 'mer de glace', and which Victor renders to Walton in the form of direct speech. Again, our extract comes from the beginning of this narrative, as the daemon entreats Frankenstein to listen to his appeal:

> 'I expected this reception,' said the daemon. 'All men hate the wretched; how, then, must I be hated, who am miserable beyond all living things! Yet you, my creator, detest and spurn me, thy creature, to whom thou art bound by ties only dissoluble by the annihilation of one of us. You purpose to kill me. How dare you sport thus with life? Do your duty towards me, and I will do mine towards you and the rest of mankind. If you will comply with my conditions, I will leave them and you at peace; but if you refuse, I will glut the maw of death, until it be satiated with the blood of your remaining friends.'
>
> 'Abhorred daemon! fiend that thou art! the tortures of hell are too mild a vengeance for thy crimes. Wretched devil! you reproach me with your creation; come on, then, that I may extinguish the spark which I so negligently bestowed.'
>
> My rage was without bounds; I sprang on him, impelled by all the feelings which can arm one being against the existence of another.
>
> He easily eluded me, and said –
>
> 'Be calm! I intreat you to hear me, before you give vent to your hatred on my devoted head. Have I not suffered enough, that you seek to increase my misery? Life, although it may only be an accumulation of anguish, is dear to me, and I will defend it. Remember, thou hast made me more powerful than thyself; my height is superior to thine, my joints more supple. But I will not be tempted to set myself in opposition to thee. I am thy creature, and I will be even mild and docile to my natural lord and king, if thou wilt also perform thy part, the which thou owest me. Oh, Frankenstein, be not equitable to every other and

trample upon me alone, to whom thy justice, and even thy clemency and affection, is most due. Remember, that I am thy creature; I ought to be thy Adam, but I am rather the fallen angel, whom thou drivest from joy for no misdeed. Everywhere I see bliss, from which I alone am irrevocably excluded. I was benevolent and good; misery made me a fiend. Make me happy, and I shall again be virtuous.'

'Begone! I will not hear you. There can be no community between you and me; we are enemies. Begone, or let us try our strength in a fight in which one must fall.'

'How can I move thee? Will no intreaties cause thee to turn a favourable eye upon thy creature, who implores thy goodness and compassion? Believe me, Frankenstein: I was benevolent; my soul glowed with love and humanity; but am I not alone, miserably alone? You, my creator, abhor me; what hope can I gather from your fellow-creatures, who owe me nothing? They spurn and hate me. The desert mountains and dreary glaciers are my refuge. I have wandered here many days; the caves of ice, which I only do not fear, are a dwelling to me, and the only one which man does not grudge. These bleak skies I hail, for they are kinder to me than your fellow beings. If the multitude of mankind knew of my existence, they would do as you do, and arm themselves for my destruction. Shall I not then hate them who abhor me? I will keep no terms with my enemies. I am miserable, and they shall share my wretchedness. Yet it is in your power to recompense me, and deliver them from an evil which it only remains for you to make so great, that not only you and your family, but thousands of others, shall be swallowed up in the whirlwinds of its rage. Let your compassion be moved, and do not disdain me. Listen to my tale: when you have heard that, abandon or commiserate me, as you shall judge that I deserve. But hear me. The guilty are allowed, by human laws, bloody as they are, to speak in their own defence before they are condemned. Listen to me, Frankenstein. You accuse me of murder, and yet you would, with a satisfied conscience, destroy your own creature. Oh, praise the eternal justice of man! Yet I ask you not to spare me: listen to me; and then, if you can, and if you will, destroy the work of your hands.' (*F* 102–104)

This is the first time that we hear the daemon's voice. His task in this extract is to induce Frankenstein to listen to his story, and he speaks in three paragraphs, interrupted by brief replies from Victor. We will follow our usual practice, summarizing the daemon's three paragraphs, to gain an overview:

1. I am miserable and hated. We are bound together as creator and creature. If you do your duty to me, I shall do mine towards you. If not, I shall destroy you.
2. Please listen. I am stronger than you, but I will be docile if you do your duty to me, which you owe me. I was good. Misery made me wicked. Make me happy, and I shall again be virtuous.
3. I was created good, but I am terribly alone, cast out by mankind, and forced to live in bleak and empty places. I should revenge myself on mankind, but you, and only you, can prevent this. Listen to my story first, then decide whether to condemn me or help me. Defendants in courts can speak in their own defence, so I only ask what any felon is allowed.

The first feature we notice is the repetition of the argument. Roughly, the daemon's case falls into four related parts. First, a statement: there is a mutual bond and obligation between Frankenstein and the creature he has brought to life. Second, an appeal for pity, because the daemon's life is misery caused by loneliness. Third, a threat: misery causes him to become wicked, and will lead him to murder Frankenstein, his relatives, and thousands of others. Finally, an offer: if he becomes happy, he will again become good, and thousands of lives will be saved.

Notice that all four parts of the daemon's argument are expressed in all three of his paragraphs. It is a brilliant combination, appealing in turn to justice, sympathy, fear, and hope. The daemon first gives Frankenstein responsibility, then paints vivid pictures of misery and disaster, then brings out the tempting offer: Frankenstein can avert disaster, because the solution is within his power. Our summary, however, already shows that the daemon's discourse is different from those of Walton and Victor: his paragraphs vary only in emphasis and tone. Rather than changing from reflection to narrative and back again, as Walton does, or rambling, as Victor does, the daemon builds upon the same material, without altering his subject between the three paragraphs of the extract.

Turning our attention to the daemon's sentences, we find a greater variety than in either Walton's or Victor's narratives. There are numerous rhetorical questions, beginning with the telling accusation, 'How dare you sport thus with life?', and including the series of four, appealing for compassion, at the start of the final paragraph. Sentence-length is also extremely varied between the very short (such as 'But hear me.') and comparatively long (such as the 46 words beginning 'Yet it is in your power . . .' in the final paragraph). What is most marked, however, is the tight and logical structure of the daemon's language. In terms of sentences, this shows in two features: first, the number of what we can call 'balanced' sentences – those which consist of two parts which equally balance each other; and secondly in the number of 'paired' sentences – that is, two sentences which balance each other.

Perfect examples of balanced sentences occur in the first paragraph: the daemon constructs his sentence around a pivotal comma: 'Do your duty . . ., and I will do mine . . .'; then, expanding the same balanced statement in his next sentence, he constructs this around a pivotal semi-colon: 'If you will comply . . .; but if you refuse . . .'. There are further examples, as the daemon re-iterates his double-pronged attack of threat and lure, stick and carrot. Paired sentences are used for the same purpose, with the added advantage of condensing the argument into a terse, pithy style: 'I was benevolent and good; misery made me a fiend. Make me happy, and I shall again be virtuous.'

The daemon's style intensively emphasizes logic, the explanation of cause and effect. For example, he follows the statement, 'These bleak skies I hail', with an explanation *because*: 'for they are kinder to me than your fellow beings'; and his appeal, 'Oh, Frankenstein, be not equitable to every other and trample upon me alone', is completed with the explanation: 'to whom thy justice, and even thy clemency and affection, is most due'. Every part of the daemon's discourse is thus heavy with reasoning. Listen first, then judge, the daemon implores. Why? *Because* 'The guilty are allowed . . . to speak in their own defence'. Our first encounter with the daemon, then, creates a powerful impression. Every rhetorical device is used to strong effect; the argument is elaborated to emphasize different parts of the appeal; constructions are relentlessly logical throughout; and a balance of good and evil consequences is hammered home in the structure of many sentences.

We may remember, at this point, what we found in Victor's narrative: that he hands responsibility for his own 'happiness or misery' to his parents; mentions the principles he was taught, casts doubt on their effectiveness, and leaves us there. In other words, having assembled all the elements of an argument, he fails to connect them and fails to express a judgement. We now notice a strong contrast between Victor and the daemon: where Victor fails to draw his ideas together and judge, the daemon does so insistently and repeatedly.

Turning to the daemon's diction, we should notice the wide range of tones at his command. These range from the patient fatalism of his opening phrase: 'I expected this reception'; to outrage: 'How dare you sport thus with life?'; to cutting irony: 'Oh, praise the eternal justice of man!'; to appeal: 'How can I move thee?' To illustrate the range and flexibility of this language, notice the contrast between a placid tone, 'leave them and you at peace', and the sudden viciousness of both sound and image in the daemon's threat to 'glut the maw of death'. From studying Walton, we distinguished a self-justifying tone with a whining overtone of self-pity, as the dominant 'voice' of that narrator. Victor's style appeared – on the surface – noticeably calm and clear, more like a written than a spoken narrative. Now, in the daemon's discourse, we are for the first time in the presence of a truly flexible 'voice', a narrative in which we can hear the natural alterations of emotion, as we read. So the daemon's diction provides another contrast to Victor's 'framing' story.

So far, our analysis has led us to admire the daemon: we are impressed by the natural power of his rhetoric, and by the emotional appeal of his language. We now turn to consider the content of his argument more closely. This will lead us to a fuller appreciation of the moral and logical problems he poses and the consequently problematic nature of our response to him. He is problematic because he has to be considered in two separate contexts: an ethical/logical, or 'philosophical' context and a simultaneous emotional context. We will consider these in turn.

First, notice that the daemon and Frankenstein agree that parents are responsible for the 'happiness or misery' of their children, and have a duty to those children to provide them with happiness if that is possible. The daemon expresses this opinion forcefully in each of his paragraphs. In the first, he claims the creator–creature (or, father–son) bond, saying he is one 'to whom thou art bound by ties only dissoluble by the annihilation of one of us', and further talks of Frankenstein's 'duty' to him. The idea that he and Victor are tied to each other for life is prophetic of the story's ending, but for the moment we simply note the assertion of bond and duty.

In the second paragraph, the daemon develops two other metaphors for their relationship. First, he describes himself as 'devoted', 'mild and docile', and describes Frankenstein as 'my natural lord and king'. This idea is then elaborated using the language of seventeenth- and eighteenth-century debates about monarchy and society, and in particular the theories advanced by Locke and Rousseau. The daemon challenges his 'king' to give him his rights, for the Social Contract demands that a monarch should be 'equitable', rule with 'justice', and 'even clemency and affection'. The daemon offers his part of the contract in return – that is, to be 'mild and docile'. The framework of the daemon's ideas, then, derives from a contractual concept of the father–son relationship. Notice also, however, the implication of the metaphor: comparing Frankenstein to a 'lord' and 'king' confers upon him absolute power. This passes all responsibility to Victor, but is also flattery of a heady kind, and – in psychological terms – echoes a child's exaggerated perception of the father's power. The 'king' metaphor, then, carries multiple connotations and a flattering temptation to Victor. The daemon's next metaphor is even more extreme, for he likens them to God and Adam. This takes flattery to a new level, although his purpose in raising this analogy seems to be his subsequent mention of himself as Satan rather than Adam, of which more hereafter.

In the third paragraph, there is renewed mention of Frankenstein's obligation, for other people 'owe me nothing' while, by implication, Victor should 'look [on the daemon] with a favourable eye' and show 'goodness and compassion', still in a quasi-biblical diction that implies a religious analogy. As he continues, however, the daemon changes the metaphor again, and casts Frankenstein as a judge and himself as a guilty defendant. This time, his appeal is not to the relationship of creator and creature that binds them nor to a Social Contract of mutual duties, but to the rules governing justice in human courts.

These statements of the relationship between them are powerful, but all are flawed. First, if their fates are tied together for life: Victor readily offers a solution to this, saying 'let us try our strength in a fight in which one must fall'. Secondly, if they are parties to a contract: which party to a contract can make his compliance conditional on the other's? Surely, a contract must be willingly entered into by both parties; and the force of Locke's and Rousseau's arguments derived from their assertion that the contract on which society is founded furthers the self-interest of both government and individual. Finally, if Victor is judge and the daemon defendant: the judge should listen first, and condemn after. This is a sound legal principle, but notice that the daemon says, 'then, if you *can*, and if you will' (my italics), enforce the sentence. In his second paragraph, he has already pointed out that Victor is weaker than he is. So, the courtroom analogy falls down, because the judge is powerless to punish the guilty.

In ethical and logical terms, then, the daemon's argument is internally consistent and powerfully argued, but his analogies are of varied quality. Those founded on Frankenstein's responsibility as his creator, and on a form of contract, are stronger; while the religious analogy is specious (was Satan banished from heaven 'for no misdeed' and was the murder of William 'no misdeed'?), and the courtroom analogy, from the unpunishable murderer of William and framer of Justine, is flagrant sophistry. However, the daemon's argument is founded on an underlying philosophical stance. The daemon re-states or adjusts his case many times, but his view of life remains consistently, even relentlessly, determinist. That is, he believes that people are formed by their environment: people have natural qualities, but these are weaker than environmental influences, so it is society, not nature, that makes everyone what they become. Consequently, if a person has become evil, society should correct its mistake, so that they become good. The daemon states this plainly: 'misery made me a fiend. Make me happy, and I shall again be virtuous'. Further, the daemon specifies society's error: social exclusion and loneliness are the culprits. These will, inevitably, breed hatred and violent revenge. He puts forward a simple stimulus and response model for the formation of character: stimulus = rejection, response = fiend; stimulus = affection, response = benevolent creature.

The daemon goes further. Notice that he twice asserts that he was born virtuous, saying 'I was benevolent and good' and 'I was benevolent; my soul glowed with love and humanity'. This belief in natural goodness echoes beliefs of the Romantic poets, such as Wordsworth's 'not in utter nakedness, but trailing clouds of glory do we come from God, who is our home. Heaven lies about us in our infancy ...'.[1] The daemon, then, agrees with the Romantics, that a newborn creature is naturally good. How omnipotent, then, must be environmental influence, which can change goodness to its opposite. This is a strong determinist statement: that our very nature can be transformed into its opposite by environmental forces. It is remarkable that Mary Shelley, writing at the very beginning of the century of the great determinist trinity, Darwin, Marx and Freud, should have articulated the daemon's outlook so powerfully.

These are the philosophical assumptions that lie behind the daemon's argument, then, and they clearly distinguish him from both Victor and Walton. They have crucial implications for other topics that we can call themes of *Frankenstein*, such as nature, science, responsibility, and fate. So, for example, we notice that Victor places responsibility for his own 'happiness or misery' on his parents, ironically just as the daemon places responsibility upon him. Yet the contexts of these two statements differ widely. Within ten pages Victor asserts that 'Destiny' was the responsible party (*F* 43); he fails to complete his own logic, and shies away from judgement. The daemon, in contrast, follows his ideas through to clear conclusions.

We now turn to the daemon's emotional appeal. We have remarked that his argument appeals to justice, fear, sympathy and hope; we should now notice how effectively his voice enforces these appeals. In the simple case of justice, he uses outrage ('How dare you sport thus with life?'), persistent and repeated balance in sentences, and cutting irony ('praise the eternal justice of man!'), to urge his plea for justice; while even his desires for retribution are shot through with the concept of fairness: 'Shall I not then hate them who abhor me?' The appeal to fear is reinforced by threats, of which there are two in this extract. Notice that the promised destruction grows from 'your remaining friends' to 'you and your family, [and] thousands of others', and that both threats are expressed in metaphors of eating: first, to 'glut the maw' of death until it be 'satiated'; then, that thousands will be 'swallowed up'.

The most effective appeal in the daemon's speech, however, is to sympathy. If we select those words and phrases which call upon us for compassion, we quickly find that they make up by far the largest element of his speech. From his observation, 'all men hate the wretched; how, then, must I be hated, who am miserable beyond all living things!', to the apogee of his appeal in the third paragraph ('How can I move thee? ... The desert mountains ... the caves of ice ... These bleak skies ... arm themselves for my destruction.'), the passage repeatedly returns to ideas of 'suffered', 'misery', 'anguish', 'trample upon me', 'bliss ... I alone am irrevocably excluded', and 'am I not alone, miserably alone?'. This appeal is effective in eliciting the reader's compassion. Victor echoes our response when deciding to hear the daemon's story. First, he 'weighed the various arguments he had used', and felt 'curiosity', but it was 'compassion' that 'confirmed my resolution' (*F* 104).

The daemon's narrative is, therefore, deeply problematic not only for Victor Frankenstein, the nominal listener, but also for the reader. We recognize the arguments used and the philosophy behind them. These arguments and the determinist outlook driving them are flawed, ethically questionable, and possibly repugnant to us. Certainly we may feel badgered and blackmailed by the daemon's use of alternating threats and promises. On the other hand, we feel sorry for him, understand his pain and loneliness, and commiserate his outcast condition, which is vividly represented.

Our 'problem' may be put another way. The argument so strongly advanced by the daemon is clearly incomplete and unsatisfactory to us as a whole; yet each part of his reasoning seems natural and sound in isolation. To illustrate this point, we can ask some questions: does the daemon's rejection by society explain his misery? Yes. Does this excuse the murder of William and the framing of Justine? No. If misery made him a fiend, would happiness make him good? Theoretically, yes.

So, we are faced with a system of thought that is deeply flawed, strongly imposed upon us, but is put forward without being rebutted.

It is, however, the daemon's attempt to find an explanation for his existence and his experiences. We can understand, and sympathize with, the genesis of these ideas in his life-story as he relates it in the succeeding chapters; but the daemon's argument remains one of several in *Frankenstein* that are proposed but never effectively rebutted, and this gives rise to a doubt about the process of interpreting experience.

Concluding Discussion

A Journey to Revelation, or to the 'Centre'

We have now sampled the three major narrators of *Frankenstein*, each of whom acts as a 'frame' for the core of the story. What effects are produced by this form of narration?

First, let us consider the reader's position in relation to the story. The opening encourages us to identify with Mrs Saville, implicitly inviting us to adopt a feminine viewpoint, sceptical of male ambition. We remain with Mrs Saville, receiving the rest of Walton's letters, but our relation to Victor's narrative becomes complicated, because it is in direct speech. A further complication is added when the daemon's narrative is also couched in direct speech. One effect of this structure is that the only *written* narrative – Walton's to his sister – is progressively relegated to the background while the bulk of the novel speaks to us first in Frankenstein's, then in the daemon's, voice. We are therefore simultaneously with Mrs Saville in England reading letters, with Walton in the Arctic listening to Frankenstein, and eventually also with Frankenstein above the glacier, listening to the daemon. This is a bewildering series of locations, and serves to underline the 'misdirection' of the novel's opening: that the ultimate destination of the story could not be predicted and was not signalled.

In her study of the frame structure of *Frankenstein*, Beth Newman remarks, '... it might seem that the purpose of a narrative technique that transfers a story from teller to teller is to direct the reader to questions of point of view',[2] but goes on to suggest that, because each listener accepts each narrative, 'without question ... we are given no new perspective'. She also asserts that the different narratives are given in 'a sameness of voice that blurs the distinction between tellers instead of heightening them', and reaches the conclusion that in *Frankenstein* 'a story is emphatically separable from the character who first tells it'.[3] We noticed, above, that there are unresolved questions, which create the impression of a gap opening up between actual life and the way we attempt to interpret life, or, if you like, between a story and its teller. However, is a 'sameness of voice' and a blurred 'distinction between tellers' what we have found in our study of three narrators?

The answer must be an emphatic no. We have found an insecure and argumentative idealist (Walton); an evasive snob whose moral and philosophical reflections are remarkably incomplete or opaque (Victor Frankenstein); and a powerful rhetorician with a forceful, single, determinist argument (the daemon). Each of these narrators has a distinctive voice, and there is a particularly noticeable contrast between Victor's and the daemon's 'points of view', despite the fact that they do not contradict each others' versions of events. The story does exist independent of its tellers, as Beth Newman remarks, because it remains one story no matter who tells it, and events remain unchallenged; but at the same time, the contrasting voices focus the reader's attention onto differences between the narrators' points of view. These are exploited in several ways.

First, some crucial events are reprised in Victor's and the daemon's narratives. Different accounts are not contradictory, but a brief examination of one example shows how important the question of point of view can be. When William is killed and Victor sees the daemon, he tells us that 'No sooner did that idea cross my imagination, than I became convinced of its truth ... Nothing in human shape could have destroyed that fair child. *He* was the murderer! I could not doubt it', and he reflects that the daemon must be 'a depraved wretch, whose delight was in carnage and misery' (*F* 78). The daemon's version, on the other hand, reveals a much more complicated situation. He seizes William with the thought that an unprejudiced boy may have no 'horror of deformity', and may become his companion. His words to William are 'Child, what is the meaning of this? I do not intend to hurt you; listen to me', clearly still appealing for friendship. It is only when William echoes adult fears, saying 'you wish to eat me and tear me to pieces', and when he shows himself as great a social snob as Victor ('he is a syndic . . . You dare not keep me'), that the daemon resorts to violence. Even then it is not clear that he intends murder, for he says, 'I grasped his throat to silence him' (all quotations are from *F* 144).

What does this second account reveal? First, it tells us that the event appeared very differently to these two narrators. Secondly, however, the re-telling of William's murder raises important thematic questions. William's childishness and innocence are frequently referred to by Victor, Elizabeth, and Victor's father, and his appearance of innocence impressed the daemon. The re-telling reveals that William's innocent appearance was false: he was already socialized – disgusted and frightened by the daemon's looks, and fully trained in family pride and snobbery. He threatens the daemon with punishment and calls him names which, the daemon tells us, 'carried despair to my heart'. Clearly, although the event is unquestioned, the two accounts present entirely different points of view, exploited by Mary Shelley to develop her critique of romantic and social conventions. The murder of William highlights the class divisions in society, and contributes to the theme of the daemon's social exclusion. It also criticizes the concept of childhood innocence, an idea that was dear to romantic poets including Percy Shelley himself. William's behaviour reveals that he has already been corrupted by his social training. By implication, therefore, this second account of William's murder supports the daemon's determinism, against romantic idealism.

Secondly, Victor's and the daemon's direct speech narratives provide the author with opportunities for characterization through extended, self-revealing speeches. In our analysis of extracts, we have been provoked to ask questions about the psychology of each of them, and even from these limited studies, we have formulated critical conclusions about each narrator. For example, we noticed how Walton uses grandiose language to bolster his own confidence, and to exclude the depression to which he is intermittently prey. We noticed that Victor evades his own story to the point where he fails to mention being born, and has to backtrack awkwardly. Finally, we noticed the daemon's flawed argument and the unevenness of his metaphors set beside the relentless demand for sympathy that is the most powerful element of his appeal. Having studied only short extracts so far, we are confident that further complexities of character in all three of our narrators will be revealed as we read on.

Thirdly, the themes treated by the three narrators, and their circumstances, are very closely interwoven, so that we are provoked to compare them with each other, and notice ironic similarities and differences. For example, we have read of Walton's idealistic mission, motivated by paternalistic benevolence and vainglory. A more extended treatment of a very similar mission, with similar motives, comes when Victor describes his scientific enthusiasm, in Chapters 3 and 4. So, where Walton writes of the 'inestimable benefit which I shall confer on all mankind', Victor dreams that 'a new species would bless me as its creator and source' (*F* 55). The novel repeatedly returns to explorations of male idealism, irrespective of the narrator. Another example of a theme echoing between narratives comes with Victor's statement that parents are responsible for the 'happiness or misery' of their offspring. Even from our study of these limited extracts, we have remarked that the daemon echoes this idea in his demand that Victor should 'Make me happy'. These are two very noticeable examples, where successive narratives further explore the same themes.

Mary Shelley has woven her different narratives together so densely that there are also many subtle effects to be found on every page: slight echoes continually jog our minds to make comparisons or realize ironies. One such example begins with Walton's rhetorical question: 'Do I not deserve to accomplish some great purpose?' When we read the daemon's argument, we are bombarded by similar rhetorical constructions: 'But am I not alone, miserably alone?' and 'Shall I not then hate them who abhor me?' What is the implication of two such different creatures, in widely different circumstances, both justifying their needs in such an echoing manner? Such effects occur on every page, so that it seems as if the different narratives are continually placing further overlays upon the same themes. The themes themselves therefore increase in complexity and substance, as if they are being built steadily throughout the novel – irrespective of the differences between narrators.

This close linking of the narrators to a limited range of recurrent themes and situations has an effect that counters what we might normally expect from 'framed' narratives. As Beth Newman remarks, one effect is that the story itself – never challenged – exists independent of its narrators and therefore acquires a power of its own. Another effect is that the reader is allowed no escape: for we find each new narrator trapped within the same system of ideas and events as the one before, so that eventually, a feeling of being irrevocably enclosed by the story and themes is transmitted to us as well.

We will briefly discuss some further effects of 'framed' narratives, before drawing conclusions from the beginning of our study.

First, a frame commonly introduces a distance, insulating the reader from the story. However, in some celebrated cases, and particularly where direct speech is extensively used, the frame acts paradoxically: the power of the story bursts through the frame and speaks directly to the reader, so that the breaking of the frame actually enhances the immediacy of the story rather than interfering with it. This happens, for example, with Heathcliff's and Isabella's narratives in *Wuthering Heights*. What do we find in *Frankenstein*? The answer seems to be that the framing structures here work in both of these ways. First, the structure sets up distance: reading about an explorer's ship caught in the ice of the northern ocean, then about a hut above an Alpine glacier, from Mrs Saville's home in civilized England, emphasizes the distance and isolation of Walton, Frankenstein, and the daemon, and impresses upon us that these events take place far away, in an extremely remote setting. The opening misdirection we have remarked upon increases the reader's disorientation, adding to an impression that the story takes place somewhere unpredictable, but definitely beyond the limits of civilization. Then, reading with Mrs Saville encourages us to read sceptically, sharing her 'evil forebodings'. So distance, and the isolation of the characters, is one effect of the frame structure of the novel.

When the daemon begins to speak, on the other hand, we hear a highly distinctive and powerful voice; and as we have found, his appeal is internally consistent and relentlessly presented. This is a sharp contrast to the evasiveness of Victor's 'framing' narrative. The daemon's voice is so much stronger than the less forthright narrators whose accounts supposedly enclose his, that his narrative breaks through the structural restraints set around it. When we consider that this voice speaks to us from a hardly imaginable geographical distance (and from the human distance of his difference, his daemonhood), it is clear that the final effect is greatly to magnify the potency of his narrative. In short, when an elaborate double frame has been set up, nothing is so powerful as to break it.

This discussion of distance, and of the daemon's voice, shows how the structure of narratives in *Frankenstein* takes us on a journey towards the 'centre', or the 'core' of the novel and its story. As we are taken first to the northern ocean, then to Geneva, Ingolstadt, Geneva again, and finally to the *mer de glace*, the frames and the story build up suspense as well as distance and isolation. The daemon's narrative is situated at the centre of the novel: it is the revelation we have been waiting for. It has been advertised by Victor's references to horror, disgust, and fear, so that the reader approaches it with trepidation. In this way, the frame structure plays upon suspense, so that the daemon's narrative gains status as the ultimate or central revelation. To put this in another way, the daemon, speaking to us through so many frames from the very centre of the novel, has an authority denied to the two outer narrators, whom we read with scepticism.

The final surprise is the nature and style of the daemon's story. What do we expect from him? Grunts, the gnashing of teeth, and blood-thirsty threats, perhaps. What, then, is our surprise when he speaks in cultured language and pleads his case with an appeal that engages our sympathy? We could say that the daemon's voice, when it finally comes, is the second major misdirection of the novel: first, we find ourselves reading a science-fiction horror story instead of an account of polar exploration; then, the inhuman fiend turns out to be the most articulate and intelligent speaker, and the one to whom we feel most drawn.

Conclusions to Chapter 1

As we leave this chapter, we should draw some tentative conclusions, which may be confirmed and further developed in the succeeding chapters. Our analyses have indicated certain *themes* that seem likely to be major concerns in *Frankenstein*.

1. *Masculine and feminine*: We noticed that Walton writes argumentatively to his sister; and that the opening of his letter reveals some specifically male characteristics, such as the simile in which he compares his project to a childish game and the possible sexual *double-entendre* that he hopes to 'discover the wondrous power which attracts the needle'. Walton also sees himself, in patrician manner, able to 'confer' benefits on all mankind. In Victor's narrative there are further signs that Mary Shelley is placing male attitudes under a critical spotlight. For example, Victor comments on Caroline Beaufort's 'mind' as 'of an uncommon mould', and that his father has to 'approve' of her before loving her, whereupon he shelters her 'as a fair exotic', and her 'mind' suddenly becomes 'soft and benevolent'. Looking at Victor's hope from his great discovery, we read that 'No father could claim the gratitude of his child so completely as I should deserve theirs'. In short, there is a continuing vein of gendered references and attitudes in both Walton's and Victor's narratives, signalling that a critique of masculine attitudes is likely to be a theme of the novel.

2. *Science and the pursuit of knowledge*: So far, we have only met Walton's ideal of exploration, and briefly referred to Victor's scientific endeavours. However, we can be confident that enthusiastic projects like Walton's are to be a theme of the novel. Walton's idealisms are already satirized by his grandiose references (to rivalling Homer and Shakespeare, for example), and are clearly the subject of controversy between him and his sister. Furthermore, Walton already appears insecure, and argues to bolster his ego. Grandiose idealistic undertakings, whether in science or exploration, are clearly set to become a theme in *Frankenstein*.

3. *Nature*: We can include nature in our list of potential themes, because of Walton's descriptions of the region of the pole, on the first page of the novel. We remember that he tried to believe it 'the seat of frost and desolation', but his imagination saw instead

'the sun ... diffusing a perpetual splendour' and 'a land surpassing in wonders and in beauty every region hitherto discovered'. It is clear from this that nature, and misperceptions of nature, is a subject closely allied to Shelley's interest in the masculine projects of Walton and Victor. Inevitably, then, nature will develop into a major concern or 'theme' of the novel.

We have discussed the *framing structure* of *Frankenstein*, almost all of which comes to us in the words of *three narrators*. Having studied a sample from each narrator, and considered the relations between them and between them and the reader, we suggest that the effect of this structure is dual and paradoxical:

1. First, we found that the text reveals three distinct characters, and that their voices do vary (with the most marked contrast in 'voice' between Victor and the daemon). On the other hand, the use of a small range of 'touchstone' terms common to all three narrators ('benevolent' and 'ardour' are good examples); the fact that no narrator's story is challenged by another; and the continuous play upon a specific group of themes in all three narratives minimize the narrators' differences, and *enhance our impression of the unity of the text*. These elements also have the effect of separating the story from its particular teller, so that the story appears to exist independently of the narrators.

2. On the other hand, we have found that the frame structure emphasizes distances and isolation, and is used by Mary Shelley to incorporate *two daring misdirections*: first, from polar exploration to Swiss and German science-fiction; then, by reversing our expectations of the daemon's speech. So, the frames encourage *uncertainty* in the reader, and enhance the *unpredictability* of the story. As we read the frames towards the centre of the novel, the effect of gradual revelation or 'journey towards a centre' heightens authenticity and suspense. Paradoxically, the ability of the daemon's voice and appeal to *break through the frames* directly to the reader, while *speaking from so far away* both within the elaborate frames and in terms of geographical distance, enhances his power and the authority of his narrative.

Methods of Analysis

We have approached the analysis of three extracts, using a range of analytical techniques:

- We made a brief summary of the extract, paragraph-by-paragraph, then considered our summary in order to understand the structure of the narrative. This technique revealed, for example, Walton's argumentative purpose and Victor's evasiveness.
- We focused on sentences, analysing the kinds of sentences used, their length, and variety. Using this analysis as a basis for asking further leading questions has brought insights into the narrator's character. For example, we noticed how Walton's sentences lead from depression to delight, or vice versa, as his moods alternate or his language bolsters his hopes; that Victor's reflections are some-times incomplete; and the logical cause-and-effect reasoning densely worked in to the daemon's style.
- We examined diction – the choice and use of words – and found this a particularly fruitful area of inquiry into our extracts. In particular, we noticed that all three narrators use significant repetition of what we have called 'touchstone' terms, such as Walton's 'delight' and 'fervent', Victor's and the daemon's 'benevolent'; and how Walton's avalanche of first-person pronouns underlines his self-absorption.
- We considered imagery – similes and metaphors – and examined these both critically (e.g., we noticed that the daemon's judicial analogy is flawed, inferior to his contract analogy; and we noticed Walton's mixed metaphor of the soul's 'intellectual eye') and for their interpretation (e.g., we noticed the recurrence of an eating motif in the daemon's threats).
- Finally, we turned our attention to the particular concern of this chapter, asking of each passage:
  - What kind of a narrative is this?
  - What relationships between language, thought about life, and life itself, are represented in this narrative?
  - How does it function as a frame or within the novel's structure?
  - As readers, in what relation do we stand to this narrative and this narrator?

- After analysing the extracts, we surveyed the three analyses we had carried out, and discussed some of the topics that had arisen, seeking to develop our ideas further in a *concluding discussion*. Again, this involved formulating and then pursuing questions about the text, focusing on this chapter's main concern. In other words, we asked questions to explore just how the structure of 'framing narratives' works, and what effects it generates, in *Frankenstein*.

Suggested Work

Using the approaches and techniques demonstrated in this chapter, analyse *either* Alphonse Frankenstein's letter to Victor (pp. 73–75) *or* Elizabeth's letter to Victor (pp. 191–192). Your analysis should include consideration of the context of each letter (i.e., where Victor reads it, in what circumstances, and how he receives the content) as well as content.

Consider how these letters contribute to the narration of the whole story; whether they present any different personalities as narrators, and how they relate to all three main narratives.

You may then look at Elizabeth's letter to Victor, pp. 65–68, analysing this in a similar manner. This letter is often criticized as an awkward narrative device, a clumsy way for Mary Shelley to introduce the character of Justine Moritz. What do you think?

2

Characterization

This chapter looks at the way people are presented in *Frankenstein*: How are the people who inhabit the story built up for us? Do the characters appeal to us as fully realized individuals? We will focus on each of the main figures at a moment of crisis.

Analysis: Walton, pp. 215–218

We start with Walton's reception of the crew's deputation, since this is clearly a time of crisis for him. Here are the most relevant passages from pages 215 to 218:

September 2nd.

MY BELOVED SISTER,

I write to you, encompassed by peril, and ignorant whether I am ever doomed to see again dear England, and the dearer friends that inhabit it. I am surrounded by mountains of ice, which admit of no escape, and threaten every moment to crush my vessel. The brave fellows, whom I have persuaded to be my companions, look towards me for aid; but I have none to bestow. There is something terribly appalling in our situation, yet my courage and hopes do not desert me. Yet it is terrible to reflect that the lives of all these men are endangered through me. If we are lost, my mad schemes are the cause.

And what, Margaret, will be the state of your mind? You will not hear of my destruction, and you will anxiously await my return. Years will pass, and you will have visitings of despair, and yet be tortured by hope. Oh! my beloved sister, the sickening failing of your heart-felt expectations is, in prospect, more terrible to me than my own death. But you have a husband, and lovely children; you may be happy: Heaven bless you, and make you so!

My unfortunate guest regards me with the tenderest compassion. He endeavours to fill me with hope; and talks as if life were a possession which he valued. He reminds me how often the same accidents have happened to other navigators, who have attempted this sea, and in spite of myself, he fills me with cheerful auguries. Even the sailors feel the power of his eloquence; when he speaks, they no longer despair; he rouses their energies, and, while they hear his voice, they believe these vast mountains of ice are molehills, which will vanish before the resolutions of man. These feelings are transitory; each day of expectation delayed fills them with fear, and I almost dread a mutiny caused by this despair . . . .

September 5ᵗʰ.

We are still surrounded by mountains of ice, still in imminent danger of being crushed in their conflict. The cold is excessive, and many of my unfortunate comrades have already found a grave amidst this scene of desolation. Frankenstein has daily declined in health: a feverish fire still glimmers in his eyes; but he is exhausted, and when suddenly roused to any exertion, he speedily sinks again into apparent lifelessness.

I mentioned in my last letter the fears I entertained of a mutiny. This morning, as I sat watching the wan countenance of my friend – his eyes half closed, and his limbs hanging listlessly – I was roused by half a dozen of the sailors, who demanded admission into the cabin. They entered, and their leader addressed me. He told me that he and his companions had been chosen by the other sailors to come in deputation to me, to make me a requisition, which, in justice, I could not refuse. We were immured in ice, and should probably never escape; but they feared that if, as was possible, the ice should dissipate and a free passage be opened, I should be rash enough to continue my voyage, and lead them into fresh dangers, after they might happily have surmounted this. They insisted, therefore, that I should engage with a solemn promise, that if the vessel should be freed I would instantly direct my course southwards.

This speech troubled me. I had not despaired; nor had I yet conceived the idea of returning, if set free. Yet could I, in justice, or even in possibility, refuse this demand? I hesitated before I answered; when Frankenstein, who had at first been silent, and, indeed, appeared hardly to have force enough to attend, now roused himself; his eyes sparkled, and his cheeks flushed with momentary vigour. Turning towards the men, he said –

'What do you mean? What do you demand of your captain? Are you then so easily turned from your design? . . . .'

He spoke this with a voice so modulated to the different feelings expressed in his speech, with an eye so full of lofty design and heroism, that can you wonder that these men were moved? They looked at one another, and were unable to reply. I spoke; I told them to retire, and consider of what had been said: that I would not lead them farther north if they strenuously desired the contrary; but that I hoped that, with reflection, their courage would return.

They retired, and I turned towards my friend, but he was sunk in languor, and almost deprived of life.

How all this will terminate, I know not; but I had rather die than return shamefully – my purpose unfulfilled. Yet I fear such will be my fate; the men, unsupported by ideas of glory and honour, can never willingly continue to endure their present hardships.

September 7th.

The die is cast; I have consented to return, if we are not destroyed. Thus are my hopes blasted by cowardice and indecision: I come back ignorant and disappointed. It requires more philosophy than I possess, to bear this injustice with patience.   (*F* 215–218)

These extracts relate a period of crisis for Walton: the forces that operate at this decisive time are fully explained, and we wait to see which way the conflict will be resolved. We can begin by considering how the narrative is structured. One short paragraph and most of Frankenstein's speech to the crew have been omitted, but otherwise the extract is continuous, and is divided into three letters dated 2nd, 5th and 7th September. The first two letters are further divided into paragraphs.

Here is a summary, which will help us to see how the narrative and Walton's character are constructed:

2 September (First letter):

1. We are in terrible danger, due to my mad schemes, but I still hope.
2. If I die, you will grieve, having no news of me; but your family may make you happy.
3. Frankenstein raises everyone's spirits temporarily when he speaks, but I fear a mutiny.

5 September (Second letter):

1. We are still in danger of being crushed in the ice, and Frankenstein is weakening.
2. A deputation of sailors came to me, asking for my promise to turn back, if the vessel should be set free.
3. I hesitated, unsure what I should or could answer. Frankenstein spoke to the sailors.
4. (Frankenstein's speech: urging glory and heroism, and sarcastic about cowardice).
5. The sailors could not reply. I said I would turn back if they insist, but I hoped they would change their minds.
6. Frankenstein had fainted.
7. I would rather die than turn back; but I shall probably have to turn back.

7 September (Third letter)

1. It is unfair and unjust! I have had to agree to turn back.

At first glance, this may appear a confusing list of statements and topics, as Walton considers himself, his sister, Frankenstein and the crew by turns; and as he thinks of their current danger, his hopes and their future course. In short, a number of topics are crowding in upon Walton's mind. However, we can still gain a useful overview by studying our summary.

The first letter consists of three paragraphs, and our summary highlights that all three hinge upon 'but', and focus upon thoughts and emotions that swing from extreme to extreme. For example, the first paragraph mentions Walton maintaining his 'courage and hopes', yet within two lines he calls them his 'mad schemes'. In the second paragraph he imagines the 'sickening failing' of Margaret's hopes, before conceding that she 'may be happy'. These extreme swings of mood or opinion are exemplified by the comment on Frankenstein's oratory, which makes it seem that 'these vast mountains of ice are molehills, which will vanish before the resolutions of man'. We know, and Walton tacitly agrees, that they are still 'vast mountains of ice', despite anything Frankenstein may say.

The second letter relates the story of the sailors' deputation. Our summary of this narrative is clearer than the mood-swings of the first letter, yet two accounts are given simultaneously. First, there is the story of Walton and his crew (he knows he cannot force the crew, as they would mutiny; he feels they have justice on their side; he hesitates, then asks them to think again; he fears they will not change their minds); secondly, there is the story of Frankenstein and Walton's crew (he is growing weaker, clearly near to death; he speaks of glory, honour and fame, and calls the sailors cowards, but urges them to be heroes; he faints). This letter, in fact, seems to juxtapose the responses of Walton and Frankenstein to contrast Walton's practical against Victor's enthusiastic answers to the crew.

The third letter is only one paragraph: Walton's emotional outburst at the sailors' decision to turn back, which he calls 'cowardice' and 'injustice'. This isolated paragraph is the first in which Walton expresses an unmixed emotion, and consequently has an enhanced effect. Walton's outburst is, at the same time, both powerful and childish and unfair: it is clear from his own preceding narrative that the sailors are not cowards, nor can their decision be called 'injustice'. This paragraph, then, shows Walton lashing out like a child in a tantrum.

We notice that Shelley has organized the incident into three stages. The first letter is *before*: a confusion of contradictory fears, hopes and ideas, ending with fear of mutiny. The second letter is *during*: it relates the story of the incident (the sailors' deputation). The third letter is *after*, giving the outcome and Walton's intemperate reaction. Walton's character thus moves from confused vacillations (Letter 1) towards a single view (Letter 3). In many other novels, such a structure might demonstrate the character's increasing maturity, or learning from experience. Shelley does not suggest this in Walton's case, however. Rather, the simple *before/during/after* structure of the episode highlights for us just how non-sequential the different attitudes are.

A simple comparison of before and after shows this clearly. In the first paragraph, Walton shows consciousness of his responsibility, and awareness that his 'brave fellows' are looking to him for leadership he cannot provide: they 'look towards me for aid, but I have none to bestow'. Their lives are 'endangered through me', and Walton calls his voyage to the pole 'my mad schemes'. In short, there is a welcome breath of sanity running through Walton, and one only wonders how he can say, in the same paragraph, 'yet my courage and hopes do not desert me'. Afterwards, however, Walton brings together 'hopes blasted', 'cowardice', 'indecision', 'ignorant', 'disappointed', and declares that he cannot 'bear this injustice with patience'. The contrast is stark: 'brave fellows' are now cowards, and no awareness of responsibility remains. In Letter 3, everything is done *to* Walton (his hopes are 'blasted'; he suffers 'injustice' and is rendered 'ignorant and disappointed'); where in Letter 1, everything was done *by* him (he persuaded the sailors, he endangered their lives).

As character-development, this seems to go backwards: Walton moves away from a wider awareness of responsibility as an adult, and moves back into the self-centred narrowness of childish petulance. Does Walton grow down, rather than up?

Before answering this question we need to look at the content of this extract more closely. In Chapter 1 we noticed that Shelley uses repetition to focus our attention on certain terms. In the present extract, the word that stands out because of its repetition is 'justice'. First, the sailors urge that Walton cannot, in 'justice', refuse their request; then, Walton thinks about whether he could 'in justice, or even in possibility', refuse; finally, Walton rails against turning back as an unbearable 'injustice'.

Where is 'justice' in this situation? One could say that the crew
have 'justice' on their side: Walton is responsible for their lives, so they
have the right to demand that he helps them to survive. On the other
hand, perhaps Walton has 'justice' on his side: the sailors knowingly
embarked upon a dangerous voyage, and they are simply changing
their minds out of cowardice. Walton is right to complain that they
are breaking their word. So, the crew's assertion of 'justice' and Walton's hesitant thoughts are equally hollow: repetition of the word only
highlights the brittleness of abstract terms and the high-flown concepts they denote. In the present passage, the concept of 'justice' is
undermined in three ways. First, it appears in a context where it is
ambiguous, as we have remarked; secondly, Walton's final use of 'injustice' is as a childish synonym for 'frustrating to *me*'; thirdly, several
elements of the narrative show us what is really happening, which has
nothing to do with 'justice', and everything to do with power. So,
Walton wonders whether he can 'even in possibility' refuse the sailors'
demand, knowing perfectly well that he cannot. He already admitted, 'I almost dread a mutiny'. For the same reason, the sailors call
their request a 'requisition' and 'insist' that Walton should 'engage' his
promise because he 'could not refuse'. They, too, colour their demand
with the concept of 'justice'; but it is plain that this term is mere
colouring. The sailors are really warning Walton that they will mutiny
if he refuses to turn back.

Another term used three times in this extract is 'despair'. First,
the crew do not 'despair' while Frankenstein speaks; then, Walton
fears the crew's 'despair' will lead to mutiny; finally, Walton hears the
crew's demand and tells us, 'I had not despaired'. 'Despair', then, is
an important word in Walton's vocabulary. What does the context
tell us? The first and second uses of the word occur as contrast to
Frankenstein's idealism: for a short time, while Frankenstein speaks,
Walton and the sailors can believe that 'these vast mountains of ice
are molehills'. This effect is 'transitory', however. When Frankenstein
stops speaking, the sailors return to their natural state: 'despair'. The
first letter shows that Walton's natural state is also 'despair'. He tells
us that Frankenstein 'endeavours to fill me with hope' and 'in spite
of myself . . . fills me with cheerful auguries'. Clearly Walton, like the
crew, despairs when Frankenstein is not speaking. This is confirmed

by his reference to 'mountains of ice' (not molehills!) at the beginning of Letter 2.

The third time 'despair' appears therefore poses a question: having acknowledged that he can only hope while under the influence of Frankenstein's eloquence, Walton unaccountably claims, 'I had not despaired'. We are entitled to wonder: is he trying to deceive us, or himself? Or, what is the truth: does Walton 'despair' or not? These questions become more problematic when we notice how dislocated conversation is at this crucial moment. The sailors address Walton; Frankenstein answers; they cannot answer Frankenstein; Walton speaks; Frankenstein is unconscious. The effect of this disjointed discussion is that idealism comes from Frankenstein, while Walton speaks words of compromise.

How do these repetitions contribute to the presentation of Walton as a character? First, we should remember our first introduction to Walton, the conflict between his ambitions and his sister's misgivings, and his argumentative purpose. The present extract, some 200 pages later, still turns upon the same argument. That is, an argument between the sailors, who urge the value of life and survival, and the elements in Walton which acknowledge these values, on the one side; and Frankenstein/Walton on the other side, urging glory and heroism, and describing a romantic vision in which 'mountains of ice' are 'molehills' and ice is 'mutable, and cannot withstand' the firmness of human resolution.

Both sides of this argument now receive support from Walton. Most strikingly in this extract, Walton describes his voyage as 'mad schemes', and agrees that the sailors' lives are 'endangered through me'. Other signs of increased awareness are Walton's consciousness that the effect of Frankenstein's eloquence quickly fades, and his imagination of his sister's emotions. On the other hand, Walton claims he 'would rather die than return shamefully', that he 'had not despaired', and lashes out at 'cowardice' and 'injustice' when forced to turn back. Clearly, then, Walton is still caught in the same conflict he was arguing when we first met him. The oddness of his personality seems to come from the way in which the two sides of his conflict alternate. To explain this comment, let us look at the first paragraph of Letter 1.

In this paragraph, the physical situation dominates: they are 'mountains of ice, which admit of no escape'. Walton recognizes the ship's 'peril' which is 'terribly appalling'. He calls England, and his relatives, 'dear' and 'dearer'. He is responsible, for he 'persuaded' the crew, and they risk their lives 'through me'. He also seems to feel guilty, for he has no 'aid' to bestow as their leader, and their peril is the result of 'my mad schemes'. In short, it would be hard to frame a more comprehensive acknowledgement that Mrs Saville was right all along. In the course of this paragraph, however, Walton interpolates, 'yet my courage and hopes do not desert me'. His return to guilt and responsibility is then introduced with another 'Yet . . .'.

What can he mean? If he longs for England, if he finds their situation appalling, if he feels responsible for the crew, and, above all, if the voyage is 'my mad schemes', then his 'courage and hopes' have deserted him. If, on the other hand, he is telling us the truth that his 'courage and hopes do not desert me', then we can only imagine that this is in some other mind or heart, different from the mind and heart expressed by the rest of the paragraph. This impression that the two sides belong in different personalities is highlighted by the double 'yet' that frames Walton's inexplicable insertion. What is the relation between these two sides of Walton's character? We are given no real answer to this question. Instead, one contradictory phrase is inserted between two conjunctions 'yet', with no further explanation. The extract as a whole inexplicably contains both the opinion expressed by 'my mad schemes' and its opposite – that these being thwarted is 'cowardice' and 'injustice'.

In terms of character, then, we have found a continuing conundrum rather than an understandable personality. Walton is composed of different, often contradictory, aspects of the central conflict with which he is identified. These different aspects are, as it were, thrown together into his character, different emotional centres appearing at different moments, and with an absence of information as to how they relate to each other. The author remains reticent about how experience affects character. In this extract Walton's experience seems to provoke a childish outburst. Does this mean that he has regressed?

At this point in analysing character, there is a strong temptation to 'join the dots': in other words, to draw a conclusion about cause and effect, just because there is a sequence in the text. For example, we know that Walton experiences the peril of imprisonment in the ice, the sailors' deputation and their threat of mutiny. Then, we know that he lashes out at their 'cowardice' and pities himself for the 'injustice' of turning back. We also know that this represents a change in Walton's mood and opinions, from the beginning of the extract. On the other hand, there is no evidence that his change of mood is the outcome of his experience: it is not assigned a cause in the text. Perhaps Walton's reasonableness was always a false surface, covering the self-centred childishness that bursts out on September 7th? Perhaps Walton is really frightened, and wishes to turn back, but wants to be forced by the sailors, so that he can pretend to complain about his fate? Perhaps Walton sets up Frankenstein to be his stalking-horse for this purpose, so he can excuse himself both from urging the crew towards more danger and from giving in to their demands too easily?. . . and so on. All such speculations about Walton's psychology are no more than 'joining the dots': that is, inventing a connection between two elements of the text, where no connection is given.

Our study of Walton, then, has given us a number of vivid parts of a personality. We have strong impressions of his sense of responsibility in 'my mad schemes'; of his imagination of his sister's grief; and of his egocentric tantrum over 'injustice'. However, we are not allowed to connect these parts, except to say that the elements of Walton continue to revolve around the central issue with which he is involved: male ambition and idealism. For the present, Walton seems to be a number of parts, but not the sum of those parts.

Analysis: Frankenstein, pp. 170–171

We can now turn our attention to Victor Frankenstein. In the following passage, he is close to completing the task he promised to undertake: the creation of a mate for the daemon. He thinks about the consequences of this work:

> Even if they were to leave Europe, and inhabit the deserts of the new world, yet one of the first results of those sympathies for which the

daemon thirsted would be children, and a race of devils would be propagated upon the earth, who might make the very existence of the species of man a condition precarious and full of terror. Had I a right, for my own benefit, to inflict this curse upon everlasting generations? I had before been moved by the sophisms of the being I had created; I had been struck senseless by his fiendish threats: but now, for the first time, the wickedness of my promise burst upon me; I shuddered to think that future ages might curse me as their pest, whose selfishness had not hesitated to buy its own peace at the price, perhaps, of the existence of the whole human race.

I trembled, and my heart failed within me, when, on looking up, I saw, by the light of the moon, the daemon at the casement. A ghastly grin wrinkled his lips as he gazed on me, where I sat fulfilling the task which he had allotted to me. Yes, he had followed me in my travels; he had loitered in forests, hid himself in caves, or taken refuge in wide and desert heaths; and he now came to mark my progress, and claim the fulfilment of my promise.

As I looked on him, his countenance expressed the utmost extent of malice and treachery. I thought with a sensation of madness on my promise of creating another like to him, and trembling with passion, tore to pieces the thing on which I was engaged. The wretch saw me destroy the creature on whose future existence he depended for happiness, and, with a howl of devilish despair and revenge, withdrew.

I left the room, and, locking the door, made a solemn vow in my own heart never to resume my labours; and then, with trembling steps, I sought my own apartment. I was alone; none were near me to dissipate the gloom, and relieve me from the sickening oppression of the most terrible reveries.

Several hours passed, and I remained near my window gazing on the sea; it was almost motionless, for the winds were hushed, and all nature reposed under the eye of the quiet moon. A few fishing vessels alone specked the water, and now and then the gentle breeze wafted the sound of voices as the fishermen called to one another. I felt the silence, although I was hardly conscious of its extreme profundity, until my ear was suddenly arrested by the paddling of oars near the shore, and a person landed close to my house.

In a few minutes after, I heard the creaking of my door, as if some one endeavoured to open it softly. I trembled from head to foot; I felt a presentiment of who it was, and wished to rouse one of the peasants who dwelt in a cottage not far from mine; but I was overcome by the sensation of helplessness, so often felt in frightful dreams, when you in vain endeavour to fly from an impending danger, and was rooted to the spot. (*F* 170–171)

This passage narrates a crucial action by Victor: the destruction of the nearly completed female, breaking his promise to the daemon. This act sets the final phase of the novel in motion. What do we learn of Victor's character, from this account of his action?

First, we can assemble Victor's reasons for destroying the female. The preceding paragraph tells us that he was sitting 'idle', when 'a train of reflection occurred to me, which led me to consider the effects of what I was now doing'. He then imagines the possible disobedience of the female who might 'refuse to comply with a compact made before her creation', and who might 'delight, for its own sake, in murder and wretchedness'. A female might turn from the daemon 'to the superior beauty of man', echoing Milton's Eve in *Paradise Lost*, who finds Adam 'methought less faire, / Less winning soft, less amiablie milde', preferring the superior beauty of her own reflection.[1] Then Victor develops further worries: the two daemons will breed a race, a species that might threaten humanity. On the basis of this 'train of reflection', then, Victor tears to pieces the female he has been making.

This account of Victor's reasoning is both acceptable and full of gaps, at the same time. It is acceptable because the female's character, and her reactions to creator and mate, cannot be predicted; and because the long-term effects of creating a new species are equally impossible to foresee. Victor's thoughts are sufficiently reasonable that we do not immediately reject his logic, then. On the other hand, his reasoning is weak. First because it is unfounded speculation about the future; secondly because Victor contradicts the only consistent account of character in the novel – that of the daemon – and the daemon's solemn promises; thirdly, because Victor brings forward only practical, not moral, grounds for his decision.

It may be objected that Victor does have moral concerns, because he questions his 'right' to complete the female, and castigates the 'selfishness' of doing so to buy his own peace – that these are moral reflections. Let us look at the context of these thoughts more closely. Victor considers the couple breeding. He jumps from this to the assertion that 'a race of devils would be propagated'. What justification has he for this judgement? The daemon has given him none: on the contrary, the daemon declared that '[my] virtues will necessarily arise when I live in communion with an equal. I shall feel the affections of a sensitive being, and become linked to the chain of existence and events' (*F* 150); and further stated that 'I was benevolent; my soul glowed with love and humanity' (*F* 103), suggesting that a benevolent species is a more likely result, than the devil-species Victor fears. Victor attaches his question to this irrational prediction, asking whether he has the 'right' to inflict 'this curse'. It is clear that Victor does not reflect upon the morality of his actions in themselves, but only in relation to their consequences. In other words, he sees nothing wrong in making daemons, as long as they are harmless daemons.

The next quasi-moral reflection in Victor's narrative is the suggestion that it would be 'selfishness' at the expense of the 'whole human race', to comply with the daemon's request. Here, we find an additional reason for suspicion: Victor imagines that 'future ages might curse me as their pest', telling us that this is how 'the wickedness of my promise burst upon me'. Remember, however, Victor's hopes that 'A new species would bless me as its creator', and his anticipation that 'No father could claim the gratitude of his child so completely as I should deserve [a new species's]' (*F* 55). We remember, in short, that Victor failed to consider ethics, and pursued fame and glory, when making the daemon. He does the same again now, but this time in fear of becoming famously hated rather than famously loved! On closer examination, then, Victor's so-called 'moral' qualms turn out to be entangled with his ill-founded speculations, and his concern for his own reputation. His expectations are as ill-founded now as they were when he created the first daemon. Most significantly, however, we have found here – as in the earlier episode – an absence of moral reflection.

Having considered Victor's 'train of reflection', we can now look at the other ideas that seem to fuel his actions. First, we notice the melodramatic and derogatory language with which Frankenstein surrounds the daemon: he 'thirsted' for a mate, 'devils' would be 'propagated' and fill human life with 'terror'; Frankenstein was 'struck senseless' by the daemon's 'fiendish threats'; then, on seeing him, 'a ghastly grin wrinkled his lips' and 'his countenance expressed the utmost extent of malice and treachery'. Each time Victor utters one of these impassioned impressions, we are aware that his perceptions are unreliable. He assumes without evidence that a new race would be 'devils'. He renounces his former sense of the 'promise of virtues' the daemon had 'displayed on the opening of his existence' (*F* 150), and dismisses the daemon's appeal as 'sophisms'. Throughout this passage, in fact, Victor judges the daemon without evidence. For example, it is natural for the daemon to express pleasure on seeing his nearly completed mate, but to Frankenstein his expression is a 'ghastly grin'; and, always quick to interpret the daemon's ugliness as a threat, Victor next declares that 'his countenance expressed the utmost extent of malice and treachery'. In this extract, then, Victor displays an irrational prejudice against the daemon; a prejudice that is re-inforced by looking at him.

His emotions are also described. The terms denoting sensation are noticeable, first because of repetition, and then because they seem to tell a continuous story of their own. First, Victor 'shuddered', then he 'trembled', 'my heart failed within me', and he 'thought with a sensation of madness' before 'trembling with passion'. After destroying the female, he walks to his room 'with trembling steps' and suffers a 'sickening oppression of the most terrible reveries'. When the daemon returns, Victor 'trembled from head to foot' and feels 'a sensation of helplessness' which is likened to feeling 'rooted to the spot' in a nightmare.

The most obvious pattern here is that of repetition: Victor begins by shuddering, then he 'trembles' four times in the space of our short extract. Such a repetition suggests weakness, and the additional details of 'my heart failed', or of trembling 'from head to foot', underline this impression. This impression is misleading, however, for while 'trembling' Victor 'tore to pieces' the female body. How much strength is needed to tear a body apart? Consider also that the body in question is considerably larger and stronger than the norm. So, our first impressions from the 'trembling' motif may be misleading.

There are also three references to the irrational and to illusion: the reference to madness, Victor's 'terrible reveries', and the 'frightful dreams' in which you feel helpless. These are a further suggestive commentary on Victor's character at this crucial moment, but they are introduced by a most questionable phrase: 'I thought with a sensation of madness'. We know that this 'sensation of madness' is the immediate trigger of violence: he tells us as much by continuing 'and trembling . . . tore to pieces' linking thought to action by means of zeugma. There are, however, several other questions. What does the 'sensation of madness' relate to? Does it simply tell us that he was 'mad' (then) to promise making a female? Does it tell us that he is 'driven mad' (now) by realizing what he is doing? Or, does 'a sensation of madness' merely imply that his actions (now) are out of control, are irrational?

In this decisive episode, Victor's emotions are portrayed as violent and irrational, and the emphasis on him 'trembling' does not suggest physical weakness, so much as it suggests a weakness of his personality, being overwhelmed by emotions that issue in violent action as he tears the female apart in a state variously described as 'a sensation of madness' or 'trembling with passion'.

In summary, then, our extract shows the limited range and prejudice of Victor's reasoning as a process of rationalization: his mind, following its 'train of reflection', is merely picking and choosing reasons. He persuades himself that he should not complete the female. His decision is bolstered by seeing the daemon's face, whose expression his prejudice misinterprets. Simultaneously, the extract describes Victor's emotions or sensations. We are told of a kind of fit, in which violent emotions overwhelm him and, in a state without conscious reason or thought, he carries out the decisive act of destruction. Victor's action has nothing to do with right or wrong, and is on the contrary the product of violent emotion, out of his own control.

A similar episode of uncontrollable emotion occurred when Victor first animated the daemon. On that occasion he remarked, 'The different accidents of life are not so changeable as the feelings of human nature', and the suddenness of his revulsion is vividly described, 'the beauty of the dream vanished, and breathless horror and disgust filled my heart'. On that occasion, Victor's reaction was also beyond his control: 'Unable to endure the aspect of the being I had created' (all *F* 58). At both of these crisis moments in Victor's story, he is overpowered by a fit of emotion that sends him out of control and triggers unpredictable actions. Indeed, one of the most surprising features of the extract we have analysed in detail is the lack of connection between Victor's 'train of reflection' – the thin covering of rationalization with which his mind is engaged – and the 'sensation of madness' under the influence of which he acts. What we have found, then, is a character of limited and unreliable intellect, no ethical perception, strong prejudices, and subject to sudden overwhelming emotional states which lead him to act unpredictably. In both of his crises, Victor's actions have also been inconsistent (deserting the creature he laboured to create; destroying the female he had promised to make). In the simplest terms, we know why Victor does what he does: it is because he is in a passionate or 'mad' emotional state. On the other hand, this tells us no more about Victor's psychology than his own enigmatic observation: 'The different accidents of life are not so changeable as the feelings of human nature' (*F* 58). We still ask, what motives, what fears and desires drive Victor's actions?

This is the point at which analysing Frankenstein's character becomes speculative. There are several suggestive elements in the 'train of reflection' leading up to the moment of action. We can suggest that Victor fears women; that he has a horror of children; that the idea of birth is traumatic to him; that he loves himself and so cannot tolerate a female; that he cannot bear to be blamed by future generations; that he cannot endure the daemon's ugliness, which drives him mad. All these suggestions are both hinted in the text and find support from elsewhere. For example, here Victor reflects that the female may be disobedient. Later, he seems willfully to misinterpret the daemon's threat and so facilitate the murder of Elizabeth; while in the earlier episode his flight from the daemon is followed by a gruesome dream of Elizabeth transformed into his mother's corpse in his arms: clearly a deep-seated fear of the female! Here, he seems frightened by the potential for children, and we remember that he almost failed to narrate his own birth – perhaps an aversion to the thought of reproduction? Here, Victor 'shudders' at the possible judgement of humanity, and we remember his earlier pursuit of fame: even as a child he contemplated 'what glory would attend the discovery' he sought to make – is his character nothing but vainglory? Finally, here he sees 'malice and treachery' in the daemon's expression and 'a ghastly grin'; earlier, he was 'Unable to endure the aspect' of the daemon: does this revulsion drive Victor, and if so, why is it so violent?

These speculations are only some of those canvassed by different critics, who have developed a number of viable theories concerning Victor's psychology. However, they remain theories. All of them, as sub-text, contribute to a richness of suggestion in *Frankenstein* as a whole; but the author does not tell us the relative importance, or the validity, of these theories. So we are left with the impression that Victor Frankenstein is at the mercy of deep and disturbing motivations; but we cannot be sure which suggested psychological drives are really present. In other words, despite a context exceptionally rich in suggestion, we are unable to 'join the dots' and so 'understand' Victor's character.

This elusiveness of character is reminiscent of our fragmentary conclusions concerning Walton. Again, we find that the character consists of a number of strong impressions, a succession of moods or states, vividly described; but the author is reticent about whether these form a causal chain. Having looked at Victor Frankenstein's reason and emotion, we are left wondering why his reasoning is so weak, and his emotion so strong. This may explain why many readers find Victor so irritating, but we should also appreciate the unpredictable, 'momentary' effect Shelley achieves by refusing to connect the different elements of Victor's and Walton's characters.

Considered as individuals, then, both Walton and Frankenstein remain perplexing. They do not yield an understanding of psychological or emotional causality. How else, then, can we look at these two men? First, we can try assembling them as parts of a composite, a type of character built by both of them together. Then, we should consider how their admittedly dislocated thoughts and actions contribute to the novel as a whole.

It is comparatively easy to join Frankenstein and Walton together in our minds, to build a composite 'type' of ambitious, idealistic man. Similarities between their circumstances and experiences are many. For example, both of them pass through phases of absurd enthusiasm early in their development: there were Walton's poetic ambition, fired by his belief that he might equal Homer and Shakespeare (!); and Frankenstein's period of dedication to Agrippa, Paracelsus and Albertus Magnus, when he attempted 'the raising of ghosts and devils' and was 'guided by an ardent imagination and childish reasoning'

(*F* 42). Similarly, Frankenstein anticipates being blessed as the 'creator and source' of a 'new species' and yearns to be the one to 'unfold to the world the deepest mysteries of creation' (*F* 55, 49), while Walton anticipates conferring an 'inestimable benefit ... on all mankind to the last generation' (*F* 16). Also, Walton disregards his father's 'dying injunction' (*F* 16) and ignores his sister's opinion, while Frankenstein cuts himself off from his family despite knowing how his silence 'disquieted them' (*F* 56). These and many other characteristics of idealism, hubris and so on are shared between Walton and Frankenstein, so that the picture of a 'type' of ambitious male is built up by the two figures together.

There are also significant differences between Walton and Frankenstein, particularly in their circumstances. Critics have made much of the fact that Frankenstein laboured in isolation, while Walton was necessarily involved with others (the crew) in his great enterprise. They suggest that Shelley wrote an allegory proving that it is vital to work in co-operation with others, which Frankenstein demonstrably failed to do; or proving Percy Shelley's astonishing claim from the 1818 Preface, that *Frankenstein* was written for 'the exhibition of the amiableness of domestic affection' (*F* 12).

Of the two men, Frankenstein makes the more grandiose romantic claims. He asserts that 'This ice is not made of such stuff as your hearts may be; it is mutable, and cannot withstand you, if you say that it shall not', and persuades others, briefly, that 'these vast mountains of ice are molehills, which will vanish' (*F* 216–217). Walton, on the other hand, cannot maintain such beliefs, and acknowledges that he 'cannot withstand' the crew's demands for a return home and 'must return'. Frankenstein's response is to claim that his purpose is 'assigned to me by Heaven' and to mention 'the spirits who assist my vengeance', whereupon he attempts to rise, and fails (*F* 219). This may be dramatic and heroic on the part of Frankenstein; but the contrast with Walton's realism highlights how stupid it is. Frankenstein's duty has not been 'assigned by Heaven' at all – it is the result of his own disastrous past actions; and the reader knows that the 'spirits who assist my vengeance' are no other than the daemon himself, leaving food for his pursuer to keep him alive. In short, Frankenstein becomes foolishly superstitious, and Walton's more rational perception acts as a foil to set off Victor's madness in the final scenes. Certainly, the conjunction of Walton and Frankenstein at the end of the story, treats us to two different versions of male ambition and two different outcomes that highlight the characteristics of both.

We can conclude, then, that Walton's and Frankenstein's characters contribute, together, to Shelley's critique of male ambition: all the egoism, delusions of grandeur and pursuit of glory of which these two characters are guilty, fill out our understanding of a gendered type. Such men's moods and errors are demonstrated by Victor and Walton at different times, in a manner that can be called 'composite' characterization.

It is worth noting how subtly Shelley enables an element of one character to reinforce another, so that where we might be uncertain in our interpretation of either man, considering them together gives us more confidence that we understand their 'type'. For example, we noticed the possible *double-entendre* of Walton's desire to 'discover the wondrous power which attracts the needle' (*F* 15), but we are not sure that Shelley intends this image as a deliberate innuendo. When, 25 pages later, we read of Victor's 'fervent longing to penetrate the secrets of nature', and of how science had 'partially unveiled' nature's face but 'her immortal lineaments were still a wonder and a mystery' so he could not 'enter the citadel', but some men had 'penetrated deeper', and so on (all from *F* 41): when we read the dense use of sexually charged imagery, describing Frankenstein's ambitious drives, we find ourselves ascribing the sexual motive to both men, confident that Mary Shelley intends us to interpret her writing in this way. The 'composite' characterization therefore suggests the generalization that all ambitious men are motivated by a sexual drive.

How do Walton and Frankenstein contribute to the novel as a whole? We noticed that Walton is perplexingly changeable in mood, including extreme and opposed attitudes within the extract we analysed, and without explanation of how these different 'states' of mind relate to each other. Then, we noticed that Frankenstein's mind produces weak and prejudiced reasoning, while his actions seem to be triggered by an unrelated and sudden emotional state. In short, both characters are unpredictable, and both demonstrate the weakness of human reason, in contrast to the power of emotional drives. At the same time, both demonstrate how difficult it is to understand what pushes people to act in the way they do. Together, Walton and Frankenstein suggest that people are unpredictable, tossed about by obscure needs, their reasoning faculties limping far behind, and impossible finally to understand. The overall effect is to isolate the continuous rhetoric of idealism and individualism with which these two men indulge themselves, and to highlight the absurdity of such rhetoric, which is repeatedly undercut by compulsive actions, the result of lower – but still suggested rather than defined – emotional drives.

Analysis: The Daemon, pp. 136–137

We now turn to consider the daemon's character. The extract we have chosen is the final part of his interview with old Mr DeLacey, when he attempts to reveal himself to the family:

> 'Excellent man! I thank you and accept your generous offer. You raise me from the dust by this kindness; and I trust that, by your aid, I shall not be driven from the society and sympathy of your fellow-creatures.'
>
> 'Heaven forbid! Even if you were really criminal, for that can only drive you to desperation, and not instigate you to virtue. I also am unfortunate; I and my family have been condemned, although innocent; judge, therefore, if I do not feel for your misfortunes.'
>
> 'How can I thank you, my best and only benefactor? From your lips first have I heard the voice of kindness directed towards me; I shall be forever grateful; and your present humanity assures me of success with those friends whom I am on the point of meeting.'
>
> 'May I know the names and residence of those friends?'
>
> I paused. This, I thought, was the moment of decision, which was to rob me of, or bestow happiness on me forever. I struggled vainly for firmness sufficient to answer him, but the effort destroyed all my remaining strength; I sank on the chair and sobbed aloud. At that moment I heard the steps of my younger protectors. I had not a moment to lose, but seizing the hand of the old man, I cried, 'Now is the time! Save and protect me! You and your family are the friends whom I seek. Do not you desert me in the hour of trial!'
>
> 'Great God!' exclaimed the old man, 'who are you?'

At that instant the cottage door was opened, and Felix, Safie and Agatha entered. Who can describe their horror and consternation on beholding me? Agatha fainted, and Safie, unable to attend to her friend, rushed out of the cottage. Felix darted forward, and with supernatural force tore me from his father, to whose knees I clung: in a transport of fury, he dashed me to the ground and struck me violently with a stick. I could have torn him limb from limb, as the lion rends the antelope. But my heart sunk within me as with bitter sickness, and I refrained. I saw him on the point of repeating his blow, when, overcome by pain and anguish, I quitted the cottage, and in the general tumult escaped unperceived to my hovel.   (*F* 136–137)

This passage relates an emotional crisis which is also a turning point in the daemon's story. Up until his interview with old De Lacey, the daemon has been learning: he has learned to speak and to understand, and he has learned to read. He finally resolves to approach the blind man, hoping to forge a relationship with human beings. After this interview, he burns the cottage, and proceeds to murder William, frame Justine and confront Frankenstein. In other words, this crisis initiates the series of destructive events that are sustained throughout the rest of the novel. How is the daemon's character presented in this crisis?

First, this is a highly charged scene, and the daemon's diction expresses the tension he feels at this juncture. Not only does he use grand and absolute terms in his dialogue with old Mr De Lacey – such language as 'Excellent', 'you raise me from the dust', 'my best and only benefactor' and 'Do not you desert me in the hour of trial!' – but he also describes his own emotions as extreme: he 'struggled vainly for firmness' but the effort was beyond him and he 'sank on the chair and sobbed aloud'. His emotions are so powerful because he recognizes this moment as crucial: it will 'rob me of, or bestow happiness on me forever'.

The daemon's speech remains rhetorically fine. His image 'You raise me from the dust' is striking, and the periods of the remainder of that sentence provide two pauses followed by a fluent phrase, a rhythmically satisfying structure. His second speech is equally well-turned, and we notice that both, although beginning with a heartfelt expression of gratitude, lead to the daemon's purpose: that he will 'not be driven from' human beings, and that he seeks 'success' with those he is about to meet. In short, the daemon is again presented with strong persuasive powers, and a clear purpose. His speeches and actions all contribute to achieving his purpose. The only other element that appears before the young people return is the daemon's lack of confidence. Even with the old man's encouraging words, and his success so far, the daemon remains fearful of rejection – for this is the moment that could 'rob me of . . . happiness . . . forever'.

The final paragraph of the extract narrates the disastrous action with which the scene ends, and briefly tells us of the daemon's emotions. He explains that 'my heart sunk within me as with a bitter sickness' and that he was 'overcome by pain and anguish'. These two states of feeling explain, respectively, why he did not fight Felix then and there (he 'could have torn him limb from limb'), and why he ran away.

Our extract, then, shows the daemon as a consistent and logical figure engaged in the crucial attempt to which his life so far has led him. He has argued throughout that acceptance or rejection from other beings was the deciding factor in his character and life. We remember him explaining to Frankenstein: 'misery made me a fiend. Make me happy, and I shall again be virtuous' (*F* 103). We are therefore not surprised that he expresses his gratitude for the old man's kind words in grandiose language, or that he fears rejection so much that this paralyses him; nor are we surprised that rejection brings 'bitter sickness' and 'anguish', so that he withdraws rather than fight. In short, everything in the words, emotions and behaviour of the daemon emphasizes the central and supreme importance of acceptance or rejection by others. We could not say the same of the changeable Walton, or of the rationalizing Victor, with his unpredictable fits. So, the daemon is presented in a different manner from the other two main narrators, as a consistent personality whose character is never mysterious.

In the present scene, then, the daemon's character is developed exactly as we would expect. His emotion on being rejected is evocatively described, providing a clear emotional centre and a strong sympathetic appeal. Consequently, we accord him a more natural and direct response than we can give Walton or Frankenstein, in whose company we are often frustrated, irritated, disappointed and mystified. In our extract there is only one reminder of the other strand in

the daemon's character – his threat – when he states that he could have
torn Felix 'limb from limb, as the lion rends the antelope'; but in our
passage this aspect is muted as he refrains from using his power.

So, Shelley uses a different means of characterization for the
daemon. This enables us to respond to him more strongly than we
do to either of the other narrators. There is, however, another side to
this simplicity of character. We have said that everything about the
daemon in this scene highlights the one idea that is central to his life:
that affection and acceptance will make him good, and rejection will
make him evil. We remember also the single-mindedness of his appeal
to Frankenstein, which we analysed in Chapter 1. In short, everything
the daemon says, everything that happens to him, and everything he
does throughout the novel supports his argument that love or rejection are of paramount importance in life. So, we may sense that he is
a figure whose role is to prove a point: he embodies a powerful argument, and an explicit emotional appeal. He is not, however, a character
created in the naturalistic mode.

This point may also help to explain why the daemon affects readers
so powerfully. When we understand that we are not so much responding to a person, as to the embodiment of a powerful idea, and that our
emotions are awakened by an archetypal appeal to sympathy for the
lonely, then we can see how the daemon has been created as a vehicle for these forces in the novel. His character therefore has a peculiar
and ambivalent effect. First, by virtue of his contrast with Walton and
Frankenstein, he impresses us as more 'present' and more concrete than
they are. Then, by virtue of his singleness of purpose and idea, and by
virtue of the sympathy he awakens in us, he impresses us as a mythic
figure, a sort of archetype and therefore larger than life.

We should not leave the daemon without mentioning his possible
significance as a 'dark' or unconscious aspect of Frankenstein himself.
This suggestion has been widely canvassed by critics, who have developed psychoanalytical theories, explaining either Frankenstein or Mary
Shelley by this means. Several features suggest that Frankenstein and
the daemon are, as it were, two warring 'sides' of a single psyche. For
example, when the daemon approaches on the *mer de glace*, we may
notice how Frankenstein 'was troubled: a mist came over my eyes, and
I felt a faintness seize me' (*F* 101), and connect this with the dreamlike

dominance of the moon over the sea, and Frankenstein's 'helplessness, so often felt in frightful dreams' (*F* 172), when the daemon visits on Orkney. Both of these occasions suggest a dreamlike participation of Frankenstein's unconscious. Or, we may notice how Frankenstein's and the daemon's lives are bound together, from the daemon's assertion that they are 'bound by ties only dissoluble by the annihilation of one of us' (*F* 102) to the point when the daemon intones over Frankenstein's corpse: 'in his murder my crimes are consummated; the miserable series of my being is wound to its close!' (*F* 221). We already noted that Frankenstein's character is rich in suggestions and hints about his psychology, but that these hints are all more or less uncertain. The same is true of the character-pairing, light and dark or conscious and unconscious, between Frankenstein and the daemon: there is a great deal of suggestion regarding some form of duality between them, in the novel; but, as with Frankenstein's motivation, Shelley does not seem to accord one explicit significance to these suggestions.[2]

One of the most suggestive moments occurs when Frankenstein wonders whether the daemon can be seen 'nearly in the light of my own vampire, my own spirit let loose from the grave, and forced to destroy all that was dear to me' (*F* 78). This is a deeply disturbing suggestion, one of many hints that Frankenstein is a disturbed and abnormal personality. However, there is still no clear one answer, as to why Frankenstein's 'own spirit' would wish to 'destroy all that was dear to me'. We will return to some of these vexed questions later in this chapter.

Analysis: Clerval, Elizabeth and Alphonse Frankenstein

For now, we turn our attention to the second rank of characters, beginning with Clerval. He is described during Frankenstein's account of his childhood:

> Meanwhile Clerval occupied himself, so to speak, with the moral relations of things. The busy stage of life, the virtues of heroes, and the actions of men were his theme; and his hope and his dream was to become one among those whose names are recorded in story, as the

gallant and adventurous benefactors of our species. The saintly soul of
Elizabeth shone like a shrine-dedicated lamp in our peaceful home. Her
sympathy was ours; her smile, her soft voice, the sweet glance of her
celestial eyes, were ever there to bless and animate us. She was the living
spirit of love to soften and attract: I might have become sullen in my
study, rough through the ardour of my nature, but that she was there to
subdue me to a semblance of her own gentleness. And Clerval – could
aught ill entrench on the noble spirit of Clerval – yet he might not
have been so perfectly humane, so thoughtful in his generosity – so full
of kindness and tenderness amidst his passion for adventurous exploit,
had she not unfolded to him the real loveliness of beneficence, and made
the doing good the end and aim of his soaring ambition.   (*F* 39–40)

In the novel as a whole, Clerval fulfils the role of Frankenstein's friend.
He nurses Victor back to health after his 'nervous collapse'; they
study oriental languages together at Ingolstadt; they travel together to
England and Scotland. Throughout these events Clerval is friendly,
loyal and sympathetic, as his role of best friend demands. Shelley
does, however, ascribe a certain amount of separate individuality to
Clerval.

Let us look at the key terms associated with Clerval in this passage.
His interests are first described as focusing on the 'moral relations of
things. The busy stage of life . . .'. These phrases are clearly chosen
to distinguish Clerval from Victor himself, who was interested in 'the
metaphysical, or in its highest sense, the physical secrets of the world'.
When we hear of the 'moral relations of things', then, we refer back
to the preceding paragraph, where Victor admitted his lack of interest
in 'governments' or 'politics' and 'states', and we realize that the 'moral
relations of things' must refer to the ways in which states are governed –
an impression that is confirmed by the next phrase, 'the busy stage
of life'. So far, only the word 'stage' indicates any equivocal attitude
towards Clerval's interests: perhaps he sees his life as acting a part, at
the centre of public attention. This hint is then underlined: 'virtues
of heroes' and 'actions of men' are vainglorious phrases of masculine
admiration, and we are then told that Clerval hopes to be admired and
remembered: he hopes to become a character 'recorded in story' whose
attributes are to be 'gallant' and 'adventurous'. We already notice from
'stage' and 'story' the fantasy overtones of Clerval's ambition; while

from 'heroes', 'men', 'gallant' and 'adventurous', we recognize that he is telling himself a particularly masculine fairy tale about his future.

The paragraph then changes direction: in contrast to both Victor and Clerval, Elizabeth arrives with a dense cluster of religious terms. Her saintly nature is then said to soften the boys' rougher characters. With regard to Clerval, he might have been less 'humane', 'thoughtful' and 'full of kindness and tenderness' had it not been for Elizabeth. But for her influence, Clerval might have had only a 'passion for adventurous exploit' and 'soaring ambition' without the concomitant aim of 'doing good'. The change of focus from Clerval to Elizabeth, in the middle of this paragraph, completely alters the emphasis. Suddenly, we are reading words of religious gentleness, and our final description of Clerval associates him with language such as 'kindness' and 'tenderness', and 'doing good the end and aim' of his character. As a result, we may almost miss the plain meaning of Victor's remarks, which is overshadowed by the impact of Elizabeth's saintliness. Clerval, without Elizabeth, would have displayed 'soaring ambition' and a 'passion for adventurous exploit', without any moral purpose – without the aim of 'doing good' that Elizabeth taught him. We should notice the hint: what happens to an amoral man of 'soaring ambition'? The answer is, he becomes a warlord, a tyrant, a bandit, or a ruthless and crooked accumulator of wealth.

The characterization of Clerval, then, is straightforward. He is interested in 'adventurous exploits', is ambitious and focuses on 'the busy stage of life'. When he turns up at Ingolstadt, his plan is to study the Orient as 'affording scope for his spirit of enterprise' and as leading to 'no inglorious career' (*F* 70). This is the vocabulary of Imperialist expansion and exploitation: clearly Clerval has not changed. His natural character has its roughness moderated by the influence of Elizabeth. Otherwise, in the novel, Clerval simply plays the role of Victor's best friend.

What is the purpose of Clerval's simple characterization, then? Noticing how he is introduced, his interests distinct from Victor's, yet both of their natures softened by the influence of Elizabeth, it is as if their conjunction makes up an ideal and complete group: as Frankenstein remarks, 'I feel exquisite pleasure in dwelling on the recollections of childhood' (*F* 40). Victor's picture of those innocent years has unmistakable overtones of Eden. Ostensibly, this passage proposes a balance between Victor's and Clerval's masculine qualities, and Elizabeth's feminine ones, as an ideal. Many critics believe that Mary Shelley is deeply critical of Elizabeth's role, however. For Betty T. Bennett, for example, Elizabeth's privileged position 'exacts the heavy toll of a passivity that reflects her position in the family and in society'.[3] However we view Elizabeth's position, Clerval still represents a type of male ambition different from both the scientific fascinations of Frankenstein and the explorer's ambitions of Walton. Shelley's catalogue of overreaching males would have been less complete without the political and imperialist ambitions ascribed to Clerval.

Clerval, then, seems to be a figure who is present in the story to fulfil two clear purposes: first, to play the role of Frankenstein's friend; and secondly, to embody the political version of masculine ambition, in Mary Shelley's critique of male hubris. We already remarked, of the daemon, that every aspect of his character contributes to the power of his argument and that this gives him a slightly larger-than-life, or archetypal quality, rather than a naturalistic personality. Similarly, Clerval's characterization emphasizes one point in the novel's themes, and he is therefore rather a two-dimensional figure. Unlike the daemon, however, Clerval does not appeal to our emotions. Consequently, he remains a rather cardboard figure: we can say that Clerval's significance, his role in the novel's ideas, is more striking than his personality. We now turn to the other secondary characters: Elizabeth Lavenza and Frankenstein's father.

We have already made some comments on the characterization of Elizabeth Lavenza. In the paragraph concerning Clerval, her appearance transforms the language: her 'saintly soul' is like a 'shrine-dedicated lamp' and her 'celestial' eyes were there to 'bless' because she was the 'living spirit of love' revealing the 'loveliness of beneficence'. This is a remarkable cluster of neo-religious terms, but is not unusual among the descriptions of Elizabeth, whose angelic appearance ('fairer than a pictured cherub', for example [*F* 36]) and behaviour are consistent. She is repeatedly associated with 'loveliness', 'soft' and 'sweet', 'gentleness' and 'tenderness' until these terms build up a kind of litany of epithets, surrounding Elizabeth with a holy aura, and beginning with her first appearance in the story:

Among these there was one which attracted my mother far above all the rest. She appeared of a different stock. The four others were dark-eyed, hardy little vagrants; this child was thin, and very fair. Her hair was the brightest living gold, and despite the poverty of her clothing, seemed to set a crown of distinction on her head. Her brow was clear and ample, her blue eyes cloudless, and her lips and the moulding of her face so expressive of sensibility and sweetness that none could behold her without looking on her as of a distinct species, a being heaven-sent, and bearing a celestial stamp in all her features.   (*F* 36)

This passage not only initiates the practice of encircling Elizabeth's character with heavenly diction, but it also hints at two questionable elements in the judgement of her character. First, the idea that Elizabeth is from 'different stock' and the contrast between her fairness and the dark colouring of the peasant children, who were 'hardy little vagrants', introduces a snobbery of birth gross enough for feudal times, underlined by the idea that she represents 'a distinct species'. Secondly, Elizabeth's hair is like 'living gold' and is set on her head like 'a crown of distinction' – similes which imply a confusion between beauty and wealth in somebody's mind.

In whose mind are these confusions? The passage narrates Mrs Frankenstein's meeting with the peasant family, and purports to tell of her response to the exceptional child. On the other hand, Victor accompanied his mother, and must be reporting his own reactions. In any event, the prejudices are quickly reinforced. The girl is, in fact, from a 'different stock' being the daughter of a 'nobleman' and therefore not just metaphorically, but actually, 'a garden rose among dark-leaved brambles': in this manner the snobbery of the golden-haired, dare we say it – Aryan – superior race, is reinforced. Then, Mrs Frankenstein gives Elizabeth as 'a pretty present for my Victor', confirming the perception of her as an object of trade, for in Victor's mind 'all praises bestowed on her I received as made to a possession of my own'.

We should note that the passage we are studying comes from the 1831 text. The 1818 version of *Frankenstein* has no visit to a peasant's cottage, no foster-siblings; and Victor's mother does not give him a 'pretty present'. The original version has Elizabeth as Victor's first cousin, daughter of Alphonse Frankenstein's sister and an Italian gentleman, brought to live with them when Victor is four years old. However, as in the 1831 version, Elizabeth is 'the most beautiful child [Mrs Frankenstein] had ever seen', Victor 'loved to tend on her, as I should on a favourite animal', and 'Every one adored Elizabeth'. The 1818 version also includes Mrs Frankenstein's intention 'to consider Elizabeth as my future wife' (*F* 229). Mary Shelley seems to have intensified the suggestions of snobbery and commercial thinking, as well as Elizabeth's holy aura, in 1831; but they were already present in 1818.

These elements of prejudice and of social and commercial arrogance cannot be in question: in Chapter 1 we remarked that Frankenstein's family pride is the first characteristic of his narrative, and the story of their visit to the peasant cot only adds to our sense that Victor was brought up in the attitudes of a patrician class. Therefore, part of Elizabeth's role in the novel is to be the unwitting object of prejudices of which Mary Shelley is critical. On the other hand, Elizabeth does represent positive values in the novel.

Elizabeth is unfailingly good, loyal, loving, tender and considerate: by the time of her death she has demonstrated that she is the angel she originally appeared to be. Towards the end of the story, life and suffering have affected her, taking away 'some of that heavenly vivacity that had before charmed me' as Victor remarks; but she still has 'gentleness' and 'soft looks of compassion' which in his opinion make her a more suitable companion for him, now that he has become miserable. Leaving aside the persistent egoism of Victor's point of view, we still recognize that Elizabeth presents the standard of long-suffering goodness. Elizabeth's other representative role in the novel is her contribution to the three-person structure of their childhood society. Here is Victor's description of their ideal relationship:

> ... the diversity and contrast that subsisted in our characters drew us nearer together. Elizabeth was of a calmer and more concentrated disposition; but, with all my ardour, I was capable of a more intense application, and was more deeply smitten with the thirst for knowledge. She busied herself with following the aerial creations of the poets; and in the majestic and wondrous scenes which surrounded our Swiss home – the sublime shapes of the mountains; the changes of the seasons;

tempest and calm; the silence of winter, and the life and turbulence of our Alpine summers – she found ample scope for admiration and delight. While my companion contemplated with a serious and satisfied spirit the magnificent appearances of things, I delighted in investigating their causes. (*F* 38)

Poetry and nature are the benchmarks of Elizabeth's character in this account, then. She contemplates the beauties of landscape, and changes of season and weather, which give her 'ample scope' for 'admiration and delight'. These two words describe a passive or receptive response to natural wonders, and Shelley's text makes a clear distinction between Elizabeth who 'contemplated' and Victor who is actively 'investigating' nature. Elizabeth remains 'satisfied' to appreciate her surroundings. Victor, on the other hand, is active, and his scientific studies take the form of interference in nature. Clearly, Elizabeth's attitude to the world around her is healthier than Victor's; and Shelley hints here again that a balance between the two attitudes might produce an ideal 'harmony' like that Victor claims for their relationship. Further, as Shelley here and elsewhere identifies Victor's desire to discover the secrets of nature, with his masculinity, we can suppose that Elizabeth's non-invasive response to the natural world is advanced as a feminine characteristic. When, after their wedding, Elizabeth and Victor are drifting towards Evian, Elizabeth displays just this quality in order to soothe Victor's melancholy fears (see *F* 197, 'Be happy, my dear Victor . . .' etc.). This is clearly the function of a wife who seeks her husband's happiness, and Elizabeth here ministers to her man in the best way possible, by opening his mind to passive contemplation of natural beauty.

Elizabeth, then, performs two functions in the novel. First, she is the object of those snobberies and prejudices concerning gender, birth, rank and race, which we find at the beginning of Victor's narrative. This aspect of her function – that she is treated in a grossly stereotyping manner as a sort of combined treasure, servant, decoration and comforter, by the Frankensteins – is sustained throughout. Elizabeth makes no complaint: the reader is more sensitive on her account than she is herself. For example, we are shocked at Victor's self-centred rebuke to her after their wedding: 'Ah! if you knew what I have suffered, and what I may yet endure, you would endeavour to let me taste the quiet and freedom from despair that this one day at least permits me to enjoy' (*F* 197). Elizabeth does not take offence, but meekly tries to cheer up her whingeing husband.

Elizabeth's other function is to represent a standard of goodness, in the form of gentleness, and loyal and forgiving love, from which she never deviates. This goodness is described as exerting a moderating and saving influence upon both Victor and Clerval, who became less 'sullen' and 'rough' and more 'humane' and 'thoughtful' (all from *F* 40) than their merely masculine natures would have allowed. We may therefore suggest two possible interpretations: first, that Elizabeth represents a quality of femininity that Shelley proposes as a necessary antidote to male ambitions; or, secondly, that Elizabeth is a victim of her impotent feminine role, unable, despite her qualities, to avert Victor's masculine disaster. This aspect of Elizabeth's significance is underlined when Victor, in Ingolstadt, cuts himself off from her influence. He acknowledges that 'my eyes were insensible to the charms of nature' and that 'I wished, as it were, to procrastinate all that related to my feelings of affection' (*F* 56) while he was creating and animating the daemon. He describes himself as oblivious to and cut off from both the beauties of nature and 'domestic affections', and with hindsight concludes that any such activity is 'certainly unlawful, that is to say, not befitting the human mind' (*F* 56).

Elizabeth performs her two functions in the novel, almost without alteration: hers is, like Clerval's, a straightforward characterization where the qualities she represents in the novel are Shelley's purpose, and there is an absence of complexity in her personality. The only occasion when Elizabeth steps outside these two functions is during the farewell scene with Justine and in conversation with Victor afterwards. At the height of that miscarriage of justice, Elizabeth exclaims, 'I wish . . . that I were to die with you; I cannot live in this world of misery' (*F* 89). After Justine's execution, she gives a remarkable account of how she has re-assessed the world:

> I no longer see the world and its works as they before appeared to me. Before, I looked upon the accounts of vice and injustice, that I read in books or heard from others as tales of ancient days or imaginary

evils; at least they were remote and more familiar to reason than to the imagination; but now misery has come home, and men appear to me as monsters thirsting for each other's blood . . . .

. . . Alas! Victor, when falsehood can look so like the truth, who can assure themselves of certain happiness? I feel as if I were walking on the edge of a precipice, towards which thousands are crowding, and endeavouring to plunge me into the abyss. (*F* 95–96)

There is only one other passage in *Frankenstein* to equal the perspicacity Elizabeth shows here: that in which the daemon describes the 'strange system of human society' (*F* 122). Here, for once, Elizabeth expresses her own feelings in a natural and outraged criticism of the world. The horror and anger contained in 'men appear to me as monsters thirsting for each other's blood' is not spoken in Elizabeth's usual submissive tone. She is only briefly out of role, however, and quickly returns to her proper feminine function, soothing Victor. In summary, apart from the above brief abandonment of her role, Elizabeth fulfils her roles in the book, rather than being created as an individual or 'real' person.

We will complete our survey of characterization in *Frankenstein* with a brief look at Victor's father. In the following extract, he discusses the marriage between Victor and Elizabeth:

The expression of your sentiments of this subject, my dear Victor, gives me more pleasure than I have for some time experienced. If you feel thus, we shall assuredly be happy, however present events may cast a gloom over us. But it is this gloom which appears to have taken so strong a hold of your mind, that I wish to dissipate. Tell me, therefore, whether you object to an immediate solemnization of the marriage. We have been unfortunate, and recent events have drawn us from that everyday tranquillity befitting my years and infirmities. You are younger; yet I do not suppose, possessed as you are of a competent fortune, that an early marriage would at all interfere with any future plans of honour and utility that you may have formed. Do not suppose, however, that I wish to dictate happiness to you, or that a delay on your part would cause me any serious uneasiness. Interpret my words with candour and answer me, I conjure you, with confidence and sincerity. (*F* 156–157)

Reading this speech, we hear a different voice from Victor Frankenstein's narrative. The elder Frankenstein speaks in a formal and ponderous manner, his sentences are rather massively constructed, and he
expresses his thoughts in careful academic language. So, for example,
there is a vein of circumlocution as Victor's love for Elizabeth is called
'your sentiments of this subject'; the deaths of William and Justine are
'present events'; a quick wedding is 'an immediate solemnisation'; and
so on. Then, the speaker likes his terms to come in pairs. So there
are 'years and infirmities', 'honour and utility' and 'confidence and
sincerity'.

Each of the elder Frankenstein's sentences performs a clear task.
Look, for example, at his second sentence. The structure is logical,
'If . . . , we shall . . . , however . . . '. This states the speaker's confidence
that the young couple's love will vanquish temporary sadness. Sentence
3 takes up the word 'gloom' from the end of sentence 2, and states
the speaker's wish to 'dissipate' that gloom. Sentence 4 follows with
'therefore', logically supposing that the lovers' marriage might 'dissipate' the gloom. We are impressed by the clearly argued reasoning of
this speaker, as each sentence deals with an aspect of the circumstances.
Before the speech is over, Alphonse Frankenstein has composed two
sentences, one in favour of each choice, that is to say, an immediate or
a delayed wedding. This provides his speech with a balanced conclusion, leaving his son free to return either answer, only conjuring him
to speak with 'sincerity'.

This is a voice of wisdom, authority and justice, and it is the
voice with which the elder Frankenstein consistently speaks. There
is one moment when Victor criticizes his father – when he dismisses
Cornelius Agrippa's works as 'sad trash' (*F* 40) and Victor speculates
that a fuller response at that stage might have saved him from his
later errors. Otherwise, Alphonse is a standard of liberality, justice,
good judgement and balanced consideration, until his death, and we
hear those qualities in his slightly ponderous voice whenever he speaks.
Frankenstein *père* is two-dimensional and representative in the novel,
rather than complex and human: he is there to embody authority,
wisdom and justice.

As in the case of Elizabeth, our thoughts about the elder Frankenstein concern the fate of the qualities he represents, rather than his

fate as an individual, which adds nothing new to our understanding of him. The extract above exemplifies this point. We have shown how the speech displays Alphonse's justice and scrupulous consideration. Notice, however, our reaction on reading this in context, for the irony of circumstances renders all the old man's care ineffectual. He does not know about his son and the daemon; consequently, his judgement and authority are wasted. In fact, the story of Victor's father is the story of how wisdom, authority and justice become completely irrelevant, unable to counter the challenges Victor has conjured into the world. This is the effect, as, each time we hear the elder Frankenstein speak, his utterance is a little more ignorant and a little less relevant.

We can suggest, at this stage, a comment common to both Elizabeth and Frankenstein *père*. Both of them are characters who represent positive qualities, and who never deviate from their particular virtues. Both their characters tell the story of how these positive qualities fail in the world of the novel. Elizabeth's influence is curtailed by absence and ignored by Victor in his pursuit of 'Natural philosophy'; and she becomes steadily less and less influential, more and more taken for granted, until her murder brings down the curtain. Victor's father has less and less ability to govern the family as the story develops: his authority is progressively brushed aside by events. In short, both Elizabeth and the elder Frankenstein exemplify the defeat of positive or 'good' forces, by the evil Victor has unleashed.

It only remains to add that there is also an element of social satire and criticism in these characterizations. We have remarked that Elizabeth's stereotyped 'feminine' role is implicitly criticized, for her submissiveness simply underlines her role as victim. Equally, we have remarked that Alphonse Frankenstein speaks in a ponderous, academic manner. His 'wisdom and authority' and Elizabeth's 'femininity' are both old-fashioned virtues. One effect of these characters in *Frankenstein* is to demonstrate that such virtues are obsolete. The world is a more dangerous, less calculable place than can be confronted by such out-of-date virtues. This is what Elizabeth seems to realize, but only briefly, on pp. 95–96.

Concluding Discussion

In this chapter, we have considered how the different people in *Frankenstein* are presented to us, or 'characterised'. We have found that there is no single technique of characterization: rather, we have been able to identify three widely different approaches Shelley employs. One approach presents Walton and Victor; another creates the daemon; and a third creates the figures of Clerval, Elizabeth and Frankenstein *père*. The effects achieved by these three different kinds of characterization have also occupied our thoughts.

Walton and Victor Frankenstein

We have commented, variously, that both Walton and Victor are inconsistent, irrational and frustrating personalities. While affected by the 'suspension of disbelief' that allows us to think them real, we find ourselves frequently irritated by them, or even shocked. This comment particularly applies to Victor, whose monstrously egotistical reasoning is often offensive (see, e.g., his assertion that Justine, condemned to death, 'felt not, as I did, such deep and bitter agony' [*F* 89]). We are irritated while reading their narratives, then; but we noticed further and possibly more significant characteristics as well. In particular we noticed their weak reasoning, unpredictable actions, and the richness but inconclusiveness of suggestions about their psychology and motives.

These two characters, we concluded, remain perplexing: we cannot quite understand how they work, and a number of possible but shadowy theories are indicated, tempting us to think they may 'solve' the character. This must be intentional: the author wishes to emphasize how unpredictable, wild and irrational Victor and Walton are; and how many and shadowy might be the psychological sources of their actions. In short, Mary Shelley may be telling us, through the characterization of Victor and of Walton, that we will have to put up with uncertainty in a maze of suggestions, and we will have to do without a single authorial solution. In the case of Victor Frankenstein, most of the speculations about his character take us into the realm of abnormal psychology. Therefore, Shelley's refusal to be explicit, and her refusal to kill off the implicit, contributes to the unsettling overall effect of the novel.

The Daemon

By contrast, Shelley presents the daemon – and he presents himself – with clarity and singleness of purpose. His entire character is devoted to developing a single argument: that the newborn innocent is innately good, and that environmental factors will be all-powerful in determining ultimate character. The daemon puts this point succinctly: 'I was benevolent and good; misery made me a fiend. Make me happy, and I shall again be virtuous' (*F* 103). The daemon's argument turns entirely on the possibilities for love or rejection in life, and he appeals to Victor – and the reader – on the grounds of his isolation, his loneliness. We will say more regarding the daemon's beliefs – in particular his assertion of innate goodness, and his environmental determinism – in later chapters. For the present we are interested in how Mary Shelley has created him.

The effect of this characterization, we have suggested, is to exploit the contrast with Victor and Walton, thus heightening power of the daemon, for both his intellectual clarity and the potency of his emotional appeal. So, the daemon's narrative, which lies structurally at the centre of the novel's framing devices is also the core of the novel by virtue of its narrator's power as a dominant personality. It stands out in terms of both the strength of the argument it hammers home and its pull on the reader's sympathy. We also noticed a paradoxical effect: that the daemon being so single-minded and simple, yet so appealing and powerful, gains a larger-than-life, archetypal quality like that of a representative or allegorical figure.

Clerval, Elizabeth and the Elder Frankenstein

These three characters represent particular qualities, and they play their roles in the novel without deviating from each one's straightforward 'type'. So, Elizabeth is angelic and feminine, and almost her every contribution displays these qualities. The author does not examine her as a person, but rather presents her as an ideal. With Elizabeth, we are therefore reading about one of the novel's contributory ideas, and we are not in the company of a character created with a naturalistic aim. The same is true of Clerval, who represents a third kind of male ambition, and plays the role of Victor's best friend; and Frankenstein's father, who acts as the standard of authority, justice and careful judgement.

Notice that none of these three kinds of characterization creates the impression of an individual's 'reality'. The first kind leaves us full of shadowy disturbances and irrational, unpredictable drives; the second presents a figure of mythic proportions and excessive power; and the third simply uses two-dimensional figures to embody elements of the novel's meaning. In other words, although these characterizations differ from each other, they do have one ingredient in common: they all subject the individual to the structure of the work as a whole. So, we could say that people in *Frankenstein* belong to the story, to an unusual degree. The effect is of people as 'figures' rather than of psychological depth: they play their parts in a world of larger forces, because their individual psychology is less significant than the parts they play in a sort of primal 'game' with the dangers of nature and knowledge.

'Composite' Characterization

In this chapter we have mentioned 'composite' characters, by which we mean the effect when one character's situation or behaviour seems to amplify or reflect another's. This occurs frequently in *Frankenstein*, most particularly between Victor and Walton. It is acknowledged when they meet. Victor says, 'Unhappy man! Do you share my madness? Have you drunk also of the intoxicating draught?' (*F* 29). In this way the similarity of the two men's circumstances becomes the reason for Victor's narrative, and they are tied together. We noticed, in our extract concerning Walton, how the sailors appeal to him, yet Frankenstein answers them. That is one example of what becomes a curious interchangeability between them, which extends also to their baffling contradictions. So, Frankenstein claims that his story will kill Walton's ambition ('let me reveal my tale, and you will dash the cup from your lips!' [*F* 29]); yet, when he has told it, he urges the sailors to the opposite: 'Oh! be men, or be more than men. Be steady to your purposes, and firm as a rock' (*F* 217); while we have shown how Walton changes from acknowledging 'my mad schemes' to castigating the sailors' 'cowardice', five days later.

The 'composite' effect Shelley achieves with Victor and Walton is a result of densely interlocking the two men's characters, so as to provide multiple points of comparison. For example, we have mentioned the theory that Victor's isolation while he makes the daemon is his most significant mistake; pointing out that Walton is saved from disaster because he has to work with others (i.e. the crew) and so his own 'madness' is held in check. This detailed interlocking of the two figures provides Shelley with multiple opportunities to enlarge upon the dangers of male ambition and hubris.

We have suggested that another form of 'composite' is made up of opposites: Victor Frankenstein on one side, and his dark opposite, the daemon, on the other. According to such an interpretation, the daemon might represent repulsive, rejected and denied elements in Frankenstein himself: his own dark side, or unconscious. We have briefly discussed this idea and noted that the text provokes such an interpretation several times. Most of all, this theory gains credence each time either Frankenstein or the daemon asserts that they are indissolubly linked together – assertions that culminate in the daemon's peroration over Frankenstein's corpse: 'in his murder my crimes are consummated; the miserable series of my being is wound to its close' (*F* 221). The implications of this theory point in two directions. First, towards myths or morality tales or even social allegory, in which contexts the concepts of 'light' and 'dark' sides of nature can be developed. Secondly, towards the modern field of psychoanalysis, where the daemon becomes representative of some intolerable guilt or unthinkable desire that must be fled and repressed.[4] We will discuss these issues further in the chapters that follow.

Conclusions to Chapter 2

We have found different types of character, composites, fragmentary figures, and we have responded to the figures in the novel in a variety of different ways. For example, Frankenstein's snobbery and egoism have shocked us; his self-excusing obfuscations have probably irritated us; Elizabeth's dedication has exasperated us, or shaken our belief; and the daemon's narrative has wrenched our sympathy to him. Having examined so much variety, it will be helpful to re-state, in summary form, where we believe analysis of characterization has brought us:

- Some characterizations amplify each other and reflect each other, creating a suggestion of overlap, or *composite characterization* (obviously Frankenstein/Walton; and as character and shadow, Frankenstein/daemon, but also Frankenstein/Walton/ Clerval).
- Other characterizations are *sketchy and idealized* (e.g. Elizabeth, Frankenstein's father).
- The overall effect is of *people as 'figures' rather than of psychological depth*: individual psychology is less important than the part each figure plays in a sort of primal 'game' with the dangers of nature and knowledge.
- In the six main figures Frankenstein/Walton/the daemon/Clerval/ Elizabeth/Frankenstein *père*, we can see that *characterization is made to serve treatment of themes* (e.g., Victor, Walton and Clerval are three types of masculine idealism; the daemon and Elizabeth are two attitudes to predicament; Elizabeth stands for angelic self-denial, and Frankenstein *père* stands for wise authority).

So, the novel *Frankenstein* exists as a whole to which the characters contribute. We will turn our attention to the 'whole' that is *Frankenstein*, in the next three chapters.

Methods of Analysis

We have used the same range of techniques in approaching extracts in this chapter, as in Chapter 1, with the following additions. When analysing character, seek to identify and then consider:

- *The character's thoughts and reasoning.* This focuses on how the character's brain is working; on their opinions and beliefs; and on the patterns of thinking that lead the character to make decisions or reach particular conclusions. When you have identified the character's thoughts and reasoning, consider them sceptically: is the reasoning sound, or flawed? Are the thoughts fair, or prejudiced? You will often find that the character is not thinking clearly at all, and is led by emotion rather than reason. We found this in the cases of both Victor Frankenstein and Walton. When reason is led by emotion or desire, it is called *rationalization*, and typically fabricates excuses for actions the character wants to carry out anyway, or has already impulsively carried out.
- *The character's impulses and emotions.* This focuses on how the character feels at any given moment – whether they are driven by fear, desire, self-love, pride: try to identify the kind and intensity of emotion the character feels, particularly at the moment when they undertake action. In this chapter, for example, we looked at Frankenstein's emotion at the moment when he destroys the nearly completed female. We found this impossible to define in terms of *quality*: 'sensation of madness' and 'trembling with passion' tells us nothing about *what kind of emotion* overwhelms Victor at that moment. On the other hand, we are told of the extreme *quantity* of his emotions. This led us to the conclusion that Victor's character is rich in suggestions which remain inconclusive.
- *Compare the character's reasoning with his/her emotion, and both with his/her actions.* Clearly, it is enlightening to consider whether emotion or intellect is in control, and to see whether thoughts or desires trigger actions (or, the other way around, whether a character's actions reflect their mind, or heart, or neither). At this point you may also consider the *role of experience* in the character's

development: does he or she learn from experience? Does experience change him or her?

These stages of analysis develop your understanding of the character you are studying, from a psychological point of view. In *Frankenstein*, we found a great deal of suggestive psychological detail relating to Victor and Walton; but nothing consistent or conclusive. Some further approaches have also proved useful in this chapter:

- *Study the diction* in which characters are described, or in which they speak: look for repetitions, or for terms that are regularly associated with a particular person. In the case of Victor, for example, the terms 'ardour' and 'ardent' are conspicuous, particularly in the opening chapters. Elizabeth's figure is surrounded by the language of religion, repeatedly emphasizing 'angelic' qualities in her. In the case of Frankenstein *père*, we found his sentences to be particularly strong in logical structure, connections and balance, all emphasizing the quality of justice in his character.
- *Analyse and interpret imagery* also: look at metaphors and similes, as well as motifs that are associated with particular figures. For example, we noticed that Elizabeth is persistently associated with light – remember her shining golden hair, and the simile comparing her to a 'lamp'. We also noticed the simile of a nightmare, used by Victor to explain how the daemon's approach paralyses him, which could be evidence for the idea that the daemon represents a 'dark side' of Frankenstein's own psyche.

Finally, of course, it is important to pull back from the close detail of analysing extracts, and to *consider what part the character plays in the novel as a whole*. This can often lead to thoughts that seem too obvious to be worthwhile. Remember, however, that any comment is a basis on which to build, and is therefore useful. For example, it may seem blindingly obvious to any reader, that Elizabeth is gentle, unselfish, almost too good to be true. This may be obvious, but it provokes the question: why does Shelley make Elizabeth so over-perfect? Answers to this question are far from obvious. Indeed, in this chapter we have suggested two (that her feminine qualities ideally counterbalance Victor and that Elizabeth is a critical satire on the social impotence of women), without being able to decide between them.

Suggested Work

Study the daemon's account of his first days of life, pp. 105–108. Consider the presentation of the daemon as a product of his environment and experiences (some critics make much of Shelley's use of the contemporary theory of the senses). What does this tell us about the outlook on life encouraged by *Frankenstein*?

In the present chapter, we have commented that all elements of the daemon's character support his determinist belief. The daemon ascribes absolute power to love and relationship, or rejection and loneliness, as determining character. In studying pp. 105–108 you will need to consider:

- how far the sense-development and growth of perceptions described by the daemon, contribute to fostering his determinist outlook, and
- what is the status of this version of psychological development, in the philosophy of the novel as a whole.

3

Nature, Society and Science

Nature, Natural Surroundings

This chapter investigates major themes and motifs in *Frankenstein*. Clearly, nature is one of these: the grandeur of nature plays a major role in creating the ambience of the tale; and Victor's search for the 'hidden laws of nature' initiates the story's horrors. We will begin by looking at three short extracts in which nature seems to exert an influence.

Analysis, *p. 38*, pp. 97–98, p. 99

Here is a description of Elizabeth's and Victor's childhood responses to their surroundings:

> . . . She busied herself with following the aerial creations of the poets; and in the majestic and wondrous scenes which surrounded our Swiss home – the sublime shapes of the mountains; the changes of the seasons; tempest and calm; the silence of winter, and the life and turbulence of our Alpine summers – she found ample scope for admiration and delight. While my companion contemplated with a serious and satisfied spirit the magnificent appearances of things, I delighted in investigating their causes. The world was to me a secret which I desired to divine. Curiosity, earnest research to learn the hidden laws of nature, gladness

akin to rapture, as they were unfolded to me, are among the earliest sensations I can remember.   (*F* 38)

Nature is presented as a powerful positive force in this extract, with the adjectives 'majestic', 'wondrous', 'sublime' and 'magnificent'. At the same time, nature is not only pretty; on the contrary, Shelley emphasizes its 'changes' and includes 'tempest and calm'. So, it is all aspects of nature including the wild and violent, that are fit subjects for Elizabeth's 'contemplation', leading her to 'admiration and delight'. In the final part of the paragraph, however, Victor's perspective is described, and nature becomes something else: 'a secret' with 'hidden laws'. This nature inspires Victor's 'desire' and 'curiosity', leading to a 'gladness akin to rapture' when he makes discoveries.

Of course, Shelley is beginning to define Victor's error; but if we focus on this extract alone, we may be struck by the sheer contrast it achieves. Nature is first 'wondrous', 'majestic' and 'sublime', then 'a secret I desired to divine'. It is as if a tableau of natural beauty has been painted for us, then the lights go out: Victor looks into some darkness behind, seeking its 'causes'. Indeed, when Victor looks at the world, he sees nothing – because 'a secret' is not visible. So, this passage not only tells us that Victor has a scientific interest in natural laws, but it also creates for us a kind of blindness from which Victor suffers, by the very suddenness of its descent on the word 'secret'. Before moving on, we should note that the context of this extract is a description of the 'harmony' in which Elizabeth and Victor grew up: the assertion that their 'contrast' drew them 'nearer together'.

Let us now look at Frankenstein's journey to Chamounix, part of which is described as follows:

> The weight upon my spirit was sensibly lightened as I plunged yet deeper in the ravine of Arve. The immense mountains and precipices that overhung me on every side – the sound of the river raging among the rocks, and the dashing of the waterfalls around, spoke of a power mighty as Omnipotence – and I ceased to fear, or to bend before any being less almighty than that which had created and ruled the elements, here displayed in their most terrific guise. Still, as I ascended higher, the valley assumed a more magnificent and astonishing character. Ruined

castles hanging on the precipices of piny mountains; the impetuous Arve, and cottages every here and there peeping forth from among the trees, formed a scene of singular beauty. But it was augmented and rendered sublime by the mighty Alps, whose white and shining pyramids and domes towered above all, as belonging to another earth, the habitations of another race of beings. . .

. . . A tingling long-lost sense of pleasure often came across me during this journey. Some turn in the road, some new object suddenly perceived and recognized, reminded me of days gone by, and were associated with the light-hearted gaiety of boyhood. The very winds whispered in soothing accents, and maternal nature bade me weep no more. Then again the kindly influence ceased to act – I found myself fettered again to grief and indulging all the misery of reflection. Then I spurred on my animal, striving so to forget the world, my fears, and more than all, myself – or, in a more desperate fashion, I alighted and threw myself on the grass, weighed down by horror and despair.　(*F* 97–8)

This is certainly a fine description: we can visualize the scenes as we read, and Shelley puts together 'raging', 'dashing', 'hanging', 'impetuous' and 'towered', filling the landscape with energy and movement. The passage also shows a chorus of words denoting power: 'immense', 'mighty', 'Omnipotence', 'almighty', 'ruled', 'mighty' again. The description thus conveys the energy and power of the landscape. How does this affect Frankenstein?

First, nature's effect upon Frankenstein is clearly positive. His feelings are 'sensibly lightened' as he undertakes the climb; but when he summarizes his state during the journey, he records only intermittent relief: that he often felt a 'sense of pleasure' related to 'the light-hearted gaiety of boyhood', and at these times 'maternal nature bade me weep no more', but that at other times nature's 'kindly influence ceased to act' and he was plunged back into despair. The mechanism by which nature acts upon Frankenstein is also explained. Nature is 'immense', and the river 'raging' and 'dashing' impresses him with 'a power mighty as Omnipotence'. Nature is shown in its 'terrific guise', and as he ascends, it becomes 'more magnificent and astonishing' and is then even 'augmented and rendered sublime' by the mountain peaks above. Responding to nature's power, Victor ceases to fear any being less than God, or as he puts it 'less almighty than that which had created and ruled the elements'. This passage, then, suggests that God can be found in nature, and can influence the individual through his response to nature. Shelley stops short of personification, however: she is clear, that it is his appreciation of God's power – His Omnipotence – as displayed in the great powers of nature, that puts Frankenstein's fear of the daemon into perspective.

Two further touches are added to the motif of nature, in this extract. First, Victor describes the high peaks as 'pyramids and domes', metaphors which suggest religion, but 'pyramids' certainly suggest pagan religion; 'white and shining', which suggests both beauty and purity, but perhaps also remoteness and cold; and as on 'another earth', 'the habitations of another race of beings', which furthers the suggestion of remoteness and strangeness. Then, Frankenstein associates his periods of relief from despair with memories of 'boyhood', and he personifies the favourable influence as a maternal figure: 'The very winds whispered in soothing accents, and maternal nature bade me weep no more.'

What, then, does nature represent in this extract? We have a range of indications, starting with a conventional God in his aspect of omnipotence, but also including a hint at pagan worship of different 'beings', and personification as a 'soothing . . . maternal' influence. We may well be surprised at this variety, and particularly that both male and female gender-typing of nature occurs within the one extract. On the other hand, all three influences of nature contribute to raising Frankenstein's spirits. Omnipotence begins, by removing his fears; then the 'sublime' and 'mighty' mountains impress his mind; and finally nature's 'maternal' influence soothes his misery. These powers are further described on the next page:

> . . . These sublime and magnificent scenes afforded me the greatest consolation that I was capable of receiving. They elevated me from all littleness of feeling; and although they did not remove my grief, they subdued and tranquillised it. In some degree, also, they diverted my mind from the thoughts over which it had brooded for the last month. I retired to rest at night; my slumbers, as it were, waited on and ministered to by the assemblance of grand shapes which I had contemplated during the day. They congregated round me; the unstained snowy

mountain-top, the glittering pinnacle, the pine woods, and ragged bare
ravine, the eagle, soaring amidst the clouds – they all gathered round
me and bade me be at peace.   (*F* 99)

Here are the same influences again. Victor describes the high mountains elevating him from 'littleness of feeling', and on the next page
adds that 'The sight of the awful and majestic in nature had indeed
always the effect of solemnizing my mind and causing me to forget the
passing cares of life' (*F* 100); he says that his mind is 'diverted from' its
previous thoughts – just as before he claimed that lesser fears vanished
when nature's grandeur revealed God's omnipotence. Finally, nature
'subdued and tranquillised' his grief. Finally, Frankenstein suggests a
divine influence: he is 'ministered to' by nature, which 'congregated'
around him bidding him 'be at peace'.

During Victor's journey to the 'mer de glace' we also meet an
opposing aspect of nature. Power and grandeur are part of nature's positive influence, as we have remarked. Mist, rain, darkness and cloud,
on the other hand, inspire Victor's melancholy thoughts again. So,
when he wakes the second morning, 'dark melancholy clouded every
thought. The rain was pouring in torrents, and thick mists hid the
summits . . .' (*F* 99); later that day he saw that 'vast mists were rising
from the rivers which ran through it [the valley] and curling in thick
wreaths around the opposite mountains, whose summits were hid in
the uniform clouds, while rain poured from the dark sky, and added
to the melancholy impression I received . . .' (*F* 100). The important element here seems to be visibility: mist and darkness hide the
mountains which are Victor's 'mighty friends', and bring melancholy.
When he can see the mountains – when 'their icy and glittering peaks
shone in the sunlight' – then Victor's heart 'swelled with something
like joy' (*F* 101). So, nature visible is a healing and cheering influence;
while nature hidden brings melancholy. This connection between
Frankenstein's mood and visibility seems to be consistent. For example, even on the evening of his wedding day, when 'the clouds swept
across [the moon] swifter than the flight of the vulture and dimmed
her rays . . . Suddenly a heavy storm of rain descended', we find Victor's
emotions at the mercy of nature's change: 'I had been calm during the
day; but so soon as night obscured the shapes of objects, a thousand

fears arose in my mind' (both from *F* 198). Shelley's insistent use of 'mist', 'clouds', 'dimmed' and 'obscured' emphasizes how visibility determines Frankenstein's mood.

We have found that the grandeur of nature can exert a quasi-religious influence over the individual. However, looking back to the distinction between Elizabeth and Victor with which we began, we can also conclude that there are harmonious ways of responding to nature, and ways which bring disaster – in other words you can have a good or a bad relationship with the world around you. This point is underlined by Victor's inability to achieve any lasting escape from his guilt and misery, after he has broken nature's laws by creating the daemon. So, in the present episode Victor remembers the 'gaiety of boyhood' and a past when his soul could 'soar from the obscure world to light and joy'. Elsewhere, Frankenstein contrasts his own and Clerval's pleasures as they voyage down the Rhine: 'I seemed to drink in a tranquillity to which I had long been a stranger. And if these were my sensations, who can describe those of Henry? He felt as if he had been transported to Fairy-land and enjoyed a happiness seldom tasted by man' (*F* 160). Clearly, Victor's scientific crime has made him an outcast from nature's influence: the breach that occurs with the making of the daemon is stronger than nature's power to heal. Frankenstein remains unable to restore harmony between himself and the world around him, and can only feel nature's comforts intermittently, before losing them again.

Nature, Human Nature

So far, we have discussed nature in the sense of natural surroundings; but *Frankenstein* also raises important questions concerning human nature. The story explores the borders of what may be called natural and unnatural behaviours. Shelley also questions the 'natural' or innate in human beings, and considers how far environment determines character and fate. In other words, an important subject in *Frankenstein* is the age-old debate between Nature and Nurture.

We have already met the argument for *nurture* in more than one context. For example, Frankenstein allocates responsibility to his parents, his happiness or misery resulting 'according as they fulfilled their duties towards me' (*F* 35); and, of course, the daemon consistently argues determinism: 'I was benevolent and good; misery made me a fiend. Make me happy, and I shall again be virtuous' (*F* 103). The cause of nurture provokes the moral question that is always leveled against determinism: If the daemon understands the difference between good and evil, why can he not choose to be good? The daemon answers that he cannot choose. If evil is done to him, he will do evil in return. This is an inevitable consequence of circumstances, and there is nothing the daemon can do about it. So, following Felix's rejection, 'my feelings were those of rage and revenge. I could with pleasure have destroyed the cottage and its inhabitants, and have glutted myself with their shrieks and misery' (*F* 138); or, he asks, 'Shall I not then hate them who abhor me? . . . I am miserable, and they shall share my wretchedness' (*F* 103). Still, when the daemon threatens Frankenstein that he will become 'the scourge of your fellow creatures, and the author of your own speedy ruin' (*F* 104), he sounds decisive, as if he is choosing his actions rather than being forced into evil by vengeful passion. It is this sense that he is 'using' threats and bribes that leads us to suspect his determinism: if he is 'using' threats, then his mind is in control, and he is not at the mercy of 'nurture'. This view is presented by Frankenstein, who describes the daemon's argument and its effect thus: 'I had before been moved by the sophisms of the being I had created; I had been struck senseless by his fiendish threats' (*F* 171).

The determinist argument is asserted by the daemon, then: according as he receives love or hate from others, so he will return love or hate to them. In this he claims to be driven by his emotions of revenge and despair. Frankenstein is suspicious of this argument, believing that the daemon speaks 'sophisms' and is full of 'malice and treachery' (*F* 171). The daemon's sincerity is never tested: because Frankenstein destroys the female, the daemon will never prove that he would become 'virtuous' if he were 'happy'. The cycle of rejection/revenge continues until Victor's death and the assumed subsequent suicide of the daemon.

We can now turn to the argument for *nature*: that is, the argument that we are born with innate qualities, which we can develop by choosing our actions in life. How is this view presented in *Frankenstein*? To answer this question, we can examine what various characters say about freewill, and in particular what is said about Frankenstein's enthusiasms which lead to the creation of the daemon; and we should examine how the daemon himself describes his nature to Walton, in his final appearance.

First of all, notice that Frankenstein judges the daemon on the basis of the *nature* argument – that is, that he can choose between evil and good; that he chose evil, and should therefore be punished: 'He showed unparalleled malignity and selfishness, in evil . . . that he may render no other wretched, he ought to die' (*F* 220). This, Frankenstein calls the judgement of 'reason and virtue'. However, his thoughts about his own error are more confusing. Frankenstein says that his childhood was happy 'before misfortune had tainted my mind', which changed 'bright visions of extensive usefulness into gloomy and narrow reflections upon self' (*F* 40). To what 'misfortune' does he refer? The first 'misfortune' in Victor's life was the death of his mother, but at this point in the narrative she is still alive. Or, does he refer to the 'misfortune' of having created the daemon – another event still years in the future? If so, it is a peculiar use of the word: making the daemon could be described in many ways, but not as bad luck. Victor then considers the source of his miseries for the second time in the same paragraph:

> . . . I also record those events which led, by insensible steps, to my after tale of misery: for when I would account to myself for the birth of that passion, which afterwards ruled my destiny, I find it arise, like a mountain river, from ignoble and almost forgotten sources; but, swelling as it proceeded, it became the torrent which, in its course, has swept away all my hopes and joys. (*F* 40)

Frankenstein was led towards the disaster of creating the daemon by 'insensible steps', then; and his passion for Natural Philosophy originated in 'ignoble and almost forgotten sources'. The simile of a mountain torrent is ambivalent: it successfully conveys the power with which his enthusiasm sweeps away 'all my hopes and joys'; on the other hand, how can the source of a mountain river be 'ignoble'? So, something negative is the source of his catastrophe, but

Frankenstein does not clarify whether that something is a token of guilt ('ignoble') or bad luck ('misfortune'). He does not choose between personal responsibility and freewill (*nature*) and a 'misfortune' (i.e. an environmental influence beyond his own control, or the *nurture* argument).

Frankenstein's narrative continues to waver between hinting at personal guilt and blaming others or external factors. So, for example, he quite outrageously blames his father for his ruin (see *F* 41); and he conceives of himself as a battlefield for the conflict between good and evil supernatural powers, when he is almost saved by changing to the study of mathematics: 'It was a strong effort of the spirit of good; but it was ineffectual. Destiny was too potent, and her immutable laws had decreed my utter and terrible destruction' (*F* 43). These efforts of Frankenstein's hindsight, and particularly the superstitions which have become pathetic delusions by the end of the novel, all tend to apportion responsibility onto something external – a force acting upon Frankenstein, that he could not resist ('the torrent which . . . has swept away all my hopes and joys') or that was inevitable ('Destiny was too potent'). On balance, then, Frankenstein appears to favour explanations based on the idea that he has been blown about by forces more powerful than he can control; although there are incomplete hints of some other more shameful and personally guilty explanation.

It is in the nature of this age-old debate, of course, that every point can be argued from both sides. For an example, consider Frankenstein after creating the daemon: this one action has trapped him and removed his freedom to direct his own life. Frankenstein frequently complains that he cannot escape the consequences of the daemon's existence. Is this determinism? We can argue that making the daemon was an act of freewill: so, our actions in life make our own destiny. Or, we can agree with Frankenstein that it was 'the evil influence, the Angel of Destruction, which asserted omnipotent sway over me' (*F* 47). Ultimately, Frankenstein fudges this question. He hints at some obscure shame or guilt in himself, but he also throws blame around onto others and onto events, and he expresses superstitions which absolve him of responsibility. Discussing Frankenstein's character in Chapter 2, we found just this kind of final effect: contradictory ideas and intellectual confusions, disturbing hints and suggestions, but no conclusive revelation of his psychology.

Analysis, p. 222

We now turn to the daemon's final account of himself:

> ... Think you that the groans of Clerval were music to my ears? My heart was fashioned to be susceptible of love and sympathy; and when wrenched by misery to vice and hatred, it did not endure the violence of the change, without torture such as you cannot even imagine.
>
> After the murder of Clerval, I returned to Switzerland, heart-broken and overcome. I pitied Frankenstein; my pity amounted to horror: I abhorred myself. But when I discovered that he, the author at once of my existence and of its unspeakable torments, dared to hope for happiness; that while he accumulated wretchedness and despair upon me, he sought his own enjoyment in feelings and passions from the indulgence of which I was forever barred, then impotent envy and bitter indignation filled me with an insatiable thirst for vengeance. I recollected my threat, and resolved that it should be accomplished. I knew that I was preparing for myself a deadly torture; but I was the slave, not the master, of an impulse, which I detested, yet could not disobey. Yet when she died! – nay, then I was not miserable. I had cast off all feeling, subdued all anguish, to riot in the excess of my despair. Evil thenceforth became my good. Urged thus far, I had no choice but to adapt my nature to an element which I had willingly chosen. The completion of my demoniacal design became an insatiable passion.   (*F* 222)

We can begin by remarking that the daemon's speech is characteristically fine and persuasive. Notice, for example, the rhetorical question with which our extract opens, and his ability to juxtapose his misery and Frankenstein's happiness, twice, as he leads up to the natural consequence of such injustice: 'then impotent envy and bitter indignation filled me'. However, the aspect of the daemon that is described more fully here than elsewhere is his nature: the goodness and innocence that were his innate qualities. He tells us that his nature was 'wrenched by misery' to evil, and that it was unimaginable 'torture' to 'endure the violence of the change'. Previously, the daemon has emphasized inevitability – that rejection determines his reaction. Here, particularly in the verb 'wrenched', he emphasizes the violence of the conflict as his natural self became distorted. The persistence of this conflict is also emphasized, and we find a motif of self-hatred and self-torture running through the passage, from 'I abhorred myself' to 'preparing for myself a deadly torture', 'an impulse, which I detested' and 'riot in the excess of my despair'.

At the same time, the daemon repeatedly expresses how the negative consequences of his suffering were stronger than his innate goodness. So, he had an 'insatiable thirst for vengeance' and 'an insatiable passion'. Despite the pain it caused him, 'I was the slave, not the master, of an impulse', he 'could not disobey', and eventually he 'had no choice but to adapt my nature to an element which I had willingly chosen'. These phrases carry us through the process which overwhelmed the daemon's innate goodness, and distorted his nature. He finally declares that his nature has been 'wrenched' into its opposite, when, in an echo of Milton's Satan, he says that 'Evil thenceforth became my good'. The whole of this passage, then, suggests a hard-fought conflict between the daemon's natural goodness and the even greater strength of his despair. In the end, in a sentence curiously combining determinism and freewill, he claims to have 'had no choice but to adapt my nature' because he had 'willingly chosen' evil. This, perhaps, expresses the ethical inversion to which his nature was subjected; but 'willingly chosen' may also suggest the overwhelming power of his despair and his 'thirst for vengeance' to drive him to such a 'willing' choice, despite the 'deadly torture' of doing what he 'detested' and the unnatural effort with which he 'cast off all feeling, subdued all anguish'. This extract conveys the torturing power of the daemon's conflict to us vividly. Notice that the phrases become shorter, and throw us backwards and forwards between 'resolved that it should be accomplished', 'preparing for myself a deadly torture', 'slave', 'master', 'detested' and 'could not disobey' more and more rapidly, imitating the growing violence of the conflict up to the decisive climax: 'Yet when she died!'.

In this passage, then, Shelley fully portrays the daemon's conflict. It is a violent battle that rages in him, between the goodness that was born in him naturally – his *nature* – and the evil influence of the way others treat him, or the determining forces of *nurture*. This battle is crucial to our understanding of the world, also. For if the battle is always won, as in the daemon's case, by the forces of the environment, then we have no free will; and all our pretence of choosing good or evil is a sham. A further disturbing question is raised by the daemon's self-revelations: if those environmental forces, as in the daemon's experience, are always cruel and unjust, then natural goodness – the benevolence with which all creatures are born – will always be defeated, and 'wrenched' into violent vengeance. These unsettling questions arise from Shelley's persistent references to a determinist outlook.

Putting this account of human nature together with the account of the natural environment discussed earlier, we notice that Shelley portrays both as innately good. The natural environment displays beauty, and benevolent qualities which 'elevate' and 'solemnise' the soul as well as 'maternal' care which 'soothes'; and in 'harmony' with this nature, people may find 'admiration and delight' and the 'soul' may 'soar'. With regard to human nature, the daemon's account is of a natural inclination towards love and sympathy, a natural benevolence and lack of suspicion that would harmonize with the beauties and grandeur of the world. In short, Shelley presents *nature* as innocent and good. In this, her novel suggests the potential for a resolution of the world's ills. We can tentatively suggest that it is the oppression, distortion and defeat of nature, both inanimate and human, that constitutes the tragedy of *Frankenstein*.

One further aspect of the concept of nature in the novel needs some discussion, before we move on. In the last chapter, we commented about Elizabeth that the fair-haired girl turns out to be, literally, from a 'different stock', and that 'in this manner the snobbery of the golden-haired, dare we say it – Aryan – superior race, is reinforced'. On other occasions, we have had reason to remark on Frankenstein's own social snobbery. This admiration of the high-born or high-ranking appears in one or two other places in the novel. For example, we may be struck by Walton's use of religious diction to describe Frankenstein, echoing the language in which Frankenstein describes Elizabeth: 'like a celestial spirit, that has a halo around him, within whose circle no grief or folly ventures' (*F* 30). Walton makes numerous comments

admiring of Frankenstein's personality. So, his 'manners are so con-
ciliating and gentle, that the sailors are all interested in him', and 'he
must have been a noble creature in his better days' because even now
he remains 'so attractive and amiable' (*F* 28). In particular, Frankenstein's voice and language are praised: 'He is so gentle, yet so wise;
his mind is so cultivated, and when he speaks, although his words are
culled with the choicest art, yet they flow with rapidity and unparalleled eloquence' (*F* 28–9); and Walton exclaims, 'What a glorious
creature must he have been in the days of his prosperity, when he is
thus noble and godlike in ruin!' Frankenstein agrees, saying that 'I
possessed a coolness of judgment that fitted me for illustrious achievements. This sentiment of the worth of my nature supported me . . .'
so that he 'could not rank myself with the herd of common projectors'
(all from *F* 214). The daemon adds his voice, calling Frankenstein
'generous and self-devoted being!' (*F* 221) and 'select specimen of all
that is worthy of love and admiration among men' (*F* 224). In short,
Frankenstein's manners, voice and cultivated speech make him appear
a higher or more refined kind of human being than, for example, the
sailors; just as Elizabeth immediately appeared a higher kind than the
'hardy little vagrants', her foster-siblings. One other person referred to
as a superior creature is William. Frankenstein believes that William's
beauty would keep him safe: 'Nothing in human shape could have
destroyed that fair child'. However, the daemon's account reveals that
William relied on his social position, rather than beauty, for safety.
He boasted of his father's rank and claimed, 'You dare not keep me'
(*F* 144).

All of these comments suggest that there is a natural hierarchy
among human beings, and that Victor Frankenstein, Elizabeth and
William are of a superior kind. On the other hand, most of these
comments come from Walton and Victor, both characters whose
judgement and wisdom we question. For example, we surely cannot
accept Walton's idea that 'no grief or folly ventures' within Victor's
'halo'! Only the daemon's remark about Frankenstein carries more
conviction. Perhaps Victor was a man of abilities and charm, but we
suspect that much of his impressive personality derives from his class,
and from the admiration social inferiors are conditioned to accord.
Shelley does not imply that there is a difference in *nature* between

superior and other human beings, but some of her characters do make this mistake.

Society

Analysis, pp. 122–123

We will begin our discussion of the society depicted in *Frankenstein*, with a close look at how the daemon first learns about the world beyond one isolated cottage family. He watches and listens as Felix teaches Safie from Volney's *Ruins of Empires*:

> Through this work I obtained a cursory knowledge of history and a view of the several empires at present existing in the world; it gave me an insight into the manners, governments, and religions of the different nations of the earth. I heard of the slothful Asiatics; of the stupendous genius and mental activity of the Grecians; of the wars and wonderful virtue of the early Romans – of their subsequent degenerating – of the decline of that mighty empire, of chivalry, Christianity, and kings. I heard of the discovery of the American hemisphere and wept with Safie over the hapless fate of its original inhabitants.
>
> These wonderful narrations inspired me with strange feelings. Was man, indeed, at once so powerful, so virtuous, and magnificent, yet so vicious and base? He appeared at one time a mere scion of the evil principle, and at another as all that can be conceived as noble and godlike. To be a great and virtuous man appeared the highest honour that can befall a sensitive being; to be base and vicious, as many on record have been, appeared the lowest degradation, a condition more abject than that of the blind mole or harmless worm. For a long time I could not conceive how one man could go forth to murder his fellow, or even why there were laws and governments; but when I heard details of vice and bloodshed, my wonder ceased, and I turned away with disgust and loathing.
>
> Every conversation of the cottagers now opened new wonders to me. While I listened to the instructions which Felix bestowed upon the Arabian, the strange system of human society was explained to me. I heard of the division of property, of immense wealth and squalid poverty; of rank, descent, and noble blood.

> The words induced me to turn towards myself. I learned that the pos-
> sessions most esteemed by your fellow creatures were, high and unsullied
> descent united with riches. A man might be respected with only one of
> these advantages; but without either he was considered, except in very
> rare instances, as a vagabond and a slave, doomed to waste his pow-
> ers for the profits of the chosen few! And what was I? Of my creation
> and creator I was absolutely ignorant, but I knew that I possessed no
> money, no friends, no kind of property. I was, besides, endued with a
> figure hideously deformed and loathsome; I was not even of the same
> nature as man.   (*F* 122–3)

Here, Shelley exploits the opportunity to observe, as it were from
the point of view of an innocent alien; the daemon's uniquely ignorant standpoint enables her to strip away our over-familiarity with
human society, and describe it as if newly perceived. This exploitation of a fresh viewpoint is a common feature of Science Fiction, a
genre said to have been founded by *Frankenstein*. However, such a
technique exploited for the critical analysis of society already had a
distinguished pedigree. See, for example, Friday's comments on the
Religion Robinson tries to teach him, in Defoe's *Robinson Crusoe*,[1]
or the astonishment with which Gulliver's descriptions of Europe are
greeted by those he meets on his travels.[2]

Shelley's daemon focuses his meditation upon two central questions:
the existence of evil people and the organization of human society. He
focuses upon these two issues because they are the facts he finds most
difficult to accept. In other words, Shelley implies, these facts do not
make sense. To an innocent and virtuous person, evil does not make
sense; and to a reasonable person, the organization of human society
does not make sense.

The passage expresses wonder, and emphasizes the wide contrast
between virtue and vice. The daemon experiences 'strange feelings' and
says that 'for a long time I could not conceive' of evil. Two statements
argue the senselessness of evil: first, that to be good seems 'the highest
honour' and to be evil 'the lowest degradation'; therefore, the daemon
believes, every man would seek to be good and avoid being evil. The
daemon therefore cannot understand wickedness. He has no knowledge of the motives that lead people to vicious actions, being innocent.
So, when he is finally convinced that evil does happen, all he can do

is turn away 'with disgust and loathing'. Shelley works one further aspect of society into this analysis: not believing in the existence of evil, the daemon did not, at first, see the need for governments and laws. Clearly Shelley's suggestion is that the purpose of law and government is to control evil.

When he comes to the 'strange system of human society', the daemon lists what he learns: 'of the division of property, of immense wealth and squalid poverty; of rank, descent, and noble blood'. These are 'new wonders' and it is a 'strange system', still emphasizing the daemon's innocence. The list tells us that the inequality of human society is an astonishing shock to the daemon: he cannot understand why one is rich and another poor; why society is divided into ranks; why birth matters; or what difference there is between common and noble blood. These are all radical and egalitarian criticisms of society for Shelley's time, but we should also notice that she includes the very 'division of property'. This is an extremely radical critique, cutting at the foundation of capitalist Europe and the basis of the state. The idea that the world belongs to everybody in common seems, even in the present day, impossibly idealistic. On the other hand, to a being raised as the daemon has been raised, private ownership of the woods, mountains, trees – or even the cottage – would not make any sense.

It is natural that the daemon's next intellectual act will be to compare himself with those about whom he learns. Before doing so, however, he makes one more devastating observation, reporting what he 'learned' from Felix. Society values birth and wealth and you can be respected if you have one or both of these advantages, but as to the man with no advantage: 'he was considered, except in very rare instances, as a vagabond and a slave, doomed to waste his powers for the profits of the chosen few!' This comment takes the analysis a further step so that Shelley's critique becomes a socialist statement. It is not only that property is divided, or that society is unequal: the problem is much more deeply ingrained than this, for the poor are exploited, and it is their labour and poverty that keeps the rich rich.

It would be hard to find as trenchant a critique of nineteenth-century capitalism outside the pages of Marx. Shelley not only attacks the contemporary targets of unjust inequalities in wealth and rank. She pushes her analysis to its logical conclusion, citing the origin and bedrock of the economic system, 'division of property', and exposing the exploitation of the poor for 'the profits of the chosen few'. The passage is rendered particularly effective by the daemon's tone of innocent astonishment, and by his earnest effort to make sense of what he learns. In the context of the daemon's understanding, the facts appear absurd. In this way, society is satirically ridiculed, and if we were not more inclined to turn away 'with disgust and loathing' as the daemon does, we might be tempted to laugh.

There may be another layer encoded in Shelley's satire, when she exploits the daemon's naïveté to expose the unreason of human society. Her father William Godwin was a radical philosopher who believed in reason, and who believed that states and laws would be unnecessary in a society organized according to the dictates of reason. Percy Shelley was in many ways equally idealistic, and naïve: a believer in free love and, like Godwin, an opponent of marriage and private property. So the daemon's analysis is satirical in two senses: not only does it provide a devastating critique of social injustice; but also it satirizes the innocence of those – like Percy Shelley and William Godwin – who try to live by radical ideals.

Much of the daemon's early narrative partakes of this quality, where Shelley exploits his innocence to highlight the strangeness, to him, of a society with which we are cynically familiar. However, at the end of our extract he brings himself into the analysis: without family or property, his position in society must be that of 'a vagabond and a slave'; or, as he is also 'deformed and loathsome' and 'not even of the same nature as man', an even more rejected position – that of a 'monster, a blot upon the earth'.

Turning to consider the daemon's social significance, we need to think about the novel as a whole, and the daemon's part in it also as a whole. We begin to do this by making a list of the major features of the daemon's existence, in the form of notes which may suggest further ideas. Here are some notes:

• The daemon is ugly and deformed – a 'monster' of disproportion.
• The daemon was manufactured by a patrician, a scion of the ruling class, who is immediately horrified at what he has made.
• He was produced by the misuse of science.

- The daemon is dangerous, frightening and stronger than his creator.
- The daemon is clever, eloquent and plausible.
- The daemon destroys his creator's family.
- The daemon is hated and rejected by the rest of society.
- The daemon becomes violent as a response to being cruelly treated.

We could go on: there are further thoughts about the daemon that could belong with this list (e.g., the daemon is made from different body-parts unnaturally joined together). However, the above thoughts are sufficient to help us think about the figure of the daemon in the novel as a whole. Now, we can try to frame ideas of his significance, using as many of the above thoughts as we can incorporate.

What is ugly, has been made by the ruling class, by the misuse of science, is stronger than the ruling class, potentially dangerous, and becomes violent in response to being oppressed? One answer to this question is, the industrial working class – a section of society that was already large and growing rapidly in Mary Shelley's time. Another answer to this question could be, the revolutionary mob, in France: a group repeatedly referred to as 'monsters' and 'monstrous' in the public literature of the time.[3] It does not matter greatly which answer we choose, since the important characteristics are common to both: the idea is of a monster with an enormous capacity for danger and destruction, created by the ruling class but then rendered rebellious by cruel oppression. Furthermore, many feared that revolution would spread from France to England, or believed that it was doing so, in the form of the luddite industrial troubles of the time. Such a reading of the daemon's significance is not stretching a point. Remember his own description of the class of the dispossessed: 'considered . . . as a vagabond and a slave, doomed to waste his powers for the profits of the chosen few' (*F* 123).

There are further parallels between the monster and the social group he seems to represent. For example, the impact of industrial development was everywhere ugly. Huge factories, black dust and fire and noise, ugly towns made up of ugly rows of slum dwellings, and an ugly population dressed in shapeless clothes, and including miners with blackened faces: these were the appearances of industry, and Walton's words could express a common middle-class response to their ugliness:

'Never did I behold a vision so horrible...of such loathsome, yet appalling hideousness' (*F* 221). There was also a superstitious mistrust of machines, and a tradition that they were a kind of sorcery; or that factories, furnaces and mills were hellish places filled with devilish scientific fires and engines; attitudes which fuelled the luddite machine-breaking of 1811–17. The gothic trappings of Frankenstein's laboratory; his season spent in 'vaults and charnel-houses' (*F* 53), in researches into death and decay; and his pale, emaciated and fanatical person, all echo the mistrust of science that was a feature of industrial politics at the time when *Frankenstein* was composed.

We can read the daemon as representing either a revolutionary mob or the industrial working class, then. His superhuman strength, and the threat he poses, reflect middle-class anxieties about possible revolution; but his analysis of society, his argument and his appeal develop a critique that goes far beyond expressing anxiety, for it highlights both the foolishness and the selfish injustice of the ruling class. We recognize the political potency of the daemon's rhetoric, and we should also recognize the political significance of his existence and his story, as being thoroughly subversive of the establishment of Shelley's time. Let us now look at the daemon's effect upon society, as shown in the novel.

Legal authority appears four times in *Frankenstein*: first, in the form of the court that condemns Justine; secondly as the French court that tries the De Laceys; next, as Mr Kirwin, the Irish magistrate; and finally in the person of the magistrate Victor consults after the murder of Elizabeth.

Before the trial of Justine, Frankenstein's father advises Elizabeth to 'rely on the justice of our laws' (*F* 82), confident that the system will arrive at a correct verdict. We know that he was wrong: the planted locket decisively fools the court. Justice is blinded by deceit, then, and the innocent is found guilty. Thus the judiciary's first tangle with the daemon ends in a rousing defeat for society. At the same time, Frankenstein *père* loses some of his mantle of wisdom, for he explicitly trusted the court.

The French court that tried the De Laceys was motivated by a government which sentenced the Turk on grounds of 'flagrant' injustice, probably in order to confiscate his wealth, and was then so 'greatly enraged at the escape of their victim' that they came to a punitive judgment on the De Laceys. In short, this is a judiciary corrupted by treachery and greed.

Mr Kirwin is, partly, an exception: Frankenstein's trial for the murder of Clerval is the only case where the law arrives at a correct verdict. On the other hand, the legal authorities in Ireland are no more successful than those in Switzerland, when it comes to indicting the murderer. Mr Kirwin is 'old, benevolent' with 'calm and mild manners' (*F* 179), and he 'ardently desired to relieve the sufferings of every human creature' (*F* 183). On the other hand, how and why does he come to believe Frankenstein innocent? The initial examination of witnesses points only to Victor's guilt, and ends with him effectively confessing to Clerval's murder, on seeing the body. On page 183, Mr Kirwin is said still to regard Victor as 'a murderer'. Then, on the next page, he suddenly finds the murder 'unaccountable' and the body planted on Victor 'as it were, by some fiend' (*F* 184). This is one occasion in *Frankenstein* when Mary Shelley appears to have left a gap in the narrative. It is an interesting case, as it suggests a conflict between the novel's wider concerns, and its nuts and bolts. As we have seen, in the world of *Frankenstein*, justice and judicial authority are failing to control a corrupt and shortsighted society. The disastrous scene in which Victor is arraigned and every circumstance tells against him appears to have been written in this spirit. On the other hand, the plot insists that Victor must be acquitted.

There is one possible explanation for Mr Kirwin's *volte face*, but the text does not suggest this except by coincidence. It is believable that Mr Kirwin's opinion of Victor is changed when he meets the impressive and patrician Alphonse Frankenstein. Certainly, when he visits to announce the father's arrival is also when he suggests that 'some fiend' framed Victor. It is impossible that Mr Kirwin, or Victor's father, should know of the fiend. Possibly, then, Mr Kirwin is giving voice to a polite fiction, which absolves his upper-class prisoner of guilt, and sets himself free from the embarrassment of accusing a man from such a high-ranking family. If this is the case, Mr Kirwin is another example of failed judicial authority: biased in favour of high birth and unable to find the guilty. Although it explains some anomalies, however, this theory is not supported by any textual evidence.

The fourth appearance of judicial authority is a damning failure. The magistrate to whom Frankenstein finally tells the truth listens 'with attention and kindness' and then became 'more attentive and interested', eventually evincing 'horror' and an air 'unmingled with disbelief' (*F* 202–203). Up to this point, it appears that Victor is convincing the magistrate of the truth of his story. However, when he then seeks judicial action, he says of the magistrate that 'the whole tide of his incredulity returned' (*F* 203). The outcome is twofold. First, the magistrate points out that he is unable to capture and punish a being as strong and agile as the daemon. Secondly, he concludes that Frankenstein is mad. In this final appearance, although there was temporary hope that authority might face the daemon's challenge, the conclusion is that society has failed. Frankenstein speaks government's epitaph: 'Man . . . how ignorant art thou in thy pride of wisdom!' (*F* 204).

We have suggested that the daemon represents the poor, the oppressed and exploited, and we have discussed his connection with both the French revolutionary mob and the threat of rebellion seen in the English working classes of the time. The failures of judicial authority in the novel amplify Shelley's picture of society. Judicial authority is shown to be easily deceived and willing to convict on circumstantial evidence, relying on a forced confession extracted under threat of damnation (at Justine's trial); then, judicial authority is the toy of a corrupt government; next, a magistrate perhaps fabricates evidence to acquit Victor, influenced by his social rank, and in any event cannot solve the crime; and finally, authority admits that it cannot contain or control the daemon, while at the same time denying its existence. In the last chapter, we commented that Alphonse Frankenstein, representative of wisdom and a public servant, becomes increasingly ineffectual as the novel proceeds. To show this, we need only remember his statement before Justine's trial, promising 'the activity with which I shall prevent the slightest shadow of partiality' (*F* 82), and the outcome of that resolution.

In *Frankenstein*, society is depicted as sick or in decline. Its authorities are either corrupt and venal, biased and cruel, impotent and irrelevant or simply ignorant. In any case, they lack the power to meet the threat represented by the daemon. In this sense, the novel can be said to act as a warning to early nineteenth-century Britain: a warning that the sheer strength and power of the mob is potentially greater than the forces of the establishment. A warning, therefore, of impending violent revolution.

One further feature of society in the novel needs remark before we move on. Victor was raised in the patriarchal family ruled by Alphonse Frankenstein. It is noticeable that the Frankensteins selectively rescue others, adopting those who deserve adoption and bringing them within the magic circle of comfort and wealth in which the family lives. First, Alphonse rescues Caroline Beaufort, but only after she has shown that he can 'approve highly to love strongly'; then she rescues Elizabeth Lavenza, who earns her place by seeming to bear 'a celestial stamp in all her features' (*F* 36). Finally, they rescue Justine Moritz, and lavish on her an education superior to her station in life. We are told that 'the benefit was fully repaid; Justine was the most grateful little creature in the world' (*F* 67). This, then, seems to be a successful exercise of charity. Alphonse Frankenstein and his family exemplify an ideal belonging to a patrician past, a time when the ruling class believed in its duty to care for those under its sway. Alphonse's largesse can be likened to that of a lord of the manor in feudal times; or may remind us of seventeenth-century theories of government, stressing the monarch's duty of care.

The novel exposes this family model as too weak to withstand Victor's fatal errors and the daemon's attack: the Frankensteins are lost or murdered, one by one. The novel again conveys a warning: that an obsolete and complacent attitude among the ruling class will do nothing to head off destruction from the forces represented by the daemon. In conclusion, then, the novel *Frankenstein* issues a stark and dire warning of revolution, as well as a heartfelt plea for greater equality and natural goodness in society. The analysis, from the exploitation of the working class for profit of the 'chosen few' to the obsolescence of patrician values and the breakdown in judicial order, is recognizably proto-Marxist. *Frankenstein* is therefore very radical for its time.

Science

Frankenstein founded a genre: that of science fiction. The appearance of *Frankenstein* prefigures the works of Verne, Wells and the many twentieth-century practitioners in this field. We begin this section by noticing some features of Shelley's novel that have become typical of science fiction.

First, the scientific element in the novel faces general disbelief, so we read of a complacent society, unaware of its peril; and the isolation of the 'hero' – the one person who understands the science on which the story is based. Secondly, the text includes some pseudo-scientific terms, and describes equipment and research in a vague manner, in order to link the fictional with science regarded as possible at the time. Percy Shelley makes this point in his 1818 Preface, that the animation of a creature 'has been supposed, by Dr Darwin, and some of the physiological writers of Germany, as not of impossible occurrence' (*F* 11). In this way, the author sets up a 'suspension of disbelief': for in a science-fiction novel, we do not demand the same kind of realism as in other fiction. The reader of general fiction demands a level of realism that makes the story *likely*. In science fiction, the story will convince as long as the science seems *possible*. Finally, in the mainstream of the science-fiction tradition that was initiated by *Frankenstein*, science itself provokes ethical questions concerning interference with nature, and the dangers, uses and abuses of knowledge.

Analysis, pp. 48–49

Our first extract focusing on science tells of M. Waldman's lecture:

> This professor was very unlike his colleague. He appeared about fifty years of age, but with an aspect expressive of the greatest benevolence; a few grey hairs covered his temples, but those at the back of his head were nearly black. His person was short, but remarkably erect; and his voice the sweetest I had ever heard. He began his lecture by a recapitulation of the history of chemistry and the various improvements made by different men of learning, pronouncing with fervour the names of the most distinguished discoverers. He then took a cursory view of the present state of the science, and explained many of its elementary terms. After having made a few preparatory experiments, he concluded with a panegyric upon modern chemistry, the terms of which I shall never forget: –
>
> 'The ancient teachers of this science,' said he, 'promised impossibilities, and performed nothing. The modern masters promise very little;

they know that metals cannot be transmuted, and that the elixir of life is a chimera. But these philosophers, whose hands seem only made to dabble in dirt, and their eyes to pore over the microscope or crucible, have indeed performed miracles. They penetrate into the recesses of nature, and show how she works in her hiding-places. They ascend into the heavens: they have discovered how the blood circulates, and the nature of the air we breathe. They have acquired new and almost unlimited powers; they can command the thunders of heaven, mimic the earthquake, and even mock the invisible world with its own shadows.'

Such were the professor's words – rather let me say such the words of the fate – enounced to destroy me. As he went on I felt as if my soul were grappling with a palpable enemy; one by one the various keys were touched which formed the mechanism of my being: chord after chord was sounded, and soon my mind was filled with one thought, one conception, one purpose. So much has been done, exclaimed the soul of Frankenstein, – more, far more, will I achieve: treading in the steps already marked, I will pioneer a new way, explore unknown powers, and unfold to the world the deepest mysteries of creation.

I closed not my eyes that night. My internal being was in a state of insurrection and turmoil; I felt that order would thence arise, but I had no power to produce it. (*F* 48–9)

This is a crucial episode because it is Waldman's lecture that sets Frankenstein upon his fatal course. We are interested in just how this extract presents science, and its effect on Frankenstein.

First, notice the clear structure: there are three main paragraphs, which could be called preparatory, lecture and effect. The first paragraph introduces M. Waldman, and establishes a contrast with M. Krempe (a 'little squat man, with a gruff voice and a repulsive countenance' [*F* 47]). Not only is Waldman more prepossessing, with 'an aspect expressive of the greatest benevolence' and 'his voice the sweetest I had ever heard', but this paragraph also establishes his approach to science as calmer than that of his colleague. Most of the terms describing Waldman's lecture are matter-of-fact: 'recapitulation', 'various improvements', 'took a cursory view', 'explained . . . elementary terms', 'a few preparatory experiments', 'concluded'. All of this sounds organized, knowledgeable and informative. Significantly, this moderate academic language contrasts with Krempe's over-expression ('every instant', 'utterly', 'entirely' [*F* 47]) and his elephantine sarcasm ('Good God! In what desert land have you lived . . .' [*F* 47]). However, even this preparatory paragraph suggests Waldman's enthusiasm: he pronounces the names of distinguished chemists 'with fervour', and he concludes with a 'panegyric'. Therefore, although on the surface this paragraph appears to present a calmer scientist contrasted with the over-excitable and opinionated Krempe, there is already an undercurrent of enthusiasm present. We should not miss Shelley's application of the term 'fervour' to Waldman – a quality frequently mentioned in connection with both Walton and Frankenstein.[4]

The second paragraph is Waldman's panegyric. His speech begins in the reasonable register of the first paragraph. Modern chemistry no longer chases the foolish aims of the alchemists of the past: Waldman sounds eminently sensible as he dismisses 'the elixir of life', and asserts that 'metals cannot be transmuted'. So modern chemists promise little, he says. However, when he turns to what modern chemists have achieved, his language suffers an abrupt change. There is no more moderation, and the style overflows with metaphors. Modern chemists have 'performed miracles'; they 'penetrate into the recesses of nature, and show how she works in her hiding-places', and they 'ascend into the heavens' acquiring 'new and almost unlimited powers'. Among these powers they can 'command' thunder, 'mimic' earthquakes, and even 'mock the invisible world with its own shadows'. What, we may ask, do any of these claims – particularly the last – actually mean? The only definable claims Waldman includes are about the circulation of blood and the composition of air. We may well ask, how have we been carried to such a pitch, from so reasonable a beginning? The answer is, simply, that Waldman has thrown off all restraint of language and indulges in a riot of metaphors.

What are these metaphors? It is worth listing them, for they tumble from Waldman's mouth with abandon. First, chemists appear to 'dabble in dirt' and the contrast to this personifies them as deities, for they perform 'miracles'. Secondly, nature, a female, has 'recesses' or 'hiding-places' and chemists 'penetrate into' these to show 'how she works'. Third, chemists rise to heaven. Presumably once they are there, they have 'almost unlimited power', and are able to 'command', 'mimic' and 'mock' various powerful and mysterious aspects of nature (thunder, earthquake and 'invisible world').

These metaphors show two dominant ideas. First, there is the portrayal of science as a gendered masculine pursuit which will 'penetrate into the recesses' of a feminine nature. Next, there is a whole series of images in which the chemist plays a godlike role with 'almost unlimited' power. Looking at the metaphors also tells us how the scientist will use power once he has it; and as soon as he has power, Waldman's chemist will not be idle, he will use it: he will 'command', 'mimic' and 'mock'. We cannot miss the significance of these words to the *Frankenstein* story. Victor's creation of the daemon is clearly 'mimicry' of nature, and becomes a 'mockery' – ironically both of nature and of Victor's science.

The third paragraph of our extract describes Frankenstein's reaction to the lecture. After a brief mention of 'fate', he tells us his feelings on hearing Waldman's claims. Victor felt 'as if my soul were grappling with a palpable enemy'. This simile vividly conveys his extreme excitement, and the ferocity of his inner conflict; on the other hand, he does not specify on which side his soul, and on which side science, were fighting. Was his 'soul' struggling against the corrupting influence of scientific ambition, or was it the other way around? As is often the case with Victor, we receive a powerful impression, but no conclusive clarity. A new metaphor now takes over: Frankenstein is compared to a musical instrument, and Waldman's lecture is the musician playing him. This idea portrays Frankenstein as helpless: it is, again, a determinist conception of his character. As the musician plays, the passive verbs denote Victor's passive role: 'keys *were touched*', 'chord after chord *was sounded*' and eventually 'my mind *was filled*'. The final part of this paragraph has a chilling hubris. First, there is a chiming repetition of 'one', ringing in the end of the sentence like a bell of doom: 'one thought, one conception, one purpose'. Elizabeth's influence has taught us to sense the dangers of this single-mindedness. Then, with a scant nod in the direction of Waldman's miracle-workers, in whose steps he will be 'treading', Frankenstein declares that he will achieve 'more, far more'. He will do this by exploring 'unknown powers' enabling him to 'unfold to the world the deepest mysteries of creation'.

Frankenstein's hubris is obvious – his vanity is on open display. Notice also, however, that it is 'the soul of Frankenstein' that makes his most grandiose claims. This may answer our earlier question: it would appear that Frankenstein's soul was fighting for scientific ambition, against the 'palpable enemy' of reason, proportion, harmony and so on. In short, Waldman's lecture enables Frankenstein to defeat that which he called 'the guardian angel of my life' or 'the spirit of preservation' (*F* 43). In so doing, his 'soul' appears to have changed sides.

To what concept of science does Frankenstein dedicate himself in this passage? The answer is, surely, that he is excited by the gendered metaphor Waldman proposes, a metaphor Victor has long cherished. Even as a child, he thought the world 'a secret' with 'hidden laws', and he experienced a sensation of 'gladness akin to rapture' when such secrets were 'unfolded' (all from *F* 38). Frankenstein's (and Waldman's) fundamental misconception is related to the gendered image and language of penetration, secrets, mysteries, recesses, hidden, unfolding, unveiling, revealing and so on. Science is not, of course, hidden. Some of it has not yet been understood; that is the extent of its so-called secrecy. Frankenstein's vaunting declaration, however, echoes the gendered idea: he pursues 'unknown powers', and the facts he discovers have to be not discovered but 'unfolded', and are not mere facts but 'deepest mysteries'.

There is no question, then, that Shelley presents a concept of science, that displays two dominant errors, and that she fully intends us to be critical of Waldman and Frankenstein. Shelley depicts male scientists whose studies are sexually driven, and who desire to achieve a godlike power. These two errors are closely related – indeed, many people argue that the male sexual drive and the male drive to dominance and power are one and the same. Scientists seek to control nature, just as men have traditionally sought to control women. *Frankenstein* implies that such a masculine attitude towards science, unchecked, will bring disasters upon the world.

In our brief description of science fiction, we commented that the fictional science is normally connected to contemporary knowledge, in order to provoke the 'suspension of disbelief' on which a science-fiction work relies. In the passage above, Shelley relies on Sir Humphry Davy's *A Discourse, Introductory to a Course of Lectures on Chemistry*

(1802), which she read in 1816. Davy's and Waldman's claims for chemistry are similar. So, Davy tells us that chemical knowledge 'has bestowed upon [the chemist] powers which may be almost called creative' so that he can 'interrogate nature with power, not simply as a scholar, passive and seeking only to understand her operations, but rather as a master, active with his own instruments'; and that nature has 'profound secrets' and 'hidden operations' and is consistently 'she' and 'her'. Davy even distinguishes between the good chemist who will 'slowly ... lift up the veil concealing the wonderful phenomena of living nature' and the bad one who has 'presumptuously attempted to tear it asunder' (Davy, *op.cit.*, pp. 16, 17 and 19 respectively). Clearly, Shelley made use of her knowledge of contemporary science to make her chemist's lecture convincing. At the same time, however, she is putting forward a feminist critique of one of the major scientific authorities of her day. For, when we conclude that Waldman's and Frankenstein's motives are gender-related, guilty of an irresponsible hubris, and driven by sexuality, we pass the same judgement upon Sir Humphry Davy. He too depicts nature as feminine, her 'secrets' as 'hidden', the chemist as 'a master, active' and powerful and so on.

This critical depiction of scientists' motives embodies another of the features we mentioned in connection with science fiction: that science itself appears morally ambivalent. In this passage we have found scientists who are able to wield enormous power ('almost unlimited', we remember) by interfering with nature. The verbs describing their actions – they 'command', 'mimic' and 'mock' – do not inspire us with confidence. On the contrary, Shelley already implies that such irresponsible power is dangerous, presumptuous and immoral.

Analysis, p. 55

We can now follow the theme of science through Frankenstein's creation of the daemon. This is narrated over some ten pages of the text, but we will again begin by looking at a short extract in detail:

> No one can conceive the variety of feelings which bore me onwards, like a hurricane, in the first enthusiasm of success. Life and death appeared

to me ideal bounds, which I should first break through, and pour a torrent of light into our dark world. A new species would bless me as its
creator and source; many happy and excellent natures would owe their
being to me. No father could claim the gratitude of his child so completely as I should deserve theirs. Pursuing these reflections, I thought,
that if I could bestow animation upon lifeless matter, I might in process
of time (although I now found it impossible) renew life where death
had apparently devoted the body to corruption.

These thoughts supported my spirits, while I pursued my undertaking with unremitting ardour. My cheek had grown pale with study, and
my person had become emaciated with confinement. Sometimes, on
the very brink of certainty, I failed; yet still I clung to the hope which
the next day or the next hour might realize. One secret which I alone
possessed was the hope to which I had dedicated myself; and the moon
gazed on my midnight labours, while, with unrelaxed and breathless
eagerness, I pursued nature to her hiding-places. Who shall conceive
the horrors of my secret toil as I dabbled among the unhallowed damps
of the grave or tortured the living animal to animate the lifeless clay? My
limbs now tremble, and my eyes swim with the remembrance; but then
a resistless, and almost frantic impulse, urged me forward; I seemed to
have lost all soul or sensation but for this one pursuit.   (*F* 55)

The passage opens with images of powerful natural forces: 'like a hur-
ricane', and 'pour a torrent of light' as well as the violent aim 'which
I should first break through'. Frankenstein's hubris is clear as he casts
himself as the source of light, thus comparing himself to the God of
Genesis! Hubris is further underlined by his expectation that he will
be blessed by the gratitude of a 'new species', and by his boast that
this will create a more powerful obligation than fatherhood. It is with
this combination of wild energy and swelling ego that Frankenstein
discusses life and death as 'ideal bounds' to be conquered. We should
notice that his ambition is self-extending: no sooner has he gained
power over creating life, than he dreams of overcoming death as well.
To summarize his ambition: he wants to create, to be worshipped by
his creation, and to be immortal.

The second part of our extract concentrates on portraying Frankenstein's physical and mental state during his researches, while 'these
thoughts supported my spirits'. If we highlight the verbs and verb

phrases from this passage, the mood of Victor's research is clear: 'pursued' (twice), 'unremitting ardour', 'clung', 'dedicated myself', 'labours', 'with unrelaxed and breathless eagerness', 'secret toil', 'dabbled', 'tortured', 'tremble', 'my eyes swim', 'resistless', 'frantic', 'urged'. These terms denote Victor's single-mindedness, but also progressively suggest a loss of control. So, the words 'breathless', 'tremble', 'my eyes swim' and 'frantic' suggest the growing inability of Frankenstein's own body to survive the strain. At the same time, the inflated ego of the preceding paragraph is being reduced to a frantic wreck: he is not studying science; rather, science or its study is destroying him. This idea is further underlined by his acknowledgement that he was wrecking his health: he became 'pale' and 'emaciated'; and during the episode describing the daemon's creation, the text develops Frankenstein's unnatural isolation clearly. His 'eyes were insensible to the charms of nature', his manic labours 'caused me also to forget those friends who were so many miles absent' (*F* 56), and, in the present extract, he 'seemed to have lost all soul or sensation but for this one pursuit'. Frankenstein paints a picture of himself as he was toward the end of his work, as 'nervous to a most painful degree; the fall of a leaf startled me, and I shunned my fellow-creatures as if I had been guilty of a crime' (*F* 57). At the same time, our extract reminds us of the sexual nature of Victor's frenzy, as he 'pursued nature to her hiding-places'.

This passage, then, underlines the unnaturalness and the madness of Frankenstein's scientific project. His enthusiasm and hubris are both reiterated, but above all, the passage evokes the mad and isolated wreck he becomes, illustrating the evils of such an approach to science. We notice that he is cut off from the influence of natural beauty; from communication with his family; and eventually from all his 'fellow-creatures'. The warning we heard in his repetition of 'one . . . one . . . one' (*F* 49) is echoed in this 'one pursuit'. All the positive values of harmony, moderation and community are sacrificed. Any pursuit that interferes with a man's 'domestic affections' is 'certainly unlawful, that is to say, not befitting the human mind', Shelley explains, and goes on to assert that the great evils of history would have been avoided had this rule been observed: 'Greece had not been enslaved; Caesar would have spared his country'(*F* 56). Shelley could hardly make her criticism of hubristic science more powerful.

In these two extracts, then, Mary Shelley makes use of science in a manner that has become typical of science-fiction novels; and she uses this theme to develop the view that masculine hubris, and gendered attitudes to science and nature, are dangerous, and show an unbalanced sexual drive leading to mania and madness.

Shelley draws on Sir Humphry Davy to ensure that the scientific elements of her text are convincing; and uses contemporary science similarly when the tree is split by lightning, and a 'man of great research in natural philosophy' discourses to the teenage Victor on the subject of 'electricity and galvanism' (*F* 42–3). 'Galvanism' was a theory that had become commonly known since its author, the Bolognese scientist Luigi Galvani, published his *Commentary on the Effects of Electricity on Muscular Motion*, in 1791. Percy Shelley was fascinated by electricity and carried out numerous experiments, and Mary clearly knew about galvanism.

For the reader of that time, the mention of galvanism would relate the story to numerous reports in the popular press, telling of experiments where corpses were made to jerk by being treated with electric shocks. Such experiments hoped to show that electricity could animate dead matter, and were founded on Galvani's idea that life consisted in a so-far undiscovered fluid called 'animal electricity'. Such a connection in the reader's mind makes the story of Victor's successful experiment no mere imagined fiction. Rather, it seemed at that time quite likely. In this way Mary Shelley reinforces the sense that the science she describes in her fiction is *possible*.

On the other hand, the reference to Luigi Galvani occurs in a context that is curious in two ways. First, the original 1818 text does not mention Galvani at all. Instead, it has Victor's father explaining electricity to him, and showing him 'a small electrical machine', 'a few experiments' and 'a kite' with a 'wire' which brought that 'fluid' (electricity) from the clouds. Mary Shelley must have realized that this is inconsistent with a father who was 'not scientific'(*F* 42), and in the revised 1831 text substitutes the guest expert who mentions galvanism.

Secondly and ironically, the guest's enthusiastic explanations have the effect of destroying, not inspiring, Victor's interest in Natural Philosophy. Why? Because this reaction underlines his hubris, of which Shelley is so critical. Victor listens to their guest, and concludes that 'nothing would or could ever be known'; furthermore, he is told of discoveries that have already been made by others. This kind of science is clearly not enough to satisfy Victor's ego and its monstrous cravings, and so he loses interest. After his arrival at Ingolstadt, Victor explains, 'I had a contempt for the uses of modern natural philosophy. It was very different, when the masters of the science sought immortality and power; such views, although futile, were grand' (*F* 48). Victor has no use for painstaking work focusing on small discoveries, then: these will only bring 'realities of little worth' (*F* 48). Equally, he has no use for science which seeks to understand, but does not actively interfere. When Victor makes his great discovery, he tells us: 'When I found so astonishing a power placed within my hands, I hesitated a long time concerning the manner in which I should employ it' (*F* 54). Notice that Victor's science gives him 'power' in his 'hands', to be 'employed', in contrast to knowledge in his head to be shared. He hesitates about *how* he should use his discovery, but does not even question *whether* he should use it.

Shelley thus makes it absolutely clear to us, that Victor's vanity demands the prospect of 'immortality' (from a project grand enough to satisfy his vanity), and 'power' (from a scientific act demonstrating his dominance over nature). *Frankenstein*'s critique of masculine scientific hubris shows that Victor and scientists like him are the ones of whom we should be frightened.

Conclusions

In this chapter, we have discussed the concepts of nature, society and science as they are canvassed in *Frankenstein*. We have found that each of these topics is a major theme, and that the novel expounds a clear fable under each heading. Each fable suggests a fairly straightforward moral.

So, on the subject of *nature*, Shelley proposes that both human nature and natural surroundings are fundamentally good and benevolent. The moral is to remain receptive to nature, to maintain a relationship of 'harmony' with it: then, its benevolent influences will ensure that you cannot stray too far from a good path in your life.

Frankenstein plays the villain in this cautionary fable by shutting himself away from nature (he says, 'my eyes were insensible to the charms of nature' [*F* 56]) during his scientific mania, and by breaking the tie to his creation, thus ensuring the daemon's natural goodness is 'wrenched' to evil.

On the subject of *society*, Shelley proposes that a new threat has arisen, in the form of the exploited, downtrodden and dispossessed. She pictures a society unwilling to face or understand this threat, with obsolete authorities and institutions, unable to cope with the danger. The moral is to understand how the actions of the ruling class have made this danger, and to redress the balance of society into a more equal system. In the daemon's determinist language, speaking for his class: 'make me happy, and I shall again be virtuous' (*F* 103). Frankenstein plays his part in this cautionary fable also. His actions are those of a short-sighted establishment: hostile, prejudiced and revolted, blind. The moral for the middle and upper classes is: take responsibility for the poverty and hardship you have created; for if you act as Frankenstein does and attempt to run away from the problem, there will be a violent revolution and widespread bloody destruction.

On the subject of *science*, Shelley proposes that the pursuit of knowledge should be accompanied by respect for nature, and should therefore be in harmony with nature. It is dangerous when an inflated ego and desire for power lead to scientific discoveries, and when scientists use their knowledge to interfere with nature. The moral is to be satisfied with painstaking and detailed research work, and to be satisfied to observe and understand the world, without seeking to interfere. Frankenstein plays his part in this fable also, by his persistent quest for 'immortality' and 'power' through science (*F* 48), and by 'mocking' nature with the creation of the daemon.

We have identified three moral fables, then, one on each of our themes. These fables are strongly painted into the text by Mary Shelley, who clearly writes with a didactic intention. The fables are there to warn or teach the reader, and the morals they recommend can be appended to the book. It is not enough to find these simple fables and their morals, however; for each of the topics we have discussed is, at the same time, more complex than its fable or its moral. Also, the topics themselves are inter-related in a further network of meaning in the novel as a whole.

Looking in the text for further corroboration of our three 'fables', we begin to discover complications. Is there, for example, a distinction between a non-invasive science, on the one hand, and Victor's kind of aggressive, interfering science, on the other? The answer is that Victor's science is fully depicted, but of non-invasive science there is less evidence. Victor makes one or two scathing remarks about natural philosophy, during the period between the lightning episode and his meeting with Professor Waldman, which show his contempt for seeking 'realities of little worth' (*F* 48), when he is convinced that 'nothing would or could ever be known' (*F* 43). These remarks fail to describe an alternative 'good' science, however – they merely denote scientists with less grandiose ideas than Frankenstein himself, not a non-interfering attitude to nature.

Then, Frankenstein's refusal to finish making the female raises the issue of a scientist's responsibility: perhaps that episode will propose a 'good' science for our fable's moral? Perhaps Frankenstein indicates an ethical course when he refrains from using his power? When we return to that passage, however, we remember that Frankenstein was merely worried about his reputation – 'I shuddered to think that future ages might curse me as their pest' – and that his decisions and actions at that crisis lacked an ethical dimension. In the end, we have to conclude that a 'good' science is implied, but not present, in the text of *Frankenstein*.

Is the novel, then, anti-science? Thinking about this question, we remember Frankenstein's words to Walton: first, he warns Walton against the 'madness' and 'intoxicating draught' of desire for knowledge, saying 'let me reveal my tale, and you will dash the cup from your lips!' (*F* 29); later, when refusing to reveal his discovery to Walton, he urges the listener to 'learn from me, if not by my precepts, at least by my example, how dangerous is the acquirement of knowledge' (*F* 54). These two moments in the narrative argue against all knowledge. Frankenstein's advice is, do not do it: it will only bring disaster. At the end of his life, Victor is less negative: he warns against ambition, but then remarks, 'Yet why do I say this? I have myself been blasted in these hopes, yet another may succeed'(*F* 220). These are Victor's last words, and hardly a positive endorsement of knowledge. Is there a better argument than this, elsewhere in the novel? What, for example, does the daemon say about knowledge? Here is his meditation:

> I cannot describe to you the agony that these reflections inflicted upon me: I tried to dispel them, but sorrow only increased with knowledge. Oh, that I had forever remained in my native wood, nor known nor felt beyond the sensations of hunger, thirst and heat!
>
> Of what a strange nature is knowledge! It clings to the mind, when it has once seized on it, like a lichen on the rock. I wished sometimes to shake off all thought and feeling; but I learned that there was but one means to overcome the sensation of pain, and that was death... (*F* 123)

This is a far more mature meditation about knowledge than that of Frankenstein, who typically reacts to unpleasantness by trying to forget it. The daemon, by contrast, recognizes that knowledge is inevitable. He can express the wish that he had remained in a form of primitive ignorance 'in my native wood', and had never risen above a life of the senses, because knowledge has brought 'the sensation of pain' with it. However, it 'clings to the mind': once acquired, it cannot be suppressed. In conclusion, then, we can read of the dangers, sadness and suffering that come with knowledge; but there are very few positive comments on science or learning; and there is no example in the novel, of a 'good' science: one that does not seek power to interfere in nature. Some critics play down this absence from the text, claiming that Shelley 'implicitly invokes Darwin's theory of gradual evolutionary progress'.[5] However, the fact that an exemplary form of science is not explicit does have implications for the theme of knowledge and our interpretation of the novel.

Next, we consider the question of Frankenstein's isolation. One interpretation of the novel proposes that Walton is saved from disaster because his project is a collaborative one: that is, because he has the crew and is therefore not utterly alone. Victor, on the other hand, shunned his 'fellow-creatures', hid himself away in his laboratory, worked at night and stopped communicating with his family. Victor discusses his father's theory that as long as he is on a good road in life, he will 'think of us with affection, and we shall hear regularly from you' (*F* 56), and concludes, 'I am now convinced that he was justified'. Victor then develops his idea that no pursuit should interfere with 'domestic affections', suggesting that most of the great evils of history would have been avoided ('Greece had not been enslaved . . . the empires of Mexico and Peru had not been destroyed') if this precept had been observed (*F* 56). Clearly, he believes his own catastrophe would equally have been avoided, had he shunned a labour that interfered with his 'domestic affections'. Thus the lesson of Frankenstein's isolation, and about maintaining 'domestic' ties, is clearly expounded.

But is this relevant to Walton? It is difficult to see how Walton's voyage represents a different and less doomed project than Frankenstein's science. There is the plain fact that Walton needs a crew to reach the North Pole, while Frankenstein could work alone; but this difference only generates a nonsensical moral: if you are going to be mad, be mad with others, and they will save you. Furthermore, Walton's project does not connect with the theory of 'domestic affections', at all. Walton's crew are not his family, and their function is merely to be frightened for their own lives. Walton and the crew do not cooperate, either; rather, they force him to turn back by threatening mutiny. Finally, Walton writes to his sister regularly, unlike Frankenstein, who does not answer his father's letters for a year. Walton, then, does maintain his 'domestic affections'. We can argue that Walton is saved by the mutiny, which forces him to turn back; but to propound the theory that Walton's voyage represents a communal effort, in contrast to Frankenstein's research, seems to miss the point. In fact, the most surprising truth about Walton's voyage is that Frankenstein's story does not affect its outcome at all.

Next, we may seek better definition of nature's significance: are the natural surroundings described in *Frankenstein* significant in a Wordsworthian sense? Victor sees the high Alps as 'belonging to another earth, the habitations of another race of beings', with the effect of 'solemnising my mind and causing me to forget the passing cares of life' (*F* 97, 100). Do these terms imply passing through nature's grandeur to a visionary universe, as when Wordsworth's mind is filled with 'huge and mighty forms, that do not live / Like living men', and 'No familiar shapes / Remained, no pleasant images of trees, / Of sea

or sky, no colours of green fields'?[6] Mary Shelley was intimately familiar with Wordsworth's writings, and we may compare the awe, and
forgetfulness of day-to-day life, experienced by Victor in contact with
'the awful and majestic in nature', with Wordsworth's experience when
his senses shut down and he is in contact with 'Wisdom and Spirit of
the Universe' rather than external nature.

On the other hand, Victor attributes 'maternal' characteristics to
nature as well; and his response to 'Omnipotence' comes from the
lower landscape, before he attains the high Alps. In any case, Victor
never reaches a Wordsworthian state of vision. Instead, the text suggests a religious idea as nature 'ministers' to Victor and 'congregates'
around him, but this provides only a temporary soothing effect. At the
same time, when nature is discussed in the context of scientific knowledge, it becomes gendered as feminine and burdened with secrets and
mysteries the (male) scientist seeks to 'unfold' or 'unveil'; while at
other times storms and beauties are described either as masculine or
as neuter. Our fable tells us to live in 'harmony' with nature, and
recommends Elizabeth's attitude of 'admiration and delight' as she
'contemplated with a serious and satisfied spirit' (*F* 38) her natural
surroundings. On the other hand, even Elizabeth's harmonious relationship with nature cannot survive intact: on their wedding journey,
'her temper was fluctuating; joy for a few instants shone in her eyes,
but it continually gave place to distraction and reverie' (*F* 197). The
significance of nature in the novel consists of such a variety of indications that the overall mixture remains elusive, and we should be wary
of over-definition.

Perhaps this is a warning to be heeded whenever interpreting
Frankenstein. Looking at our three 'fables' more critically, we find that
their founding concepts are increasingly elusive. The effect is that the
novel appears to set out a very simple stall; but at the same time, the
text eludes being confined within the very stall it has set out. This creates a curious effect: *Frankenstein* is a fable with a moral which is at
once recommended, and ineffectual.

In conclusion, then, we must for the present take a less didactic line,
and limit ourselves to describing the imagined 'world' of *Frankenstein*
as well as we can. In this text, nature and knowledge are both presented as inescapable facts of the world – powerful forces all human

beings have to come to terms with, because they are our and we are their neighbours on earth. The world of *Frankenstein* starts many hares about science and nature. All of these throw up critical insights, homilies and perceptions as we go along, but none of them lead to overall interpretations. Rather, the questions all turn back upon humanity, and a quality of belonging or responsiveness, that can be called 'harmony'. This quality, its presence or its absence, is a consistent element of the novel, and places responsibility on the individual for how he or she lives in the world. Frankenstein does not possess this quality; indeed, he transgresses against it. The daemon loses it as his knowledge grows, and differentiates him from his environment. To an extent, the story supports the idea that 'harmony' may be a gendered, feminine quality; and its disastrous opposite is a temptation to which men are prone. Much of the perplexity of *Frankenstein* is expressed when we say: Elizabeth possesses the quality of 'harmony', but it does her no good at all.

Our attempt to isolate a consistent value in *Frankenstein* raises a final issue. If the text suggests an ideal of people, in their natural state of benevolent goodness, living in harmony with their natural surroundings, what of society? And, in particular, what of the powerful chains of determinism that create injustice, cruelty and conflict? In short, how can a romantic concept such as 'harmony' co-exist with the iron laws of cause and effect? These questions are not really answerable. What we can suggest, however, is that both modes of thinking are present and powerfully advanced in the text. It would be possible to argue that *Frankenstein* is like an unresolved collision between romantic and materialist modes of thought.

Methods of Analysis

Our approach has used close analysis of short extracts as a starting point, as in previous chapters, and we have deployed a similar range of techniques for the analysis of the text. In addition, in this chapter, we have used leading questions to take us to related passages elsewhere in the text, for amplification and comparison, leading to *knowing the text better.*

For example, when we had studied the passage describing Victor's journey up to Chamounix, we then looked at the surrounding pages, and added points we noticed which gave *confirmation* of what we had found, or which suggested *further insights* into the significance of nature. So, on page 99, we found the religious terms 'ministered' and 'congregated', which reinforced the suggestion of God working through nature; while on pages 100–101 we noticed the significance of mist, rain and darkness, adding a new insight to our reading of the nature theme. We then thought about where else to find this feature, and turned to page 198, on Frankenstein's wedding night, when the motif recurs.

This process, of looking at other parts of the text for corroboration, more detailed evidence, or additional insights, leads to *knowing the text better*, which enables a more fully informed and wide-ranging discussion. However, it is not a matter of looking through the whole book. When you embark on this wider-ranging exploration of the text, *use common sense to point you towards the passages most likely to be relevant.* So, for example, we know that there are several pages describing the landscape and Victor's journey, just before his encounter with the daemon on the 'mer de glace'; so it made sense to look through pp. 98–101, having analysed p. 97. Also, we remembered that there is a storm on Victor's wedding-night: it was therefore easy to turn to page 198, to see whether the same idea about visibility recurs there. We could also have remembered that there is a storm when Victor visits the scene of William's murder, so it would make sense to re-read that episode as well, for further corroboration.

This two-stage method is a powerful way of approaching the text. The initial detailed analysis of an extract ensures that your ideas have a sound textual basis; then, wider research through the text amplifies and adds detail to your findings, building upon ideas that act as a firm foundation.

Suggested Work

To add further detail to your understanding of the way nature is portrayed in *Frankenstein*, make a study of journeys by water, and Victor's use of the lake when at home. Begin by re-reading the wedding-day journey to Evian (pp. 196–7), then study the journey down the Rhine towards England (pp. 160–2), and Victor's drifts on the lake (p. 94). These passages are likely to send you to other descriptions of water, lakes, rivers, and so on (particularly, of course, Victor's passive voyage from the Orkneys to Ireland!) as you amplify your understanding of this element of the novel. Use your memory of reading the novel, and common sense, to point you towards relevant passages, with the aim of *knowing this element of the text better*.

4

Symbol and Myth

Symbol

What is a Symbol?

A symbol can be anything that is literally present in a fiction, which has an added significance beyond its literal function in the story. So, one may find symbolic meaning in a person, an object, an element or a force: almost anything can be 'symbolic'. The danger is that we are tempted to over-interpret, and will see symbols everywhere and everything as symbolic. An example makes this clear. We have suggested that Walton, Victor Frankenstein and Clerval together create a 'composite' character, representative of masculine ambition: so, the ambitions of the explorer, the scientist and the conqueror/imperialist are all represented. Does this mean that these three characters are 'symbolic'? The answer is no. Why? Because these three men are ambitious. They represent ambition because they literally have it, not because they are symbols of it. On the other hand, we have also suggested that the daemon stands for or 'represents' the English industrial working class. This interpretation does suggest that the daemon is a symbol, because the daemon is not, literally, anything to do with the English working class (he is a manufactured humanoid of Bavarian origin). So, if we attach that meaning to him, and read that meaning from his character and role in the novel, then we are saying that he has an added significance, or added meaning, beyond his literal function in the story.

Symbolism and *Frankenstein*

The question we ask in this chapter, then, is, how far are we justified in applying a symbolic meaning to *Frankenstein*? And, if we can, what is that meaning? To pursue this question, we will look into certain elements of the novel that appear to encourage interpretation. These are, Frankenstein's dream; the daemon, his existence and argument; natural forces such as mountains, water, ice, storms, the moon; and the faculties of sight and hearing.

Frankenstein's Dream

As soon as the daemon opens his eyes, Frankenstein is filled with 'breathless horror and disgust', and runs from his laboratory to his bedchamber, where:

> I slept, indeed, but I was disturbed by the wildest dreams. I thought I saw Elizabeth, in the bloom of health, walking in the streets of Ingol-stadt. Delighted and surprised, I embraced her, but as I imprinted the first kiss on her lips, they became livid with the hue of death; her features appeared to change, and I thought that I held the corpse of my dead mother in my arms; a shroud enveloped her form, and I saw the grave-worms crawling in the folds of flannel. I started from my sleep with horror . . .   (*F* 59)

Dreams have traditionally provoked interpretation, of course; and Frankenstein's nightmare is no exception – clearly, Mary Shelley expects us to pay attention to this horrific fantasy. That it is horrific suits the context: Victor describes his labours over many months as 'the horrors of my secret toil', and he has just experienced the trauma of revulsion from the daemon. That the dream contains vivid images of death such as the shroud, grave-worms and discoloured skin is also suggested by the context: Victor undertook his first researches with the adage 'To examine the causes of life, we must first have recourse to death', and studied 'the natural decay and corruption of the human body' (*F* 52). So, there is a natural connection between Victor's actual experiences at the time and the elements of horror and death in his dream. The aspects of his dream that are less obvious in origin, then, ask for interpretation. These are, first, the change when Elizabeth becomes his mother; and secondly, the change when living health becomes death, which is also when sexual arousal becomes horror.

Both of these elements of the dream are susceptible to quite common-sense explanation in Victor's psychology. After Mrs Frankenstein's death, Elizabeth becomes the emotional mainstay of the family, when she 'veiled her grief, and strove to act the comforter to us all' (*F* 45), adopting the role of female carer and so taking the dead mother's place. Additionally, in a sense, Mrs Frankenstein took Elizabeth's death for herself – death called for Elizabeth first, and was transferred to her foster-mother. So, the idea that these two women may be interchangeable in Victor's mind has been thoroughly sown. The second interpretable element is the change from health to death, and here again we can suggest an interpretation: that the dream is, in a sense, prophetic. In this interpretation, Frankenstein knows he has transgressed against nature's laws. He foresees (and fears) a terrible punishment for what he has done. It would be quite natural for his guilty mind to prophesy the death of Elizabeth. This also fits Shelley's story, presaging the climax of the daemon's revenge, which is the murder of Elizabeth.

This discussion, however, simply provokes further questions. So, if Elizabeth and Mrs Frankenstein are interchangeable in Victor's mind, what does this suggest about Victor's official sexuality, his assumed desire for Elizabeth? Has Victor an incestuous desire for his mother so forbidden that it conjures the horror-image of embracing a corpse? It could be objected that we should not apply modern psychoanalytical ideas to an early nineteenth-century text. On the other hand, the idea of incest was attached to *Frankenstein* at the time of its first publication. We remember that Elizabeth was originally Victor's first cousin, and the whiff of incest led Mary Shelley to change Elizabeth's parentage for the 1831 edition.

Then, if sexual attraction turns to death, in Victor's dream: what does this tell us about his relations with the female sex? Even without entering the realm of psychoanalysis, there are connections between this element of Victor's dream and his repeated postponement of the marriage with Elizabeth, or his attempt to become a single-sex parent. We have remarked that Shelley uses Victor and Walton as vehicles to describe a gendered male ambition of which she is critical; and we have noticed that Victor's approach to science is couched in gendered language suggesting a sexual drive (to 'penetrate', 'unfold' and 'lift the veil' from female 'nature'). This interpretation of the dream may complete the picture: that Victor's sexual drives are misdirected towards science, *because* (a) he is frightened of women and equates sex with death, and (b) he has suppressed his sexuality, horrified by his incestuous feelings for his mother.

There is no guideline as to how far such interpretation can go: we are in the twenty-first century, when psychoanalysis has become a sophisticated field of knowledge. How far can we, or should we, ignore the insights we bring to a text as readers, because that text happens to have been produced in a pre-psychoanalytical time? Our study has suggested that Shelley expounds an intentional, feminist critique of male egocentricity and hubris, and of a gendered approach to science. It is also reasonable to say that Frankenstein's dream adds to this critique, showing that something about his mother, and women in general, has driven Victor's sexuality into unnatural channels. At this point, however, interpretation is likely to trespass into other areas: treating Frankenstein as if he were a real person and a case history, rather than a literary character. The dream is highly suggestive, and could have several further interpretations. As we have seen, this kind of multiple suggestiveness is typical of *Frankenstein*.

Is Frankenstein's dream symbolic? It is difficult to answer this question. The images described, of health changing suddenly to death and of foster-sister/fiancée changing to mother, are representative and interpretable; and there is a sense in which all dreams, being non-literal, are symbolic. In any event, these images express Elizabeth's role in relation to Victor, and guiltily foretell his punishment for making the daemon; and they express Victor's abnormal sexuality.

The Daemon

We have already remarked that the daemon can be regarded as symbolic of the threat from the English industrial working class, or the French – or any – revolutionary mob. This way of thinking about the story introduces a number of other suggestions of 'symbolism' that contribute to a political story lying behind the overt events of *Frankenstein*. So, if the daemon 'symbolises' the working class, then Frankenstein symbolizes a degenerate bourgeoisie. Some elements of the tale support this idea. For example, Frankenstein has carried out 'unhallowed' research and developed new technology, and so created the daemon – just as the industrial revolution used new technology to create the proletariat. And, of course, Victor Frankenstein wants to separate himself from the ugliness he has created, just as the owners of industry insulated their own privileged lives from the factories and slums they created. Some further details fill out this interpretation: we have met Frankenstein's social snobbery, his habit of equating fair beauty with goodness, and his prejudice against the daemon; we have also commented upon judicial authority as it appears in the novel.

The fable of *Frankenstein*, then, can be interpreted as symbolic of a social or political story. However, most of this interpretative structure rests upon the daemon's description of 'the strange system of human society' on pp. 122–3; while not everything in the novel fits such an interpretation neatly. For example, Frankenstein's and Clerval's contempt for commerce expresses the arrogance of aristocracy rather than the greed of industrialists. However, the daemon is powerfully symbolic of poverty, the excluded, the exploited, the dispossessed; and we can say that he presents the case of those who lose, in the injustices of society; that Frankenstein is a degenerate patrician; and that the novel is a warning to a complacent ruling class.

The daemon makes two further claims to symbolic significance, however. First, he presents a consistent case for determinism, and so we can ask whether he 'symbolises' this mode of thought, and if so, how does this affect the overall meaning of the novel? Secondly, we have remarked that the daemon may 'symbolise' a hidden or 'dark' side of Frankenstein's own nature – that is, that the characterization of Frankenstein and his daemon is a fable about a divided psyche.

Our analyses of the daemon, both as narrator and as character, have emphasized how he speaks for determinism. Philosophically, determinism is opposed to romanticism: the one believes that the environment has ultimate power over the individual, while the other believes that the individual, through vision or idealism, can escape from, nullify or liberate himself from the influences of his environment. The crucial question, therefore, is about freewill: do we, or do we not, have the freedom to choose our courses through life? The daemon believes that we do not, that outside influences can even force us to choose a path against our nature. It is in this light that he regards his own murderous actions.

We have noticed the daemon's philosophy because it is so powerfully and persuasively advanced in his narrative. On the other hand, the environmental influences that determine his actions are not predominantly material. He is not driven to his revenge by poverty, and he is not motivated by greed. Instead, his course is decided by an absence of love. In other words, the daemon is not a prototype of materialism: rather, he seeks love, as any romantic might. His emotional appeal concerns his loneliness.

The daemon's determinism is consistently hammered home in his narrative, and so it stands out. However, Frankenstein's outlook is often equally determinist. He claims that his parents could direct his life 'to happiness or misery, according as they fulfilled their duties towards me' (*F* 35); he asserts that 'Destiny was too potent, and her immutable laws had decreed my utter and terrible destruction' (*F* 43); and he attempts to struggle from his bed in Walton's cabin, telling us that 'the spirits who assist my vengeance will endow me with sufficient strength' (*F* 219). What is the difference? Why do we accord so much more respect to the daemon than to his creator?

The answer is that the daemon's case is more convincing. When Frankenstein criticizes his father's comment on Cornelius Agrippa, we feel like reminding him that his father is right: Agrippa is 'sad trash'. When he claims that 'Destiny was too potent', we feel inclined to reply, *No: your enormous ego and your vanity were too potent: don't blame destiny*. And, when he imagines spirits assisting his vengeance, our comment would be, *poor deluded fool*. Furthermore, Frankenstein is not consistently determinist. Intermittently, he espouses a romantic philosophy. So, when he declares 'more, far more, will I achieve' (*F* 49), he asserts the freedom of the individual to make and control his own fate; and, when he tells the crew that 'This ice is not made of such stuff as your hearts may be' (*F* 217), he asserts the power of a brave individual to overcome all material limits, in true romantic fashion.

When, on the other hand, the daemon appeals to us, 'But am I not alone, miserably alone?' (*F* 103), our hearts go out to him and we believe in the emotions that are acting upon him. In short, then, we really meet two forms of determinism in *Frankenstein*: one a weakness that externalizes both blame and hope; the other a real conflict in which the individual's nature is overwhelmed.

So, does the daemon 'symbolise' a system of thought? And, what of Frankenstein's determinism: is it a result of disillusionment? The answer to this second question is no: Frankenstein gave his parents responsibility for his own life, from early on; and his romantic assertions to Walton's crew are uttered long after his own romantic dreams have turned to misery. We can suggest a possible interpretation: that Frankenstein, just as he belongs to a decadent and obsolete, patrician social order, also stands for a failure of philosophy – a shifting of blame onto others or fate, interspersed with temporary spurts of romantic assertion. So, perhaps the daemon represents the more rigorous thinking required by a harsher social reality, in contrast to the inconsistent outlook of a failing ruling class.

This suggestion has the advantage that it would fit with the daemon's political significance: indeed, it might endow Mary Shelley with a far-seeing prescience, contrasting the fading influence of romanticism against the determinist philosophies which gained ascendancy as the nineteenth century progressed. In this sense, it would be possible to see *Frankenstein* as a story of evolving philosophies. Remember, however, that the daemon, although determinist, is not materialist: rather, he too is a romantic manqué, one who finds no love where he hoped for it.

The final suggestion of the daemon's significance is as the 'dark' side of Frankenstein's psyche. This idea springs from the many statements of a fate binding the two together; and the idea that they are both emanations of one personality, which is also in the text. When Frankenstein is at the scene of William's death, he meditates,

'I considered the being whom I had cast among mankind, and endowed with the will and power to effect purposes of horror, such as the deed which he had now done, nearly in the light of my own vampire, my own spirit let loose from the grave, and forced to destroy all that was dear to me' (*F* 78). This idea relates the Frankenstein/daemon duality to traditional superstitions of succubus or possession, or of good and evil spirits inhabiting the same physical body. As in tradition, one personality is cultured, beautiful and benevolent; the other is savage and primitive and malevolent.

In support of this idea, notice the dreamlike ambience of Frankenstein's meetings with the daemon. It is upon waking from his nightmare that 'by the dim and yellow light of the moon . . . I beheld the wretch' (*F* 59); then, when he visits the scene of William's death, he 'perceived in the gloom a figure', before 'A flash of lightning illuminated the object' but 'the figure passed me quickly, and I lost it in the gloom'. When he contemplates pursuit 'another flash discovered him to me hanging among the rocks' before he 'soon reached the summit, and disappeared' (*F* 77–8). Shelley's description emphasizes momentary glimpses, and endows the daemon with an almost supernatural ability to appear and disappear, thanks to flashes of lightning. Additionally, Frankenstein feels a dreamlike knowledge: the certainty that the daemon is the murderer of William. He says that 'No sooner did that idea cross my imagination, than I became convinced of its truth' (*F* 78). Notice that Victor believes this without any evidence, much as you know a fact in a dream.

The daemon's next appearance, on the 'mer de glace', prompts Frankenstein to a near loss of consciousness: 'I was troubled: a mist came over my eyes, and I felt a faintness seize me' (*F* 101); and after the daemon's narrative, Victor feels that his promise 'made every other circumstance of existence pass before me like a dream, and that thought only had to me the reality of life' (*F* 151). Finally, when the daemon appears on Orkney, Frankenstein is unable to find relief from 'the sickening oppression of the most terrible reveries' and he 'was overcome by the sensation of helplessness, so often felt in frightful dreams' (*F* 171–2). Dreams are repeatedly associated with the daemon's appearances to Frankenstein, then. Does this mean that the daemon 'symbolises' Frankenstein's dark or unconscious side?

We can tentatively answer yes to this; but it is difficult to go any further. For example, we could theorize that the daemon is a physical embodiment of the dark, sinful side of mankind. Such ideas may be tempting, but yet again, efforts to impose too pat a symbolic meaning onto *Frankenstein* leave us less than convinced.[1] Put simply, we may have associative thoughts about light and dark sides, good and evil spirits, daemons and possession, nightmares and reality and so forth; but none of these extrapolations is firmly indicated by the text. In the text, there is a daemon created by Frankenstein; their fates are linked by that act of creation; Victor has a dreamlike sensation associated with their meetings; they are irrevocably in conflict and contrast; and that is all. Once again, we meet the special quality of this novel: an unusual richness of suggestion, and an unusual absence of certainty – or, indeed, of any evidence that would help us to choose between the many suggestions.

The daemon, then, is extraordinarily rich in suggestions of 'symbolic' significance. Undoubtedly, he provokes several strands of ideas suggesting what he may 'symbolise'. However, we are left with only the broadest of conclusions – that he stands for society's poor and disadvantaged; and that he may embody 'dark' or unconscious elements of Frankenstein.

The Moon, Water, Mountains and Storms

Frankenstein contains numerous descriptions of natural scenery, and natural forces appear to exert influence. For example, we have already discussed the influence the high mountains have in 'solemnising' Frankenstein's thoughts, and how he regards them as his 'mighty friends'. We have also discussed the possible significance of nature, as a theme in the novel. Our question now is, are the forces of the natural world symbolic in the novel? In this context we will consider the moon, water (including lakes, rivers and the sea), mountains and storms.

The Moon

We begin with the moon, because from reading the novel we have noticed that there are a number of moonlit scenes. What moonlit scenes do we remember? First, we remember the daemon's description of his first days of life; then, the scene in which he fires the De Laceys' cottage; finally, the night when Frankenstein tears the almost-completed female creature in pieces. Here are the daemon's words about the moon:

> Soon a gentle light stole over the heavens, and gave me a sensation of pleasure. I started up and beheld a radiant form rise from among the trees. I gazed with a kind of wonder. It moved slowly, but it enlightened my path, and I again went out in search of berries. . . . No distinct ideas occupied my mind; all was confused. I felt light, and hunger, and thirst, and darkness; innumerable sounds rang in my ears, and on all sides various scents saluted me: the only object that I could distinguish was the bright moon, and I fixed my eyes on that with pleasure.   (*F* 106)

When he fires the De Laceys' cottage, we read that he 'waited with forced impatience until the moon had sunk to commence my operations', then:

> I lighted the dry branch of a tree and danced with fury around the devoted cottage, my eyes still fixed on the western horizon, the edge of which the moon nearly touched. A part of its orb was at length hid, and I waved my brand; it sank, and with a loud scream I fired the straw, and heath, and bushes, which I had collected.   (*F* 140–1)

After tearing apart the female, Frankenstein locks the laboratory and goes to his own apartment:

> Several hours passed, and I remained near my window gazing on the sea; it was almost motionless, for the winds were hushed, and all nature reposed under the eye of the quiet moon. A few fishing vessels alone specked the water, and now and then the gentle breeze wafted the sound of voices as the fishermen called to one another.   (*F* 171)

The first two of these extracts suggest a consistent idea. The moon is characterized as 'gentle', 'radiant', 'bright', and it 'enlightened' the daemon's path. It is associated with 'wonder' and 'pleasure' (twice). In the daemon's apprehension, then, the moon appears so lovely, and so wondrous, as to become almost an object of worship. Consequently, when he comes to enact what he calls 'a kind of insanity in my spirits, that burst all bounds of reason and reflection', the daemon feels compelled to wait until the moon has set, before he can scream and fire the cottage in a frenzy of vengeance. Shelley is particular about this, for the daemon is already dancing with fury bearing a lighted brand, but his eyes are 'still fixed on the western horizon' watching the moonset. On these two occasions, then, the moon seems to represent a powerful benevolent influence: a calming beauty in nature that is implicitly in conflict with the daemon's impulses of violence and vengeance. On the night of firing the cottage, the daemon waits for the moon to set with 'forced impatience': thus, the moon acts to restrain him in the conflict between his natural goodness and the evil into which misery 'wrenched' his character.

What, then, should we make of the peaceful scene that is our third extract? The moon is clearly important, and her influence recalls the 'gentle' and 'radiant' account of the daemon's first perceptions: 'all nature reposed under the eye of the quiet moon', so the surroundings are 'motionless', 'hushed', and a 'gentle' breeze 'wafted' sounds. Into this scene the paddling of the daemon's oars 'suddenly' obtrudes. Certainly, the moon remains benevolent and beautiful in this scene; on the other hand, she does not appear to influence the daemon at all, and her peaceful paragraph is an isolated interlude for Frankenstein between 'the sickening oppression of the most terrible reveries' and 'the sensation of helplessness, so often felt in frightful dreams' – the twin horrors of destroying the female and facing the daemon's reproaches and threats. The only suggestion that comes to mind is that the destruction of the female brings peace and clarity. This idea would link this peaceful moonlit scene with his comment on the decision, that 'I now felt as if a film had been taken from before my eyes, and that I, for the first time, saw clearly' (*F* 175). In such an interpretation clear moonlight symbolizes clear thoughts: first the daemon's innocence; then his benevolence in conflict with his vengeful fury; and finally, Frankenstein's clear-mindedness in refusing to complete the female.

Unfortunately, there are objections to the last part of this interpretation. First, we are not sure that Frankenstein is right to break his promise. When we analysed Victor's action, we found weak reasoning, no moral awareness, prejudice, and the destructive action carried out in a trembling fit of passion. Doubts about whether he now 'for the first time, saw clearly' are underlined when we read that he shut his mind to any alternative opinion: 'I banished from my mind every thought that could lead to a different conclusion' (*F* 175). A second objection arises when he disposes of the female's 'mangled' parts. He tells us that 'At one time the moon, which had before been clear, was suddenly overspread by a thick cloud, and I took advantage of the moment of darkness and cast my basket into the sea'. After this, 'The sky became clouded', but Frankenstein is 'refreshed' by the air and feels 'agreeable sensations', so he lies down in the boat and goes to sleep (all quotations are from *F* 175–6). In this episode the moon shines and is clouded over, both at the wrong times: it fails to shine on disposing of the female, and is clouded as Frankenstein feels refreshed.

Three appearances of the moon present another conundrum. On the daemon's first night alive, Frankenstein sees him 'by the dim and yellow light of the moon', when 'a grin wrinkled his cheeks' (*F* 59); then, when he is completing the female, Frankenstein sees 'by the light of the moon, the daemon at the casement. A ghastly grin wrinkled his lips' (*F* 171); and finally, while vainly embracing the corpse of the murdered Elizabeth, Frankenstein 'felt a kind of panic on seeing the pale yellow light of the moon illuminate the chamber. . . . I saw at the open window a figure the most hideous and abhorred. A grin was on the face of the monster' (*F* 200). These three occasions join the light of the moon – in two cases specifically yellow – with sight of the daemon grinning. On the first two occasions, Frankenstein's interpretation of his expression is wrong: the daemon's grin is benevolent. Only when gloating over Elizabeth's corpse is his grin a 'jeer'. These three moonlit moments are linked together by word-echoes and circumstances: perhaps to highlight Victor's misinterpretation of the daemon's expressions. They are, of course, gothic moments of shock for the reader, just as they shock Victor. On the other hand, their moonlight, if anything, is deceptive – virtually the opposite of the significance hinted at elsewhere.

In conclusion, then, we have found that the moon has a positive symbolic function, representing beauty, gentleness and benevolence at some points in the text, and particularly in terms of its influence upon the daemon; on the other hand, this function is not consistent, and the moon provokes other interpretations in other passages.

Water

We now turn our attention to water. Again, we choose to investigate this element because there are numerous passages in the text where water seems to play a significant role. In particular, we remember Victor's habit of drifting in a boat on the lake by Belrive; Victor's and Clerval's journey down the Rhine; Victor's voyage from Orkney to Ireland, then from Ireland to France; and finally the wedding-day journey to Evian. Do these passages have any special significance? We will try to assemble suggestions and implications by re-reading the relevant passages:

- p. 94: Victor allows the boat to drift, and indulges his 'miserable reflections' – in other words, he is passive. On the lake, it is a 'scene so beautiful and heavenly' and 'all was at peace around me', while Victor feels himself to be 'the only unquiet thing that wandered restless'. He is tempted to drown himself 'that the waters might close over me and my calamities forever'. This description implies that he is out of harmony: on Victor's death, the natural beauty around would return to a 'peace' which his existence disturbs. Water would 'close over me', that is its beautiful and peaceful surface would be healed.
- p. 160: Victor tells us: 'I lay in the bottom of the boat, and, as I gazed on the cloudless blue sky, I seemed to drink in a tranquillity to which I had long been a stranger'. However, the majority of the passage is given over to an encomium on Clerval's appreciation of nature. Victor's position, passive and watching the sky, is sandwiched in between two descriptions of the part of the Rhine near Mayence, its rural life and its beauty; the first from Victor and the second from Clerval. Here again a water scene, with Victor completely passive, emphasizes nature's peace: 'a tranquility to which I had long been a stranger'. This time, however, it soothes Victor rather than provoking suicidal thoughts.

- pp. 175–7: Victor sets out from Orkney at moonrise, and sails about four miles from the shore. There, in a cloudy moment, he throws the mangled remains of the female body into the sea. It remains cloudy but the air is refreshing: Victor has 'agreeable sensations', so he lies down in the bottom of the boat (again!): 'Clouds hid the moon, every-thing was obscure, and I heard only the sound of the boat, as its keel cut through the waves; the murmur lulled me, and in a short time I slept soundly' (*F* 176). Here again, perhaps, we meet water's soothing peacefulness. However, the remainder of Victor's voyage to Ireland describes the sea in different terms: the 'waves continually threatened', and if he turned into the wind 'the boat would be instantly filled with water'. He felt 'a few sensations of terror' at the prospect of being 'swallowed up in the immeasurable waters', and 'I looked upon the sea, it was to be my grave'. Then, the breakers die down into 'a heavy swell' which induces nausea. Finally, on sighting land, Frankenstein remarks, 'how strange is that clinging love we have of life even in the excess of misery!' (quotations are from pp. 176–7).

  What are we to make of this passage? Victor's sleep, lying in the bottom of the boat, is reminiscent of the earlier episodes: when drifting, Victor can achieve some soothing harmony with his surroundings. On the other hand, the storm associates water with death: he will be 'swallowed up' and it is 'my grave'; and Victor discovers that he still does not want to die. In this voyage, in fact, we find water associated with peace and passivity, and with death. Perhaps we should also note, in passing, that water hides and closes over the evidence of Frankenstein's unhallowed labour: the torn female body.

- pp. 187–8: 'It was midnight. I lay on the deck, looking at the stars, and listening to the dashing of the waves. I hailed the darkness that shut Ireland from my sight'. Frankenstein is again lying on his back in a boat. This time, the reality of the voyage ('the vessel . . . the wind . . . and the sea which surrounded me') reminds him that the murder of Clerval is not a dream, and that it really happened. In this state of mind, he 'repassed, in my memory, my whole life' up to the night when the daemon first lived. Distressed by his memories, Victor takes a double dose of laudanum and sleeps – but he has terrible nightmares in which the daemon is strangling him. When his father wakes him, 'the dashing waves were around: the cloudy sky above; the fiend was not here: a sense of security, a feeling that a truce was established between the present hour and the irresistible, disastrous future, imparted to me a kind of calm forgetfulness' (*F* 188). Here, the voyage seems to act as a temporary sanctuary for Frankenstein's emotions: yet again, a water voyage soothes and calms.

- pp. 196–7: On their wedding journey from Geneva to Evian, Victor and Elizabeth 'enjoyed the beauty of the scene'. The text names and describes landmarks (Mont Blanc, the Jura, etc.) along their way; and when commenting on natural beauty, Elizabeth says, 'Look also at the innumerable fish that are swimming in the clear waters, where we can distinguish every pebble that lies at the bottom. What a divine day! how happy and serene all nature appears!' The end of their voyage emphasizes its gentle beauty: the air is 'soft', there is 'pleasant' motion and 'delightful scent' is 'wafted' to them. The idea that a voyage by water provides Victor with relief from his miseries is then repeated: 'as I touched the shore, I felt those cares and fears revive'. Notice that Elizabeth sees the water as transparent, whereas Victor has consistently recorded its surface as opaque: indeed, he has repeatedly referred to its ability to 'close over' and hide what it swallows. This may highlight a difference between Elizabeth and Victor – suggesting her innocence and his guilt, perhaps, or her harmony and his disharmony with nature.

These summaries suggest that voyages by water are significant: they are often portrayed as peaceful; are associated with nature's harmony and are soothing; and they show Frankenstein as passive, typically lying upon his back while the boat drifts. Twice, water is associated with death: first, when Victor feels that he should sink beneath its surface to restore the peace of nature; then, when Victor fears being 'swallowed up', and is reminded of his love of life.

Water and voyages by water have a symbolic meaning, then: they represent peace and harmony in nature. However, water is also, ominously, associated with death. As both death and natural harmony, most of the water scenes in *Frankenstein* conjure ideas of peace, sleep, restfulness, even perhaps escape from suffering.

Mountains

We have considered the significance of mountains in Chapter 3 above; and we drew conclusions about their influence on Frankenstein. They are 'mighty friends' which are 'solemnising' his mind and which give him temporary forgetfulness of ordinary cares. They are also associated with God and with religion when they 'ministered' to Victor. On the other hand, we found that this influence was all we could be sure of: that the mountains seemed to have no more definable significance than a temporary influence on Victor's mood. Their function in relation to him, then, is comparable to that of water: the mountains, like a drifting voyage, can provide a temporary respite from his misery, a temporary escape from his cares, for Victor's mind. In the case of the mountains, it is their grandeur, 'majesty' and 'awful'-ness, rather than water's 'tranquillity', that provides this relief.

Storms

There are four storms in *Frankenstein*: one which splits the oak when Frankenstein is 15 years old; one which rages where William died, and reveals the daemon in its lightning; one which blows Victor's boat to Ireland; and finally, the 'heavy storm of rain' on the night of Elizabeth's death. These four storms, however, do not seem to perform a consistent function in the text, nor does any idea of their significance suggest itself. We can say that they are all ominous of the daemon's destructive murders, except for the first one; and we can say that the second and last storms both turn a great deal on darkness or on poor visibility. So, for example, when haunting the site of William's murder, Frankenstein perceives the daemon 'in the gloom', then 'a flash of lightning illuminated' him, before he lost the figure again 'in the gloom', while the passage is heavy with terms of 'impenetrable darkness', 'darkened', 'pitchy darkness' and even the lightning 'dazzled' (all from *F* 77–8). On the wedding night, when 'a heavy storm of rain descended', Frankenstein feels that 'so soon as night obscured the shapes of objects, a thousand fears arose in my mind. I was anxious and watchful . . . ' (*F* 198). On these two occasions, then, storms perform the function of restricting visibility; so, the daemon's activities are hidden by darkness. We can think of these two storms as emblematic of the wild violence of the daemon's conflict and his murders, while the other two storms in the novel have different functions. Also, of course, storms play a recognizable role in gothic convention: they heighten the drama and enhance mystery and horror, in relation to the daemon's murders.

Sight and Hearing

Our brief consideration of the storms, however, has raised a separate issue: visibility is a significant element of two of the storms; and we have noticed before, that mist and cloud altered nature's and Frankenstein's moods in the episode leading to the 'mer de glace'. Furthermore, we know that old Mr De Lacey is blind. We should therefore think about sight and blindness, visibility and darkness: do these have symbolic significance in *Frankenstein*? To explore this idea, we will examine the episode of the daemon's approach to De Lacey, with a particular interest in how the text plays upon sight and blindness.

The daemon is clear, that sight is his enemy: '. . . the unnatural hideousness of my person was the chief object of horror with those who had formerly beheld me. My voice, although harsh, had nothing terrible in it' (*F* 134). Sound, on the other hand, may be his friend. Notice how the daemon harps upon sight in his discourse to old De Lacey: 'I *look* around, and I have no relation or friend upon earth. These amiable people to whom I go have never *seen* me'; and 'a fatal prejudice *clouds their eyes*, and where they ought to *see* a feeling and kind friend, they *behold* only a detestable monster'. De Lacey underlines the difference, saying: 'I am blind and cannot judge of your countenance, but there is something in your words which persuades me that you are sincere' (*F* 136), and the primacy of sound and hearing is underlined by the daemon: 'From your lips first have I *heard* the voice of kindness' (*F* 137).

Two other forms of judgement are associated with this 'judgment of the blind', as we might call it. First, De Lacey asserts that 'the hearts of men, when unprejudiced by any obvious self-interest, are full of brotherly love and charity'. In other words, humanity is naturally benevolent. So, although the daemon may not be able to rely on visual judgement, he should pin his hopes on 'the hearts of men' – an inner goodness: 'Rely, therefore, on your hopes', De Lacey advises. The second form of judgement is that brought about by common experience of suffering: De Lacey hears the daemon's unhappiness, and declares, 'I also am unfortunate; I and my family have been condemned, although innocent; judge, therefore, if I do not feel for your misfortunes' (*F* 137). These, then, are two forces which should enable human beings to reach a benevolent understanding: first, the natural 'love and charity' in all people; and secondly, the experiences of suffering we have in common. As we know, the daemon quickly discovers that natural 'love and charity', and common experiences, are not enough. The immediate judgement of sight horrifies Felix and the young women, just as happens with Frankenstein, the little girl's father, the villagers and William.

The daemon calls this judgement by sight a 'prejudice', pointing out that it is a delusion: instead of a 'feeling and kind friend', they see a 'detestable monster'. Prejudice means, literally, to judge before you know. This is what William does. The daemon thinks that perhaps 'this little creature was unprejudiced', but 'as soon as he beheld my form, he placed his hands before his eyes, and uttered a shrill scream' (*F* 144). The remainder of the story underlines that sight is the medium of prejudice, and dominates men's judgement. So, when Frankenstein says, 'Begone! relieve me from the sight of your detested form', the daemon responds, ' "Thus I relieve thee, my creator," he said, and placed his hated hands before my eyes, which I flung from me with violence; "thus I take from thee a sight which you abhor. Still thou canst listen to me and grant me thy compassion" ' (*F* 104). Hearing the daemon's story places Frankenstein in a sight/hearing quandary:

> His words had a strange effect upon me. I compassionated him and sometimes felt a wish to console him; but when I looked upon him, when I saw the filthy mass that moved and talked, my heart sickened and my feelings were altered to those of horror and hatred.　(*F* 149)

Walton feels the same contradictory impulses when he finally meets the daemon:

> His voice seemed suffocated; and my first impulses, which had suggested to me the duty of obeying the dying request of my friend, in destroying his enemy, were now suspended by a mixture of curiosity and compassion. I approached this tremendous being; I dared not again raise my eyes to his face, there was something so scaring and unearthly in his ugliness.   (*F* 221)

We have ample evidence, from the daemon's own narratives, that sight brings a distorted, prejudiced judgement. We can easily infer, for example, that the 'ghastly grin' that wrinkles the daemon's face at the casement on Orkney merely tells us that he is pleased – it is Frankenstein's prejudice that ascribes the expression to 'malice and treachery'. So, the motifs of blindness and sight suggest an adage very close to *don't judge a book by its cover*. The text recommends searching for inner qualities, such as 'love and charity', 'compassion' and mutual sympathy from common experience; and warns against the superficial judgements based on external beauty or ugliness.

On the other hand, the theme of sound – voice and listening – is not entirely in contrast. We looked at the interview between the daemon and De Lacey, and noted that the blind man hears 'that you are sincere', while the daemon 'heard the voice of kindness'. This promotes the idea that sound brings truer communication than sight. However, the rapprochement brought about by hearing alone, cannot survive – even the blind old man 'spurned and deserted' the daemon. Furthermore, there are several examples of misleading eloquence in *Frankenstein*. So, for example, Frankenstein refers to the daemon's 'powers of eloquence and persuasion' (*F* 223); Walton tells us of Frankenstein that 'while they [the crew] hear his voice, they believe these vast mountains of ice are molehills' (*F* 216); and Frankenstein says of Waldman that he had a 'voice the sweetest I had ever heard', but that he spoke 'the words of the fate – enounced to destroy me' (*F* 48–9). Sight and sound both seem to be unreliable guides to judgement. In short, *Frankenstein* proposes the existence of natural goodness and mutual sympathy in human nature; but the text emphasizes in how many ways our judgement is at risk from prejudice, as a result of sight or hearing.

Conclusions Regarding Symbolism

On first reading *Frankenstein*, we are struck by the power of insinuation of the fable. The creature, its creator, its rejection and vengeance played out against the grand backdrop of the Swiss Alps, or the Arctic Ocean – we are strongly impressed by the sense of an archetypal story, and we find ourselves touched, stirred and satisfied by the tale in obscure yet potent ways. Certainly some of this effect can be ascribed to a 'mythic' quality in the story, a quality to which we turn in the second half of this chapter. Also, and probably related to the tale's 'mythic' effect, there are numerous elements in *Frankenstein* that suggest psychological and sexual abnormalities, and these are equally potent, but also equally obscure. However, with a story such as this, and in such a setting, we would expect that our sense of the fable's power rests on a considerable symbolic meaning.

We have discussed a number of aspects of *Frankenstein*, considering whether they can or cannot be called 'symbolic'. We have found that there are numerous occasions, when we can say that there is a symbolic meaning in a particular passage. So, for example, when Frankenstein describes drifting in his boat: 'when all was at peace around me, and I the only unquiet thing that wandered restless in a scene so beautiful and heavenly', and he feels tempted to drown himself, we can see symbolic overtones of both death and unspoiled innocence, in the water. However, with the exception of the daemon, the elements of the text we have discussed have not suggested single, consistent significances.

Yet again, we are left in a situation where there is great richness of suggestion, coupled with a lack of confirmation or further evidence. Consequently, we find ourselves affected by numerous unconfirmed suggestions about the significance of *Frankenstein*. When we constructed three moral fables from the *Frankenstein* story, we quickly found that more complex elements undercut and enrich those simple fables. There is a comparable situation in relation to symbols: there are numerous apparent instances of symbolism in the text, but the whole is extraordinarily undogmatic. The text, in fact, seems to withdraw its own apparent significance, becoming more complex and opaque, the more we try to think about it.

Myth

There are two major topics for us to consider under this heading. First, how *Frankenstein* refers to traditional myths. Secondly, how and why the *Frankenstein* story has gripped public imagination since it was published, so that the novel has developed an attendant 'myth' of its own (in politics, in science fiction, in film, in popular consciousness).

Frankenstein and Earlier Myths

This discussion will consider *Frankenstein* in relation to four previous myths: those of Prometheus, Oedipus, Narcissus and the Christian mythology from Milton's *Paradise Lost*. We begin with the one that appears on the novel's title-page.

Prometheus

Mary Shelley subtitled her novel 'The Modern Prometheus', thus making an explicit claim that *Frankenstein* re-treats a classical myth. However, Prometheus is the protagonist of several mythological stories, any or all of which might bear some relation to *Frankenstein*. In particular, Prometheus either created humankind or breathed life into lifeless clay to animate creatures previously created by the Gods. Connected to this creation myth is the following story about Prometheus and his brother Epimetheus. When the Gods had made all the animals and humans from clay, and were ready to bring them into the light of day:

> They ordered Prometheus and Epimetheus to equip them, and to distribute to them severally their proper qualities. Epimetheus said to

Prometheus : 'Let me distribute, and do you inspect.' This was agreed, and Epimetheus made the distribution [of claws and fur and other attributes] . . . Thus did Epimetheus, who, not being very wise, forgot that he had distributed among the brute animals all the qualities which he had to give – and when he came to man, who was still unprovided, he was terribly perplexed. Now while he was in this perplexity, Prometheus came to inspect the distribution, and he found that the other animals were suitably furnished, but that man alone was naked and shoeless, and had neither bed nor arms of defence. The appointed hour was approaching when man in his turn was to go forth into the light of day; and Prometheus, not knowing how he could devise his salvation, stole the mechanical arts of Hephaistos and Athene, and fire with them.[2]

The 'arts of Hephaistos and Athene' include all branches of civilized culture and knowledge.

A second myth has it that Prometheus deceived Zeus, tricking him into choosing the bones rather than the meat of sacrificial animals, to the benefit of mankind. In fury, Zeus then took fire away from humanity; but Prometheus stole Zeus's fire again, and gave it back. In punishment for this, Zeus caused him to be chained to the mountain of Caucasus, where an eagle (or in some versions a vulture) came each day and pecked out his liver, which regenerated itself each night. Hercules eventually liberated Prometheus from this torment.

Another myth in which Prometheus plays a role is in the creation of woman: according to this story, Zeus ordered Hephaistos to make a woman, who was called Pandora, and give her to Prometheus's brother Epimetheus who then gave her to mankind. Pandora held a jar containing all the evils which might torment mortals in life. When she lifted the lid, diseases and sufferings of every kind issued forth, but deceitful hope alone remained behind. In this myth, the creation of woman, and all the consequent ills suffered by mankind, is another part of Zeus's revenge against Prometheus.

These are the three main Prometheus stories, but he appears in several other stories as well. For example, he helped the Olympians to victory over the titans, and so helped Zeus to power. His name means 'forethought', while that of his foolish brother Epimetheus means 'afterthought'. He saved humanity from extinction, when Zeus had decided to obliterate the species. In all of these many myths, Prometheus appears as a champion of mankind, and possibly a joker as well (e.g., creating homosexuality by gluing the wrong genitals onto the wrong gender, while drunk).

The first two stories about Prometheus are those most relevant to *Frankenstein*. Clearly, the image of Frankenstein bringing to life the body he has assembled from both human and animal parts has powerful echoes of the myth in which Prometheus breathes life into lifeless clay; while Frankenstein's allocation of gigantic stature to his creature is reminiscent of Prometheus and Epimetheus's 'distribution' – although Frankenstein's lack of 'forethought' makes him more of a 'Modern Epimetheus' than a 'Modern Prometheus'.

The second story seems even more relevant, however. The theft of fire and/or giving the arts of Athene and Hephaistos to man: stealing a knowledge man was never meant to have, from the rulers of the universe – this action is comparable to Frankenstein's discovery and use of the power to give life. The novel suggests that this power should belong only to God, or nature. Furthermore, the punishment Prometheus suffers for having stolen fire is suitably horrifying, as is Frankenstein's punishment at the hands of the daemon. Certainly, *Frankenstein* contains the elements of forbidden knowledge, the arrogation of godlike power, fire as a metaphor for the spark of life and nature's (or the Gods') terrible revenge on the Prometheus-figure. One encyclopaedia states categorically that Mary Shelley's subtitle 'is a reference to the novel's themes of the over-reaching of modern man into dangerous areas of knowledge'.[3]

Prometheus, then, appears in two main guises: as creator of man and as thief of fire. The main reason for choosing this latter figure as the prototype of Frankenstein is that Prometheus the thief is guilty and punished – both pervasive elements of the *Frankenstein* story. Prometheus the creator of mankind, on the other hand, was carrying out the will of the Gods. Frankenstein's account of his scientific labours makes clear that he was committing a crime against nature, and therefore a crime against God. It is also appropriate that Prometheus is credited with giving man knowledge of science. By association with the theft of fire, all scientific studies take on an aura of danger in Mary Shelley's re-casting of the myth.

Like all myths, the Prometheus story centres on elements that lie deep within our racial history, our instinctive natures. Myths are said to be grounded in the basic forces of life and survival, basic elements we will call archetypes. Such are the sun, the seasons, rain, rivers, thunder, the stars, the planets and so on: and in every culture there are myths which explain the actions of all these archetypes. Fire belongs in this category, because it is a crucial power enabling mankind to survive. At the same time, it is an elemental destructive force. Language is another crucial possession. Consequently, there is a range of myths concerning the theft of fire from various gods, of which the Prometheus story is but one;[4] equally, there are many myths which explain the gifts of speech and language, or which tell the origin of any branches of knowledge that have enabled human beings to control their environment. In founding her story on the Prometheus myth, then, Mary Shelley taps into racial memories that are called up when we respond to archetypes. The story of *Frankenstein* thus becomes more powerful and of wider significance than it would be, were it simply the story of one scientist's misfortune. It becomes instead a story of universal significance, touching on the boundaries of human and divine power; the line between natural and unnatural; transgression against the natural order; the dangers of human hubris and so on.

It is noticeable that Shelley includes an enactment of the discovery of fire, and of the dangers of knowledge, in the daemon's account of his early life. With regard to fire, the daemon discovers its ambivalent nature immediately: '...and was overcome with delight at the warmth I experienced from it. In my joy I thrust my hand into the live embers, but quickly drew it out again with a cry of pain. How strange, I thought, that the same cause should produce such opposite effects!' (*F* 107). Here, the daemon enacts an allegory of Victor's mistake with the 'fire' of scientific knowledge: by analogy, Victor ignorantly thrusts his hands into dangerous knowledge. It would have been better for him to respect the dangerous nature of knowledge, as the daemon learns to do with fire.

Mary Shelley incorporates the Prometheus myth into the story of *Frankenstein*, then. She calls her novel the 'Modern' Prometheus, because she is presenting a 'modern' version of the myth: her own re-casting which she conceives as appropriate to her own time. The most noticeable 'modern' element in Shelley's version of Prometheus is that her tale morally supports Zeus rather than the generous titan, champion of mankind, who was a hero to the ancient Greeks. In other words, Shelley's re-casting turns the ethics of the myth upside down.

The 'fire' Frankenstein brings to earth and uses – the power to create life – is something human beings should not meddle with. However, it is also something that is becoming accessible to humanity, in the modern world. Because of scientific discoveries, Shelley seems to be saying, mankind now has access to powers that have previously belonged to God and nature alone. The 'Modern Prometheus' can steal such powers and use them irresponsibly. In this way he will bring down a terrible punishment upon the world. It seems to be in this sense that Shelley calls her fable 'the Modern Prometheus'. Her Prometheus figure is the irresponsible scientist, author of catastrophe; not the champion of humanity celebrated in classical myth.

Oedipus

Oedipus unintentionally killed his father and married his mother. When he discovered what he had done, Oedipus tore out his own eyes. This myth bears a different relation to *Frankenstein*: it is not on Mary Shelley's title-page or mentioned in her text. Rather, discussing the traces of Oedipal story found in *Frankenstein*, acknowledges the novel's rich psychoanalytical suggestiveness.

Put simply, the Oedipus story and therefore the 'Oedipus complex' is basic to Freud's analysis of early childhood. Psychoanalysis holds that all male infants desire their mothers, and hate their fathers. The infant is quickly taught that these feelings are taboo, and suppresses them: literally, the forbidden feelings are put away in the unconscious. It is what those forbidden feelings do after they have been hidden away, that psychoanalysis focuses upon. A number of psychoanalytical critics build theories about Victor Frankenstein, based on Oedipal elements of his story.

One of these is the age difference between his mother and father, which exaggerates the distance from his father, and brings him closer to his mother. Notice that Victor mentions intimate 'tender caresses' from his mother, and his father's more distant 'smile of benevolent pleasure'

(*F* 35). Then, Victor's mother provides him with a sex-object, even saying: 'I have a pretty present for my Victor' (*F* 37), called 'cousin' but in Victor's words 'more than sister'. With the gift of Elizabeth Lavenza, Mrs Frankenstein virtually acknowledges her duty to respond to and satisfy her son's desire. That she is giving Victor, in effect, a version of herself – an incestuous present – is underlined when she speaks from her deathbed: 'She joined the hands of Elizabeth and myself: – 'My children,' she said, 'my firmest hopes of future happiness were placed on the prospect of your union . . . Elizabeth, my love, you must supply my place to my younger children' (*F* 44); and the identity of Victor's desire for Elizabeth, with an incestuous desire for his mother, appears in his dream – a dream in which embracing his mother is accompanied by all the horror and death-imagery attendant on such a taboo. We may also notice how Victor's actions steadily deprive his father of judgement, authority, and therefore potency; and eventually of life.

There are some outstanding elements of Victor Frankenstein's story, which seem to cry out from the text, to be interpreted in terms of his early psycho-sexual development. We will mention three, in passing. First, there is Victor's misdirected sexual drive, channeled into penetrating nature's secrets rather than healthy heterosexual love. Secondly, there is Victor's achievement of masculine-only reproduction, excluding the female and the maternal from procreation, goaded onward by the perverted idea that 'no father could claim the gratitude of his child so completely as I should' (*F* 55). Thirdly, we notice the extraordinary lengths to which Victor goes, to postpone his union with Elizabeth – the girl he declares that he loves and desires. Many critics have pointed out that the daemon's wedding-night threat is obviously aimed at Elizabeth: how perverse is Victor when he ignores this clear indication, and believes himself the target! How does this willful mistake delay and then obviate the need for him to join her in bed!

There are psychoanalytical elements in some of the critical theories in Chapter 8. For the present, we note that there are elements of an Oedipal myth, in the form of a powerful motif of incest and of the punishment that attends its indulgence; and a powerful motif in which Victor seeks to out-father, replace, or gradually destroy, his father. These elements, like the references to Prometheus, form a connection between Mary Shelley's text, and universal drives and taboos laid down in our deepest layers of memory.

Narcissus

Narcissus was a beautiful young man who fell in love with himself, or, who fell in love with his identical twin sister, depending which version of the myth you take. A nymph named Echo fell in love with Narcissus, but could not attract his attention and so she pined away until only her voice remained. Narcissus became captivated by his own reflection in a stream, either thinking it was his sister, after her death, or simply because he fell in love with himself. He loved his reflection so much that he could neither break it, to drink, or move from the sight of it; so he died where he was, still transfixed. He turned into the flower that bears his name.

Here again, we are discussing a myth much mentioned by psychoanalytical critics, many of whom diagnose Victor Frankenstein as suffering from a 'narcissus complex'. As with the undercurrents of incest in the Oedipus story, so the self-love of the Narcissus story is strongly suggested by numerous elements in *Frankenstein*. Victor's beauty, his misdirected sexuality and the sheer persistence of his oblivious self-absorption as he passes through his own story in an increasing hell of his own making; his attempt at male-only reproduction; his selection of 'beautiful' features for his creature, his other self; his dream; his refusal to create a female; and again, his avoidance of Elizabeth – all these features suggest the relevance of narcissism to his character.[5]

The most persuasive evidence for the relevance of Narcissus, however, is Victor's creation of the daemon: 'His limbs were in proportion, and I had selected his features as beautiful. Beautiful! – Great God! His yellow skin scarcely covered the work of muscles and arteries beneath; his hair was of a lustrous black, and flowing; his teeth of pearly whiteness; but these luxuriances only formed a more horrid contrast . . .' (*F* 58). Victor, in short, tries to bring to life a reflection of himself, driven to do so by narcissistic desire; but the outcome is revolting. The 'reflection' Narcissus desires becomes an opposite self, tied to Victor by fate: a part of or an emanation of himself that Victor is never able to escape. Victor dies, having spent his final years in a sort of ghastly contemplation of his 'reflection'.

Milton's Paradise Lost

In the text of *Frankenstein* there are several allusions to the story of creation and fall, as found in Milton's epic poem *Paradise Lost*. In his first speeches, the daemon makes explicit references to Milton, after Victor has greeted him as 'Devil' and 'fiend', and stated that 'the tortures of hell are too mild a vengeance for thy crimes' (*F* 102). The daemon's reply to Victor's flurry of fire and brimstone language is to say:

> Remember, that I am thy creature; I ought to be thy Adam, but I am rather the fallen angel, whom thou drivest from joy for no misdeed. Everywhere I see bliss, from which I alone am irrevocably excluded. (*F* 103)

When summing up his career of murders to Walton, in the final scene, the daemon twice alludes to Milton. First, he describes how 'Evil thenceforth became my good'. In *Paradise Lost*, Satan persuades himself that he can never repent and return to Heaven:

> So farewel Hope, and with Hope farewel Fear,
> Farewel Remorse: all Good to me is lost;
> Evil be thou my Good;
>
> (*Paradise Lost*, Book IV ll. 108–10)

That Satan, in this passage, bids farewell to hope, adds to our understanding of the daemon who, in murdering Elizabeth, did so to 'riot in the excess of my despair' (*F* 222). The second allusion occurs when he explicitly revisits his identification with Satan:

> When I run over the frightful catalogue of my sins, I cannot believe that I am the same creature whose thoughts were once filled with sublime and transcendent visions of the beauty and the majesty of goodness. But it is even so; the fallen angel becomes a malignant devil. Yet even that enemy of God and man had friends and associates in his desolation; I am alone. (*F* 223)

Between these two episodes, the daemon gives an account of finding
and reading *Paradise Lost*, and devotes two paragraphs to a discussion
comparing himself to Adam and *Paradise Lost* to Victor Frankenstein's
notes. The daemon sees a similarity between himself and Adam, as
both were created alone, 'united by no link to any other being in
existence'; but then sees a contrast, for Adam:

> ... had come forth from the hands of God a perfect creature, happy and
> prosperous, guarded by the especial care of his Creator; he was allowed
> to converse with and acquire knowledge from beings of a superior
> nature: but I was wretched, helpless, and alone.   (*F* 132)

The daemon then considers that Satan is 'the fitter emblem of my condition', because he recognizes an emotional link with Satan: 'for often,
like him, when I viewed the bliss of my protectors, the bitter gall of
envy rose within me' (*F* 132). With regard to Frankenstein's notes, the
daemon finds the description of his own manufacture sickening, where
'the minutest description of my odious and loathsome person is given,
in language which painted your own horrors' (*F* 132–3), and considers
his ugliness a further reason to identify with Satan rather than Adam.
Indeed, he regards himself as more unfortunate even than Satan: 'Satan
had his companions, fellow-devils, to admire and encourage him; but
I am solitary and abhorred' (*F* 133). We notice that his comparison of
himself to Satan repeatedly stresses one difference: his loneliness.

Here, then, are clear indications of a parallel between Shelley's daemon and the figures of Adam and Satan as they appear in *Paradise Lost*.
There are also, however, some further similarities between the accounts
of creation given in *Paradise Lost* and those given in *Frankenstein*.
These less explicit allusions to creation raise the most troublesome
questions, for they are largely references to the creation of Eve, while
the daemon is clearly a male creature.

We will begin by considering the daemon's explicit identification
of himself with Satan, the fallen angel. This parallel casts Victor
Frankenstein in the role of God, a role he clearly coveted. We remember his ambition that he would, like the God of Genesis, 'pour a
torrent of light into our dark world'; and his imagination that 'A new
species would bless me as its creator and source' (both from *F* 55).

The daemon also casts Frankenstein in this role because of his power to exclude him from 'bliss'. The daemon identifies himself with Satan because they share an emotion: the 'bitter gall of envy' is their common lot, when they see happier creatures. The parallel, and the consequent dynamic of the daemon's character, is very simple. When he realizes that his rejection is irrevocable, the daemon's 'bitter gall of envy' turns to despair. It is this despair that creates amoral chaos, so that, like Milton's Satan, he bids: 'Farewel Remorse: all Good to me is lost; / Evil be thou my Good'. The myth of Satan, then, amplifies our understanding of the daemon.

In *Paradise Lost*, Milton intended to 'assert Eternal Providence, / And justifie the wayes of God to men' (*op. cit.,* Book I, ll. 25–6). In other words, Milton wrote in support of God's wisdom, and he expects the reader to see through Satan's self-justifying blandishments: we are expected to recognize Satan's evil despite his subtlety. Certainly, when the daemon first compares himself to Satan, and accuses God/Frankenstein of driving him from joy 'for no misdeed', we are expected to remember that Satan rebelled in Heaven, from the sin of pride; and that the daemon has murdered William and framed Justine: were these not 'misdeeds'?

However, we must ask ourselves whether the parallel in *Frankenstein* is as simple as this: does Mary Shelley refer to Milton, simply to alert us to the daemon's sophistry? Does she expect us to admire Victor's 'Providence' and accept his delineation of the daemon as 'fiend', 'devil' and so forth? Clearly, the answer is no. Frankenstein is no God, and his attempt to play the role of creator is heavily criticized by the author. Another allusion to *Paradise Lost*, comparing Victor and Satan, underlines this. Walton is awe-struck, thinking 'what a glorious creature' Frankenstein must have been, when 'he is thus noble and godlike in ruin' (*F* 214); whereupon, Victor explains his similarity with 'the archangel who aspired to omnipotence':

> I trod heaven in my thoughts, now exulting in my powers, now burning with the idea of their effects. From my infancy I was imbued with high hopes and a lofty ambition; but how am I sunk! Oh! my friend, if you had known me as I once was, you would not recognize me in this state of degradation.   (*F* 214)

Frankenstein's sin of pride is evident when he describes his 'sentiment of the worth of my nature', and he seems still proud after the creation of the daemon, when he 'could not rank myself with the herd of common projectors'. Then, his exclamation at his fall and the suggestion that his previous glory cannot be recognized are both strongly reminiscent of Satan in *Paradise Lost*, addressing his lieutenant Beelzebub:

> If thou beest he; But O how fall'n! how chang'd
> From him, who in the happy Realms of Light
> Cloth'd with transcendent brightnes didst outshine
> Myriads though bright:
>
> > (*Paradise Lost*, Book I, ll. 84–7)

Such a direct comparison between Frankenstein and Milton's fallen angels clearly shows that Shelley regards the manufacture of the daemon as a sin. The irony is that Frankenstein regrets his fall, yet still exults in the achievement that brought it about. This astonishing blindness is further underlined by Walton's equally ironic exclamation: 'Must I then lose this admirable being!' (*F* 214).

The comparison between Frankenstein and Satan seems a good fit, then; while the daemon's allusions to the fallen archangel highlight differences which appeal to our compassion. For example, the daemon has no hope of a reprieve from his creator, and realizes this when he confronts him on Orkney, when 'The monster saw my determination in my face, and gnashed his teeth in the impotence of anger' (*F* 172). So, the daemon's despair is justified, unlike that of Satan in *Paradise Lost*, who could repent and be forgiven. Satan explains that, were he to repent and thus regain his place in heaven, 'ease would recant / Vows made in pain' (*op. cit.,* Book IV ll. 96–7), and he would soon be back to his wicked ways again! So, the daemon's despair is sound, where Satan's is mere self-pity.

Some further questions are woven into the relationship between *Frankenstein* and *Paradise Lost*. We have said that Milton wished to 'justifie the wayes of God to men'. A central theme of *Paradise Lost* is Milton's attempt to resolve the problem of freewill – that insoluble paradox: if God is omniscient, how can man be free? Therefore, in the case of the story of the Fall, the question becomes: God must have known that Eve and Adam would fall to temptation. Why did he create them, then? What was the point of the whole business? Milton's solution is also a paradox: that man was created 'sufficient to have stood, yet free to fall'.[6] The daemon reads Milton's poem, and comments that 'It moved every feeling of wonder and awe, that the picture of an omnipotent God warring with his creatures was capable of exciting' (*F* 132). Here, the daemon describes *Paradise Lost* in terms which point up the problem of freewill, and its absurd illogic: if God is omnipotent, why is he constantly 'warring with his creatures'? There can only be one logical conclusion: God must enjoy 'warring', otherwise, being omnipotent, he would not do it. For the daemon, this is particularly redolent of 'wonder and awe', in the context of his own creator's whimsical illogic. Frankenstein, like Milton's God, plays with his power irresponsibly, so that the daemon objects: 'Why did you form a monster so hideous that even *you* turned from me in disgust?' (*F* 133). Clearly, the daemon is disturbed by creation's lack of logic, and is sceptical about freewill. We can see that these issues lead into the daemon's determinist pattern of thought: the argument he advances throughout his narrative. He has been forced to become a 'fiend'; he has had no choice; he was created without freewill.

Milton's intention was to support 'Eternal Providence'. However, by the time Mary Shelley was writing, the opinion was gaining ground, particularly among the Romantics, that Milton had failed. The characterization of Satan in *Paradise Lost* was so vivid and attractive, and the scenes set in Heaven so didactic and dull by contrast, that Satan, the excluded and tragic figure, was properly the poem's hero. So, for example, William Blake wrote that Milton 'was a true Poet, and of the Devil's party without knowing it'.[7] The daemon's discussion of *Paradise Lost* in relation to his own situation seems to support such a revisionist reading. Certainly in *Frankenstein* the creator is irresponsible, and the creature argues that his natural emotions leave him no freewill. He complains that his isolation is more absolute than that of Satan; and his life is absurd, because no good reason can be found for his existence.

The daemon then seems to go one stage further: while reading Frankenstein's notebook, he is 'sickened', and ' "Hateful day when I received life!" I exclaimed in agony' (*F* 133). This seems to be an allusion to the Book of Job, from the Old Testament: for it was Job whose torments finally led him to curse his own life, saying 'Let the day perish wherein I was born' (*Job* 3, iii). Job's sufferings were brought about by a kind of wager between God and Satan: in other words, Job suffered from the caprice of God. This allusion underlines the daemon's suggestion of an irresponsible power ruling over his life: a careless power, lacking justice, compassion or reason. Equally, in the *Book of Job* God's answer from the whirlwind arrogates a power as complete as the determining forces that make the daemon what he is. The daemon's Job-like complaint is echoed by the epigraph Mary Shelley placed on the title page: Adam, in *Paradise Lost*, regrets his creation:

> Did I request thee, Maker, from my clay
> To mould me man? Did I solicit thee
> From darkness to promote me? –
>
> (*Paradise Lost and F* 1)

The allusion to Eve's creation, as described in *Paradise Lost*, occurs when the daemon contemplates his own reflection in water:

> I had admired the perfect forms of my cottagers – their grace, beauty, and delicate complexions: but how was I terrified, when I viewed myself in a transparent pool! At first I started back, unable to believe that it was indeed I who was reflected in the mirror; and when I became fully convinced that I was in reality the monster that I am, I was filled with the bitterest sensations of despondence and mortification.   (*F* 116–7)

This is a re-enactment with differences, of Eve's account of her first day alive. She tells of waking 'Under a shade on flours, much wondring where/And what I was, whence thither brought, and how', and of lying down upon the bank of a pool in order to look into the water:

> As I bent down to look, just opposite,
> A Shape within the watry gleam appeerd
> Bending to look on me, I started back,
> It started back, but pleasd I soon returnd,
> Pleas'd it returnd as soon with answering looks
> Of sympathie and love, there I had fixt

Mine eyes till now, and pin'd with vain desire,
Had not a voice thus warnd me, What thou seest,
What there thou seest fair Creature is thy self,

(*Paradise Lost*, IV, 460–8)

Shelley appears to be playing on the similarity of situation between these two passages, saying that the daemon 'started back', as did Eve, and that he – like Eve – did not know the reflection to be himself, at first. Such a close identity of context suggests an allusion, and by calling this passage to mind, Shelley highlights the contrast between Eve's love of her reflection and the daemon's 'terrified' reaction to seeing himself, and so provides another and distorted version of narcissism.

The aim here seems to be to suggest that the daemon's creation as a parodic version of the creation of Eve. In this parody Frankenstein plays Adam, with the daemon originally intended to be an object of desire: we remember Victor's admission that 'I had selected his features as beautiful' (*F* 58). The daemon's assembly from slaughterhouses, charnel houses and graveyards may be a gruesome parody of Adam's gift of a rib: 'to give thee being I lent/Out of my side to thee' (*Paradise Lost*, IV, 483–4). Most of all, perhaps, this allusion to Eve underlines how abnormal is Victor's drive to create the daemon: how oddly misdirected is his sexuality in seeking to 'penetrate' nature and reveal her 'hiding places', and how unnatural is the form of reproduction that gives the daemon life. Comparisons between the daemon and Eve have contributed a great deal to various psychoanalytical readings of *Frankenstein*, some of which will be met in Chapter 8.

We can add that both the daemon's and Eve's encounters with their own reflections are parodies of the Narcissus myth. In Milton's version Eve does indeed fall in love with herself, and would have suffered Narcissus's fate ('there I had fixt/Mine eyes till now, and pin'd with vain desire'), had not an angel's voice led her away to Adam. Even upon meeting the first Man, Eve prefers her own reflection, saying that Adam was 'methought less faire,/Less winning soft, less amiablie milde' than her own image in the water. She turns away from Adam, who has to call her back: 'Return fair *Eve*,/Whom fli'st thou?' The daemon, however, flies from his own image. Ironically, as in the case of Narcissus but for the opposite reason, the daemon's reflection comes to be the defining fact of his existence, and his Job-like rejection of his life is echoed by the epigraph Mary Shelley placed on the title page.

It is clear from this discussion that the parallels between the two texts, and the incorporation of Christian mythology into *Frankenstein*, in both original and parodic form, lead our interpretations of the text in multiple directions, and suggest a number of rich areas for speculation and interpretation, concerning the figures of the daemon and Frankenstein.

The Modern Myth of *Frankenstein*

We now ask, how and why *Frankenstein* has generated its own, modern, mythology? The first part of an answer to this comes from the myths we have discussed, and their effect upon the text. We have suggested that the incorporation of previous myths creates a connection with elements that lie deep within the memory of our species, in our instinctive natures. As we have said, myths are grounded in archetypes; and by incorporating these myths into her fable, Shelley touches a powerful sub-stratum of response, deep within her reader's psyche. In this way, not only does *Frankenstein* recall the myths to which it refers: the text also exerts some of the elemental power of a myth, of itself.

We do not have space in this chapter to chart the production and reproductions, revisions and conflations and confusions, versions and adaptations and re-tellings, that have all contributed to the broad story that is part of popular culture and the popular consciousness today. Instead, we must confine ourselves to highlighting a few salient features of the contemporary 'myth'. We will look at some of the violences that have been done to the story; the idea of the mad scientist; and the idea of the misunderstood monster.

First among the violences done to the story is the accidental conflation of the figures Frankenstein and daemon. For example, in *Mary Barton* (1848), Elizabeth Gaskell wrote of: 'Frankenstein, that monster of many human qualities, ungifted with a soul, a knowledge of the difference between good and evil'. This mistake shows one of the first effects of a popular myth – a story that does the rounds in conversation, and is imperfectly known by those who have not read the book.

So, the monster becomes known by the name of 'Frankenstein'. More significant, however, may be the idea that the 'monster' cannot tell right from wrong. Mary Shelley's daemon has a very clear moral consciousness, but Elizabeth Gaskell's hearsay version of the story erases this. George Canning did similarly, in a parliamentary speech about the abolition of slavery, in 1824. Emancipating the slaves would be like Frankenstein making his monster, he said, where he was 'unable to impart to the work of his hands a perception of right and wrong'.

Since many of the common references to *Frankenstein* compared the daemon to a lower or exploited social class (in Gaskell's case the British working class; for George Canning, the negro slaves), it was perhaps natural that society suppressed the daemon's benevolence, and created instead a figure of amoral violence: a creature to be feared. We have suggested that the daemon is Mary Shelley's warning, to a complacent ruling class, about the danger of continuing to mistreat the poor. The transformation of the daemon into an amoral 'monster' keeps the story's exciting frisson of terror, but erases the political criticism that the ruling class might find uncomfortable.

To completely draw the political sting of Shelley's daemon, the Universal film *Frankenstein* of 1931 introduces an entire sequence in which Frankenstein's assistant is sent to steal a brain from a laboratory at night. He drops and breaks the jar labeled 'NORMAL BRAIN', and so takes that labeled 'ABNORMAL BRAIN' instead. This of course provides the film with a monster who is biologically 'abnormal', erasing the entire determinist argument, and the assertion of original benevolence, that are so important to Shelley's daemon. We have no moral qualms when such a 'monster' is burned to death by vigilante villagers at the end of the film.

A later film version, the Hammer Films production *The Curse of Frankenstein* (1957), focuses its revisionist attention on Frankenstein rather than his creature. Peter Cushing's scientist is a decadent and middle-aged aristocrat, with the title of Baron, who murders a colleague in order to steal his brain. In short, in this version Frankenstein himself becomes a violent criminal, and it is his madness that the film needs to cope with, rather than that of the creature, who is only the real villain's product. It is interesting to consider the ideological environment of each re-making of the *Frankenstein* story. For example,

Paul O'Flinn argues that Cushing's mad scientist characterization was a reflection of developments of the 1950s, such as fear of the H-bomb.[8]

It is also easy to find humour in the inventions that have been added to the *Frankenstein* story by hard-pressed movie-makers: so many of these additions, like the 'ABNORMAL BRAIN' invention, lend themselves to ridicule. The film industry has acknowledged this in comic treatments: witness Universal's *Abbot and Costello Meet Frankenstein* (1948); Mel Brooks' brilliant comedy with Gene Wilder in the title role, *Young Frankenstein* (1974); and various transferred versions of monstrous-looking creatures such as the servant Lurch, in *The Addams Family* television serial.

There is no sign, however, that the film industry's radical revisions of Mary Shelley's story will ever stop. *Mary Shelley's Frankenstein* (1994), directed by Kenneth Branagh, publicized itself as being faithful to the original book: a return to authenticity, as it were. In this film, the Walton story, which had been left out of previous films, is re-instated. On the other hand, Branagh's version takes astonishing liberties with the creation of a female: Frankenstein joins Elizabeth's head to Justine's exhumed body, to create a bride for himself, rather than for the daemon; and all this follows the murder of Elizabeth. So we see that even a director who has literary pretensions and a publicity campaign stressing authenticity cannot resist making a nonsense of the story.

The many changes that have been made to Mary Shelley's story are all really a tribute to its perennial potency. In our discussion, for example, we have shown how various revisions of the daemon's character have been superadded, which draw his political sting by erasing the proto-Marxism of his analysis of society, and his determinist outlook. What is left, in the popular imagination, is a varied and vague story. People who have not read the book, but have heard of or seen various filmed versions, are likely to have a variety of slightly different versions of a 'monster' meeting, for example, a blind man, a shepherd and a little girl; and are likely to have a variety of similar pictures in their minds, of a laboratory full of wheels and dynamos and electrical insulators, gauges and massive switches, with the huge figure of the daemon clamped to a sort of operating table with electrodes fixed to his temples. These are elements – and there are many more – of the modern myth that circulates under the name of *Frankenstein*. We will now look at two salient characteristics of this myth that seem to have established themselves, in one case despite much of the film industry's revisions.

In our discussion of myths, we noted that Mary Shelley calls her *Frankenstein* 'The Modern Prometheus', and thus re-casts the myth within the 'modern' technological age. In Shelley's time, we said, scientific discoveries were putting dangerous powers within human reach: powers that previously belonged to God and nature alone. The 'Modern Prometheus' can steal such powers from nature, and use them irresponsibly. It is a commonplace of science fiction, that with knowledge comes responsibility; and that it is in the nature of discoveries to be usable and abusable – to bring danger as well as benefits. The development of Frankenstein into the modern-archetypal figure of a 'mad scientist' plays upon popular mistrust of science and learning, the suspicion that those who know more than we do may abuse their superior knowledge. These fears are descendants of the superstitious feelings expressed by machine-breakers in the early years of the Industrial Revolution: by Luddites in the decade in which *Frankenstein* was written. In the modern world, when science deals with knowledge that is increasingly inaccessible to the layman, and when, for example, nuclear physics and genetic engineering are both coping with powers almost beyond our comprehension and certainly beyond humanity's moral control, it is not surprising that the Frankenstein myth of a mad scientist, who plays with powers beyond his moral scope, lives on and is a consistent part of popular culture.

We have briefly surveyed some of the wild changes made to the *Frankenstein* story since its first publication. We should remember that the 'mad scientist' figure does not belong among such unjustified revisions. Perhaps the pictorial details of his laboratory, in our imaginations, owe more to films than to the novel; but the mad scientist himself is a fair portrayal of the Victor Frankenstein of Shelley's text: 'Every night I was oppressed by a slow fever, and I became nervous to a most painful degree ... Sometimes I grew alarmed at the wreck I perceived that I had become'; 'My cheek had grown pale with study, and my person had become emaciated with confinement ... and the moon gazed on my midnight labours' (*F* 57, 55). Popular imagination's wild-looking, staring-eyed and starving creature, poring over the experiments in his unholy laboratory, is a direct extrapolation from Mary Shelley's text. So, we can take this 'mad scientist' figure to be a major contribution *Frankenstein* makes to modern mythology.

It only remains for us to mention the mad scientist's ancestor. The character-type Mary Shelley knew from the popular culture of *her* time, and who she developed into the 'mad scientist', was the 'mad alchemist' or 'Doctor Faustus' figure. Such a man was known to resort to unhallowed arts – such as the conjuring of devils (in Faustus's case, selling his soul in exchange for wealth, power or knowledge); and shared many characteristics with his later 'mad scientist' incarnations, such as frightening laboratories, bangs and flashes, and wild hair and eyes. Mary Shelley gives us a description of the 'mad alchemist', forerunner of her Frankenstein the scientist, when she tells of his enthusiastic experiments as a teenager: 'The raising of ghosts or devils was a promise liberally accorded by my favourite authors, the fulfillment of which I most eagerly sought' (*F* 42). It is clear that, in Shelley's eyes, the 'Modern Prometheus' or mad scientist is only a continuation of the previous mad alchemist figure into a more dangerous age of scientific discoveries.

Examples of the mad scientist figure abound in our literary history and popular culture: we need only to think of Robert Louis Stevenson's Dr Jekyll (1886), the urbane doctor whose experiments lead him to change into Edward Hyde, his primitive alter ego[9]; H. G. Wells's Dr. Moreau (1896), the physiologist who experiments with blending different animals and humans into new creatures[10]; or Peter Sellers' portrayal of the crazy Dr Strangelove, lover of the hydrogen bomb, in the film of that name (1964).[11] All such figures and many more can be traced back through the character of Victor Frankenstein.

Stevenson's *Dr Jekyll and Mr Hyde*, and Wells's *The Island of Dr Moreau*, both lead us towards our next observation: not only does Frankenstein live on in modern mythology, so does the daemon, his creature. There seem to be three particular threads from the *Frankenstein* daemon, which have been picked up by our culture, and have grown and prospered in a thousand characterizations since. These are, first, the idea of a vulnerable and tragic soul trapped within an ugly body; secondly, the idea of a dual or split personality (i.e. the idea Frankenstein expresses when he thinks of the daemon as 'my own vampire, my own spirit let loose' [*F* 78]); thirdly, the idea of an artificial or manufactured being. Stevenson's novella has become the classic split-personality tale, even giving the phrase 'a Jekyll-and-Hyde character' to the language. Prendick, the narrator of Wells's *The Island of Dr Moreau*, finds his sympathies as well as his revulsion stirred by the beast-human creatures he meets on the island, tragic artificial products of Moreau's laboratory.

These are classic literary examples dating from the nineteenth century. However, we only need to allow ourselves brief thought about more recent popular culture, to realize how many of the archetypes reproduced by the mass media today owe something to Frankenstein's daemon. Such film creations as Robocop, or the Six Million Dollar Man, or a host of others, borrow elements from Shelley's artificially created human being; and it is now a commonplace that such science-produced characters have an unquenchable spark of humanity deep inside! The film character Rambo, among others, suggests that military authorities, acting a kind of Frankenstein role, have irresponsibly turned men into killing machines. For a variant treatment, reminiscent of Shelley's daemon learning from the De Laceys, consider the robot Data, and his fascination as he seeks to develop humanity, from the television series and films of *Star Trek: The Next Generation*; or look at the sophisticated treatment of this theme in Isaac Asimov's *Robot* science-fiction novels.

Dual personalities – shy characters with powerful secret selves – abound in the comic-strip world: we need only mention Clark Kent and *Superman*, Bruce Wayne and *Batman*, or Dr Banner and *The Incredible Hulk* as obvious examples of such split identities. To show that many un-human creatures appeal for love, wailing as does the daemon, 'Make me happy' (*F* 103), we need only to remember this inimitable line from Marvel Comics' *The Incredible Hulk*: 'Is there no place for a green-skinned introvert in this modern world?', and remember that Stan Lee, joint creator of the Hulk and President of Marvel Comics, 'compared The Hulk to the misunderstood creature Frankenstein's Monster'.[12]

As even such a brief discussion amply demonstrates, both of the central figures of Mary Shelley's fable, Frankenstein and the daemon he creates, have entered modern mythology, and are constantly being reproduced in variant forms. We have discussed the enduring fear of 'mad scientists', and the ethical puzzles set by each new scientific discovery. Variant daemon figures seem to express two particular fascinations. First, the idea of a fundamental, inner humanity. This is present even when obscured by the extreme ugliness (Shelley's daemon, the Incredible Hulk) or extreme mechanism (Robocop) of the body within which it hides. It is variably seen as the saving grace, or the tragic vulnerability, of the character. Another manifestation of this belief in humanity is that it becomes an object of desire (e.g. for Data in *Star Trek: The Next Generation*)[13]; so, many artificial creatures in science fiction seek to acquire humanity, or accidentally inherit their maker's humanity. The modern *Frankenstein* myth, then, emphasizes a quality that can be called 'humanity': its persistence, its saving power and its desireability. We do not have the space to enter into discussion of the political role of this concept in the modern world. However, it should be obvious that an emphasis on 'humanity' – broadly conceived in Christian terms – as a quality capable of saving individuals, artificial creatures and the human race is a concept with which the Western Democratic/Capitalist nations and their established ruling groups are comfortable.

The second fascination expressed by modern daemon-figures is a fascination with dual or split personalities, and in particular with light/dark or civilized/primitive dualities. This fascination received its classic treatment in Stevenson's *Dr Jekyll and Mr Hyde*; but, as we have remarked, there are numerous examples among the Marvel Comics superheroes. Often these characters lose control over their changes to and from alter egos, just as Stevenson's Jekyll finds himself changing into Hyde with increasing frequency. This fascination is the descendant of a long tradition concerning the 'dark side' of human nature, the origin of evil and so forth: in short, all the primitive lust and destructiveness that howls hungrily in the wastelands all around us, and threatens the 'little walled city'[14] of our civilization, with its anxious protective laws. Since the turn of the twentieth century, psychological theory has predicated the existence of the 'unconscious': a submerged part of the mind where things too horrible to think, and urges too horrible to acknowledge, are hidden from consciousness, and split characterizations have received a boost from the development of such ideas. Indeed, as we have remarked, many critics have re-read *Frankenstein* in the light of psychoanalytical theory, and concentrated on questions which cast the daemon as an embodiment of Victor's unconscious. Such questions as: why would Frankenstein's 'own spirit' wish to 'destroy all that was dear to me' (*F* 78)?

Concluding Discussion

In our forays into analysis of *Frankenstein*, we seem repeatedly to meet the same experience. Analysis begins with clear signposts, leading us to obvious conclusions – often conclusions so obvious there was no need for analysis to realize them, like the three clear fables and their morals we discussed in Chapter 3. Then, just as we feel we are about to illuminate the text, we find that our analysis comes to a stop. It is not a 'stop' in the sense of a barrier, nor is there an absence of interesting leads to carry our ideas forward. Rather, we reach a stop because the text is suddenly too rich: because there are multiple suggestions, and however carefully we try to proceed, we cannot confirm or discard from among them. This is why, several times in this and previous chapters, we have remarked on *Frankenstein*'s extraordinary richness of suggestion, coupled with its resistance to final interpretation. The only conclusions of which we can feel confident are those blindingly obvious ones that are hardly more than statements of the story; and most of these are questioned or undercut, either because of multiple, but uncertain, contrary suggestion; or because of their context within one or another frame narrative. For these reasons, the world of the novel *Frankenstein* gives a particularly dense impression.

At the same time, the world of *Frankenstein* is limited. We have commented on the use of favourite terms (such as 'ardour' and 'ardent') so that the text of each narrative is punctuated by repetition; and on how the narratives overlap, and reprise events, so that the story seems to occur repeatedly also. We have also noticed that there are very few characters, while those there are exhibit a range of qualities, rather than individuality. Furthermore, the people act out their roles against a backdrop of distant and often depopulated settings, such as the alpine 'mer de glace' and the empty Arctic Ocean. In Chapter 1, we remarked that the core of the story is intensified, or rendered more suggestive and dense, by the double frame which enhances both distance and authenticity.

However, we repeatedly find ourselves thrown about from one to another path of ideas, in the richness of the novel's many suggestions. So, for example, when we considered the symbolism of aspects of nature, we found too many meanings rather than none. What is suggested by *Frankenstein* is something powerful, difficult of access and difficult to see, rendered uncertain because framed by second-hand narratives, arduous journeys and wild, desolate settings.

In this chapter we have discussed Shelley's references to mythology. Incorporating elements of myth in her fable enables Shelley to tap into responses deep within the reader's memory: we are stirred as the story touches upon mythological archetypes, such as hubris (theft from the Gods; arrogation of God's powers; transgression against the laws of the Gods or Nature); disobedience; a hostile fate and the breaking of taboos. The elemental resonances sounded by these myths add further to the rich suggestive power of the text. It is probable that these mythological elements are rendered even more potent, because of the determination with which *Frankenstein* encourages and then resists interpretation in psychological or thematic terms, and resists conclusions. Perhaps this is as near as we can come to explaining *Frankenstein*'s ability to create its own 'myth'.

5

Themes, and Conclusions to Part 1

In our first four chapters, we have repeatedly come up against the combination of suggestive richness and interpretative uncertainty that characterizes *Frankenstein*. The characters work in combinations rather than as individuals, and their psychologies raise multiple unanswered questions. The significance of major elements of the text such as nature and science remains many-stranded and inconsistent, and resists interpretation despite a plethora of powerful suggestions. The same applies to the text's analysis of society, which is radical and powerful, but applicable in several ways and several contexts. Despite a backdrop and fable ideally suited to symbolic meaning, we were not able to develop a consistent, interpretable symbolic role except for the daemon; and, we could not link one symbolic meaning to another, in order to build a sense of symbolism in the text as a whole.

Some concepts of the widest application, which are woven into the text, do survive, however. We have referred to one in particular, which we have called 'harmony'. According to this idea, human beings are born into a world alongside the powers of nature and of knowledge. If we live in 'harmony' with our environment, we will draw benefits from nature and knowledge. When once that 'harmony' is broken, and we antagonize nature or abuse knowledge, then disaster occurs. This concept of 'harmony' appears broadly relevant to *Frankenstein*.

However, as is typical of this text, the concept falls foul of some threads of the fable. How, for example, can 'harmony' apply to the De Laceys? The judgement they accept philosophically is not 'harmony' at all: it is mere corruption and judicial bullying! If 'harmony' means submitting to injustice, it becomes a nonsensical concept. So, again, we can account for some, but not all, of the elements of the text.

Having reminded ourselves that interpretation of *Frankenstein* is a limited business, because the novel is multifarious and opaque, we should return to the other characteristic we have consistently found: the richness of ideas suggested by the text. We have repeatedly found that there are powerful themes in *Frankenstein*, and that the text makes strong, unequivocal statements about these themes, in numerous places. In this chapter, our aim is to outline the main points we have found concerning each of the main themes. We will bring together conclusions under the following headings:

- Masculine/feminine, and the critique of male idealism and hubris.
- Nature and knowledge.
- Society: class and injustice.
- Nature and nurture (i.e. romanticism vs. determinism).

Masculine/Feminine

Walton's and Frankenstein's narratives told us that Shelley paints a critical picture of ambitious men. The elements she highlights in these two characters give an ugly picture of masculine hubris – *Frankenstein* is a feminist text in this respect. Here are the elements we have found:

1. *Double-entendre* suggests perverted or misdirected sexual drives in both cases. Walton seeks to discover the 'wondrous power which attracts the needle', and Frankenstein seeks to 'penetrate' nature and explore her 'hidden places', experiencing 'rapture' when he does so.
2. Both men have enormous egos. Frankenstein scorns careful study: he expects, like the God of Genesis, to 'pour a torrent of light

into our dark world'. Walton, when trying to be a poet, compared himself to Homer and Shakespeare. Both men therefore undertake arrogant and over-ambitious projects.

3. Walton and Frankenstein both seek everlasting fame, and expect to earn the gratitude of humanity. Walton hopes to 'confer on all mankind' an 'inestimable benefit' (*F* 16); while Frankenstein will be blessed by a new species 'as its creator and source' (*F* 55). These aims reveal the two men's vainglory. Such grandiose ideas add up to the classic tragic flaw called 'hubris', which Shelley thus ascribes to a certain kind of idealistic and egocentric man.

4. Both men reject the restraining influence of their families. Walton ignored his father's dying wish, and went to sea; then he undertook his polar voyage despite his sister's 'evil forebodings'. Frankenstein 'knew well therefore what would be my father's feelings', but stopped writing home, and persisted with his project.

5. Frankenstein's irresponsibility and self-centredness is shown throughout the text. He runs away from his own creature; he regularly argues himself out of confessing the truth; he magnifies his own suffering; he procrastinates about his promise to make a female; he avoids every challenge, including his supposedly beloved Elizabeth. Two examples show what a powerful indictment of male egocentricity Shelley provides. First, remember Frankenstein's comparison of his agony with Justine's: 'The poor victim, who on the morrow was to pass the awful boundary between life and death, felt not, as I did, such deep and bitter agony' (*F* 89). Secondly, we remember how steadfastly deaf Frankenstein is to the meaning of the daemon's threat against Elizabeth, believing it directed at himself.

6. The text provides a strong suggestion that Frankenstein has a restricted and stereotypical view of a 'feminine' ideal, and that he fears and mistrusts actual women. We may remember, for example, the 'train of reflection' about a female's potential for disobedience, which persuades Frankenstein that he should tear to pieces 'the thing on which I was engaged' (*F* 170, 171). Here Frankenstein clearly reflects the misogyny of the Biblical story of original sin, and, incidentally, the misogyny of Milton in *Paradise Lost*.

7. At this point our ideas can follow a number of further suggestions concerning the psychological and sexual abnormalities that would account for Frankenstein's behaviour: narcissism; an inverted Oedipus complex; a mother-fixation – we take our choice. However, all such suggestions imply inadequacy or abnormality, and therefore intensify what is a powerful feminist critique of male egoism.

8. Femininity in *Frankenstein* is mainly represented by Elizabeth Lavenza and Caroline Beaufort. Neither of these two steps outside a caring and nurturing but subsidiary role, except when Elizabeth briefly expresses disillusionment. Frankenstein acknowledges Elizabeth's value as the 'living spirit of love to soften and attract' (*F* 40) suggesting that her influence moderates male characters, and saves them from the excesses to which they are prone; on the other hand, he treats Elizabeth as the 'pretty present' (*F* 37) his mother gave to him. Caroline is a 'fair exotic', 'sheltered' (*F* 35) by her husband. Agatha and Safie, from the daemon's narrative, have equally stereotypical feminine qualities: they are caring (Agatha) and decorative (Safie).

9. Elizabeth can be said to stand out as the representative of 'harmony' (*F* 38), the quality that can contemplate the world with 'admiration and delight' and is the antithesis of Frankenstein's male egoism. It is possible that the text argues for 'harmony' as a necessary and saving feminine quality: a quality that will save the world from men.

10. Alternatively, we can argue that Elizabeth's very submissiveness, and her ineffectual victim role in the story, is Mary Shelley's way of condemning those stereotypes of femininity that Elizabeth represents.

Nature and Knowledge

These topics are pervasive in the story of *Frankenstein*, because the central action – the making of the daemon – is shown to be a sin against nature; and because the pursuit of knowledge is subjected to such critical discussion in the text. The following are some of the points that have arisen, relating to these topics:

1. Nature is portrayed with a variety of significances. There are overtones of God's power ('Omnipotence' [*F* 97]) and nature exerting a religious influence. There are intimations of an alien kind of power in the high mountains ('mighty friends' [*F* 100] and 'as belonging to another earth, the habitations of another race of beings' [*F* 97]). There are elements of nature that play a more particular role at particular times in the story, such as the moon, water, storms and lightning.

2. Occasionally, but not consistently, nature is accorded feminine qualities (e.g. 'in soothing accents, and maternal nature...' [*F* 98]). One could argue that Frankenstein's repeated pose lying in the bottom of a drifting boat is a form of womb-symbol as he floats in a maternal nature. However, nature also has masculine characteristics.

3. Feminine gender is ascribed to nature by scientists, notably by Waldman and Frankenstein. Their language exhibits *double-entendres* about nature's 'recesses', 'unveiling' and 'penetrating'. This aggressive gender-typing of nature contributes to Shelley's critique of masculine science and exists in the scientists' heads rather than the author's.

4. Nature is presented as a positive value: whether wild and violent, or gentle and soothing; whether exerting a religious power, or a pagan alien might and majesty; whether showing masculine or feminine characteristics. Nature is to be 'contemplated with a serious and satisfied spirit' and will afford 'admiration and delight' (*F* 38). This relationship with nature, which we have called 'harmony', is one of the most consistent positive values the text contains.

5. Nature is presented as benevolent and innocent, in the personality of the daemon. This chimes with Romantic beliefs in the innocence of childhood.[1] However, natural goodness is shown to be defeated in the human character, by the daemon's example.

6. Knowledge, in *Frankenstein*, is presented as both dangerous and as bringing unhappiness. There are innocent pursuits of learning in the novel, such as Frankenstein's short-lived interest in mathematics; but most knowledge in the book brings misery, or is dangerous.

7. Knowledge that serves an ulterior motive is dangerous. So, Shelley criticizes Frankenstein's and Walton's pursuits of knowledge because both of them seek personal aggrandizement from using their discoveries. Clerval's study of oriental languages is also for use: he 'turned his eyes towards the East as affording scope for his spirit of enterprise', while Frankenstein's study of oriental languages, with no ulterior motive, he finds 'soothing' and 'elevating' (*F* 70).

8. For the daemon, knowledge brings suffering. 'It clings to the mind, when it has once seized on it, like a lichen on the rock' (*F* 123). The daemon learns that only death gives relief from the pain of knowledge. The 'knowledge' discussed in the daemon's narrative, however, is knowledge of human nature and human society, which brings understanding of injustice, corruption, cruelty and suffering. We may say that this is knowledge in a different sense from the 'discoveries' in which Frankenstein and Walton are interested.

9. We can argue that both kinds of knowledge – discoveries, and understanding of the world – play a part in *Frankenstein* analogous to the tree of knowledge in Genesis: biting into knowledge is coterminous with the beginning of suffering, and with a fall. The analogy is very clear in the case of Frankenstein. The sin he commits by arrogating a power that should be nature's or God's alone is punished by his expulsion from the innocence of his Edenic childhood: the innocent garden of Bellerive is polluted, its innocent inhabitants murdered one by one.

10. The daemon also tells of a 'fall': he loses his innocence when he sees his own reflection, and when he learns of his origin. Although the circumstances and the guilt are entirely different, knowledge brings suffering, and a fall from innocence, for the daemon just as it does for Frankenstein.

Society: Class and Injustice

The daemon's narrative is the most sustained exposition of these themes in *Frankenstein*. However, there are also a large number of incidental details that contribute:

1. The daemon's analysis of 'the strange system of human society' (see *F* 122–3) is extremely radical for Shelley's time. It is a fundamental attack on European capitalism, and bases its critique on 'the division of property'. The daemon's analysis harks forward to Marxism.

2. We have also suggested that the daemon represents the exploited or oppressed class in society, and thus both the French revolutionary mob and the English industrial working class. With these political significances, Shelley seems to warn European ruling classes that they are creating a terrible nemesis for themselves, by keeping the common people in a despair that will stoke the flames of destructive fury.

3. Shelley indicts the mistreatment of the oppressed as an injustice which fuels their fury. The daemon's own exposition of this point deserves full quotation:

   'Am I to be thought the only criminal, when all human kind sinned against me? Why do you not hate Felix, who drove his friend from the door with contumely? Why do you not execrate the rustic, who sought to destroy the saviour of his child? Nay, these are virtuous and immaculate beings! I, the miserable and the abandoned, am an abortion, to be spurned at, and kicked, and trampled on. Even now my blood boils at the recollection of this injustice' (*F* 224).

4. Frankenstein is presented as a complacent social snob, member of a spoiled elite. We have found him to be prejudiced, and without a sense of responsibility for the consequences of his thoughtless actions. His philosophy vacillates, being romantic and determinist by turns. Clearly, Shelley presents Frankenstein as a type of the ruling class she indicts.

5. The institutions of society are chronically weak. Alphonse Frankenstein's authority cannot survive his ignorance of his son's actions. Trials are all failures, because judicial authorities cannot cope with the danger society has unleashed.

6. Several contributory details add to the text's presentation of a self-satisfied ruling class, unable to deal with the 'daemon' it has produced. We remember, for example, that William appeared young enough to be innocent, in the daemon's eyes. However, he was already corrupted by his family's rank.

7. The analysis of society's danger is materialist as well as determinist: oppression and mistreatment will lead to vengeful and violent revolution, and metaphysical beliefs are dismissed by Shelley's text. Frankenstein's attempts to believe in 'the spirits who assist my vengeance' (*F* 219), or to blame fate for his mistakes, are ridiculed: Frankenstein thanks good spirits for meals provided by the daemon.

Nature and Nurture (i.e. Romanticism vs. Determinism)

We noticed these themes as presented most consistently in the daemon's determinist narrative, and in Frankenstein's and Walton's idealist dreams.

1. The daemon presents a clear determinist case, insisting that the treatment he receives from humanity (his *nurture*) is the determining factor in his character and actions. He states, simply: 'misery made me a fiend. Make me happy, and I shall again be virtuous' (*F* 103).
2. The daemon relates a violent struggle between *nature* and *nurture*. He claims that evil and violence were always unnatural to him, that he was 'wrenched by misery to vice and hatred' (*F* 222). We can conclude that Shelley shows *nature* as invariably benevolent. Human beings treat each other with injustice and cruelty, and this *nurture* spreads the danger of violent revenge.
3. In *Frankenstein*, then, *nature* is positive and *nurture* is negative. The text is pessimistic: there is no instance of nature having the victory over environmental determinants.
4. Frankenstein ironically adopts a determinist position also. We noticed that he ascribes responsibility for his own character to his parents (*F* 35); that he imagines himself at the mercy of 'Destiny...and her immutable laws' (*F* 43); that he attempts to blame his father for his own ideas receiving the 'fatal impulse that led to my ruin' (*F* 41); and that he imagines a supernatural 'spirit of good' (*F* 207), that fed him during his pursuit of the daemon.

5. Romanticism is represented in *Frankenstein* by the chimerical dreams of Frankenstein and Walton. Walton imagines the polar region as 'a land surpassing in wonders and in beauty every region hitherto discovered on the habitable globe' (*F* 15). Frankenstein's dream of a beautiful creation vanishes when it moves with its own life (*F* 58).

6. Shelley's critique of romantic attitudes goes further, when Frankenstein asserts the power of such concepts as 'honour' and 'glory' to be victorious over material obstacles: 'This ice is not made of such stuff as your hearts may be', he says to Walton's crew (*F* 217), and asserts that the ice 'mountains' are 'molehills, which will vanish before the resolutions of man' (*F* 216).

7. These romantic views are expressed by the superstitious Frankenstein, who once tried to conjure ghosts and devils. We can argue that Shelley has a satirical intention, exposing such fine romantic sentiments as mad.

8. The final burden of the text in relation to *nature* and *nurture* seems to be determinist: it is the material world, and determinist cause and effect, which prove the stronger in every conflict narrated in *Frankenstein*.

Conclusion

One brief thought may provide a conclusion to the analyses we have undertaken in Part 1 of this book. It is that *Frankenstein* shows a world with many tragic elements. In particular, it shows a world in which nature is invariably good, benevolent, innocent; and a world in which human society is generally unjust, cruel, prejudiced, complacent, foolish and dangerous.

Mary Shelley's insight is to show us a world in which the wickedness of humanity can be victorious over all the wonderful benevolence and abundance of nature. In this sense her tale is of the 'Modern' Prometheus, and instigates the genre of science fiction. In this sense also, *Frankenstein* continues to be crucially relevant to us. Just think of only a few of the dangers threatening us in the present: global warming; exhausting the world's resources; a nuclear holocaust. All of these show humanity's ability to be destructively victorious over nature. *Frankenstein* is one of the first texts to be written for such a modern world, a world over which humanity holds such terrible and untrustworthy sway.

PART II

THE CONTEXT
AND THE CRITICS

6

Mary Shelley's Life and Works

The Life of Mary Shelley

All biographies of Mary Shelley and most critical works develop theories about her parents, birth and background. We will briefly discuss some of these theories in Chapter 8. For now, we will try to provide a plain account of her life.

Mary Shelley was born on 30th August, 1797, in Somers Town, a new district just north of the City of London. Her mother was Mary Wollstonecraft, a well-known radical and feminist, author of *A Vindication of the Rights of Woman*. Her father was William Godwin, also a well-known radical and author of *Political Justice*. Mary's parents married in March 1797, against their published principles and solely to legitimate their child. Her mother suffered complications following the birth, and died ten days later. William Godwin took on the upbringing of baby Mary, and his wife's three-year-old illegitimate daughter Fanny. It seems that his few months' experience of married life had altered Godwin's principles, for he soon began looking for a second wife. He was unsuccessful with several proposals, before meeting Mrs Clairmont, a widow with two children. They were married in December 1801, when Mary was four. Charles and Jane Clairmont were thus added to the family, and when a new son was born, in 1803, there were five children. Charles was a little older, and Jane a few months younger, than Mary.

It is reported to have been a fractious and crowded household. Mary admired and loved her father, but he was a cold and rational character, often preoccupied with his writing. She hated her stepmother, who lacked sensitivity and gave preference to her own children. During her childhood, Mary therefore built up an idealized picture of her dead mother. She was rebellious, proud of her exceptional parentage, and divisively hostile to her step-mother while turning to her father for comfort.

In 1807 the family moved from Somers Town to a larger house in Skinner Street, where the Godwins' publishing business and bookshop occupied the ground floor. This transported ten-year-old Mary from the relative peace and clean air of a suburb, into the crowds, smells and dirt of one of the busiest parts of the city, between Smithfield market and Newgate Prison. Godwin's reputation as leading radical and author of *Political Justice* brought many of the original thinkers of the day to his house, and Mary enjoyed listening to their conversations. There is a story, for example, that she listened spellbound as Coleridge recited his poem *The Ancient Mariner*. Not only because she was the daughter of two literary celebrities, but also probably because it provided an escape from the frictions of her daily home life, Mary became a voracious reader. Her education consisted of some short lessons with Godwin, and intermittently other lessons with tutors; but otherwise she was self-taught, able to form opinions and choose her reading for herself. The underlying conflicts did not die down, however, and as Mary became a teenager, she found home increasingly irksome, and made herself increasingly troublesome to her step-mother.

In May 1811 Mrs Godwin took Charles, little William and Mary to Ramsgate for a seaside holiday. The others returned to town in June, but left Mary at a girls' school in Ramsgate where she remained until December. This stay must have provided some welcome respite from conflict for both daughter and step-mother. The following year, one William Baxter, an admirer of Godwin's, invited Mary to stay with his family in Scotland. Mary traveled to Dundee by boat in June 1812; and when she arrived found a well-ordered family, living in bleak but beautiful surroundings overlooking the Tay estuary. Mary's two stays with the Baxter family introduced her to a domestic harmony, and stability, that was lacking in Skinner Street, which was dominated by domestic squabbles and her father's perennial money troubles. The Baxters had two daughters, and Mary forged an intimate friendship with Isabella, the younger.

In November, Mary and Isabella's elder sister Christy visited London for Christmas. Here they met Godwin's newest disciple: the 19-year-old Percy Bysshe Shelley, and his teenage wife Harriet. Mary and Christy returned to Scotland the following Spring, and Mary's second stay with the Baxters continued until she returned to London in March 1814. Soon afterwards Shelley re-appeared in London, by now estranged from his wife. Mary and he took to walking out together, their destination often St. Pancras churchyard and the grave of Mary Wollstonecraft. This was a favourite retreat of Mary's, where she would read and muse during melancholy periods in her childhood. On 26th June, at her mother's grave, Mary declared her love for Shelley, and they made love. As the daughter of Mary Wollstonecraft and William Godwin, Mary would have thought it wrong to delay physical consummation of her love. On their return to Skinner Street, Shelley told Godwin of their love. To his surprise, the famously anti-marriage philosopher was antagonistic. He urged Shelley to overcome his passion for Mary, and patch things up with Harriet.

There followed a time of tension. The Godwins tried to suppress the love between Mary and Percy, but probably succeeded only in strengthening this particularly rebellious young couple's determination and passion. Shelley paid a histrionic visit to Skinner Street: he gave Mary a bottle of laudanum, and produced a pistol for himself, declaring that they would die rather than endure separation. This tense time could not, and did not, last very long. At four o'clock in the morning on 28th July 1814, Mary left her father's house and met Shelley, who had a coach waiting. They escaped together to the continent, taking Mary's step-sister Jane with them. So ended Mary's childhood, and so began the most exciting part of her life: the eight years she shared with Percy Bysshe Shelley.

During their years together, the couple lived at various times in Switzerland, Italy and in England. Jane, who changed her name to Claire, lived with them for most of the time. Her self-dramatizing character, and habit of demanding attention from Percy, soon led Mary to regret having taken her with them when they eloped, and the problem of Claire periodically rose up to dominate their lives. These were tumultuous years for Mary, filled with pregnancies, deaths, restless movement from country to country; and even when they had settled in Italy, from region to region, and from villa to villa. It was typical of their nomadic life that the Casa Magni, at Lerici, had been the Shelleys' home for less than three months when Percy drowned, in July 1822.

But we should return to 1814. At Calais, Mrs Godwin caught up with the runaways. She ignored Mary and Shelley, but tried to persuade Jane to return to London with her. She almost succeeded, but at the last minute Jane opted to continue the adventure. Mrs Godwin returned to England alone, and the three set off for Paris together. Their ideas of travel were extraordinarily naïve: from Paris, they hoped to walk to Switzerland, where they planned to found a commune of like-minded people on the shores of Lake Lucerne. They bought a donkey for Mary and Jane to ride by turns, but the donkey turned out to be lame so they exchanged it for a mule – with some loss of money of course. At Troyes, they acknowledged their exhaustion (and Shelley had sprained an ankle), sold the mule and bought a cart, again at a financial loss. The countryside through which they travelled was devastated by the recent war. Villages had been razed to the ground, and the peasants were filthy and desperately poor. Conditions improved somewhat after Pontarlier and in Switzerland. They eventually arrived at Lucerne, finally taking lodgings in Brunnen, on 24th August, just less than a month after they had eloped. However, they were disappointed, their lodgings were ugly and uncomfortable, and the colony of free-thinkers of which they had dreamed seemed suddenly impossible to found, and less attractive than they had imagined. On Sunday 28th August, exactly a month after they ran away and just four days after their arrival in Brunnen, the trio set off to return to England, travelling cheaply by river because money was becoming short. Shelley could not afford their passage across the channel: on arriving in England, they had to borrow from his wife Harriet, to pay their debts to mariners and coachman, before they could go to a hotel.

Money troubles continued to plague the three young people throughout that Autumn. Mary was pregnant, Jane was attention-seeking and moody, and Shelley was constantly trying to raise a loan on his expectations. The worst period came towards the end of October, when Shelley had to leave their lodgings and live in hiding for six days each week, in order to avoid arrest: he and Mary could only be together on Sunday, when bailiffs were on holiday. The situation was resolved on 9th November, when Shelley finalised a £500 loan and paid off his creditors. However, troubles of various sorts continued to beset the household. During that winter they moved several times between different lodgings; Mary was irritated by Claire's demanding moods; Claire was depressed by being the third in the house, and Shelley was unwilling to encourage Claire to go, despite Mary's evident wish to be rid of her. Mary's baby daughter was born prematurely on 22 February 1815, and died on 7th March. Meanwhile, Shelley's friend Thomas Jefferson Hogg had become a regular visitor. Shelley encouraged the idea of sexual freedom and promoted Hogg's attentions to Mary, who fell in with the project, although with some reluctance at first.

During the period leading up to and following the loss of her baby, there are several batches of pages missing from Mary's journal. These were probably torn out and destroyed by Mary herself later in life, either to cover up her affair with Hogg or to hide a sexual relationship between Shelley and Claire. However, Mary's life became easier after 13 May 1815, when Claire left to go and live alone at Lynmouth in Devon; and when Shelley finalised a financial settlement giving him an annual income of £1000, and a lump sum. William Godwin had been furious when Mary ran away, refused to see her and always condemned her; but at the same time, he expected Shelley to give him money and pay his debts; and it seems that Shelley, in the spirit of the principles set out in *Political Justice*, accepted this view. On this occasion £1000 of Shelley's lump sum went to Godwin, and Godwin's imperious demands for money continued to follow Shelley around for many more years.

Mary and Shelley travelled in the West Country during the Summer of 1815, but by August had settled in a house near Windsor, and Mary was pregnant again. She gave birth to a son, William, on

24th January 1816. In May of that year, Mary, Shelley and the baby, with Claire again in tow, travelled to Geneva. The main instigator of this journey and destination appears to have been Claire, who had an affair with Lord Byron in London, and manipulated the Shelley *ménage* into following him to the continent. They took a small house on the Belle Rive shore of the lake, Maison Chapuis; and Byron rented the much larger neighbouring Villa Diodati. So began the famous Summer when two Romantic poets talked the nights away, when a reading of ghost stories prompted a horror-story-writing competition, and when the novel *Frankenstein* was born.

Mary's account of the genesis of *Frankenstein* in the Preface to the 1831 edition is broadly accepted. Biographers and critics differ as to how far Mary censored, slanted or mis-remembered events; and many have further psychological explanations for how her nightmare arose[1] as well as numerous suggestions concerning sources for Mary's other ideas. For example, Miranda Seymour notes that Byron was working on *Manfred* that Summer, writing about a magician tortured by guilt; that Matthew Lewis visited the colony on the shores of Lake Geneva, fresh from a visit to his slave plantations; and implies that discussions about slavery, as well as the contemporary theory of a connection between African people and monkeys, may have filled Mary's mind with elements from which she distilled Frankenstein's 'creature'.[2] Seymour, however, does not believe that Mary took several days to think of a story: she believes Mary began writing immediately, on the grounds that Byron's friend Doctor Polidori does not mention Mary's delay in his journal, despite being in love with her. Jane Dunn, on the other hand, tells us that 'we have her [Mary's] word that the immediate impulse came from Shelley and Byron's discussions at Diodati and her subsequent waking dream'.[3]

Whatever actually happened to trigger the ideas of *Frankenstein* was undoubtedly a much more complicated process than any single narrative can encompass. Mary acknowledges this when she writes, 'Invention, it must be humbly admitted, does not consist in creating out of void, but out of chaos' (*F* 8). What we know is that she began writing the novel in June 1816, and that it was completed on 14th May 1817. In Chapter 8, we will find that almost all critics have an answer to the question Mary poses in her Preface: 'How I, then a young girl, came to think of and to dilate upon so very hideous an idea?' (*F* 5). For the present, we must rejoin Mary's life.

The *ménage*, with Claire by now visibly pregnant, left Switzerland at the end of August and returned to England, taking lodgings in Bath. Two tragedies occurred before the end of the year. In October, Mary's half-sister Fanny Godwin, the one who stayed at home and accepted a life of domestic drudgery, killed herself by taking an overdose of laudanum. In December, Harriet Shelley committed suicide by drowning herself in the Serpentine. Custody of the two children from Shelley's first marriage was an immediate issue, and, partly in the hope of persuading the court to award them custody, Mary and Percy Shelley were married on 30th December. Despite their marriage, the court found it hard to decide in favour of a father who had paid little attention to his two children, and had deserted his family for another woman by whom he now had another child. The custody case dragged on, and the Shelleys stayed with their friends the Leigh Hunts at the Vale of Health, north of London. In March the case was decided – neither Shelley nor Harriet's family would have custody, but both would nominate guardians for the children. At about the same time, Mary and Percy settled in Albion House, Marlow; and in May, *Frankenstein* was finished. The Leigh Hunts paid an extended visit to Albion House during the Summer. In August, the Lord Chancellor ruled in favour of Harriet's family: Shelley's two children were to be brought up by a clergyman nominated by them.

Claire had borne Byron's child, who they called Allegra, in January 1817. Mary was pregnant again, and gave birth to a daughter, Clara, in September. *Frankenstein* was published in January 1818. However, a combination of reasons urged the Shelleys to move abroad. They were worried that the law might be able to take little William and Clara from them; Shelley was in poor health, and had been advised to seek a warmer climate; the scandal of little Allegra's illegitimacy made Marlow society unwelcoming, and Byron would not fetch his daughter – although he would take her if she were brought to him; finally, the house was damp and cold. As Autumn turned to Winter, mildew sprouted everywhere. By settling in Italy, the Shelleys would keep their children safe from English law, improve Shelley's health, deliver Allegra to her father, and escape the depressing damp and cold of England's climate and society. The Shelleys, Claire and her baby, newly baptized Clara Allegra, left for Italy on 11th March 1818.

At this point, we will move back a little distance from details, and look at the four Italian years as a whole.

There were four further tragic child deaths. First, the baby Clara died, in September 1818. A crisis concerning little Allegra led Shelley and Claire to rush to Venice, hoping to reach a solution with Byron. Shelley then called Mary to join them, and Clara, already ill, became worse on the sweltering four-day journey. Another hot journey followed, escorting Claire to a doctor in Padua, then taking the ailing Clara to Byron's doctor in Venice. Shelley rushed off to find the doctor, but by the time he returned Clara was dead. Mary bitterly blamed both Claire and her husband for her daughter's death. All the rushing around about Byron and Allegra was, really, unnecessary histrionics: Clara's illness was more serious, and was ignored. Next, after a relatively fast illness and decline, William Shelley died of malaria, in Rome, in June 1819. He had reached the age of three. His death was a heavy blow to Mary, who had allowed herself to hope that he would survive. In February 1819, when the Shelleys were living at Naples, a baby girl was registered as their daughter with the name Elena Adelaide Shelley. However, Mary was not this baby's mother; and the biographers are all at sea as to who the mother may have been – and there is even doubt whether Shelley was the father. Was Claire the mother? Was this baby the daughter of Elise, the Swiss nursemaid who had been with them since 1816, and who left their service to marry their Italian factotum Paolo Foggi, in 1818? In any event, Elena Adelaide was placed with foster-parents in Naples, her upkeep paid for by Shelley. She lived only two years, dying in June 1820. Finally, Clara Allegra Byron died from Typhus, aged five, in the early Spring of 1822.

One child survived: in November 1819 in Florence, Mary gave birth to a son, Percy Florence Shelley, the only one of her children who reached adulthood. Mary's next pregnancy ended in miscarriage on 16th June, 1822, and she nearly died from the consequent haemorrhage. She was saved by her husband's timely action, sitting her in an ice-bath. Only a month later, Shelley himself was dead.

During their first year in Italy, the Shelleys spent time near Venice, in Rome and at Naples: that is, in the north-east, the centre, and the far south of Italy. After William's death in Rome, in the Summer of 1819, although they continued to change lodgings and rent villas or apartments with bewildering regularity, the Shelleys' Italian rambles were restricted to Tuscany, including Livorno and Florence. Eventually they became more settled, at Pisa, where Byron again became their neighbour. In the Spring of 1822 they were living in the same building with their friends Edward and Jane Williams. Shelley and Edward Williams loved boating, and they planned to spend Summer by the sea, at La Spezia on the Bay of Lerici. However, they could not find a suitable house. Eventually they rented the Casa Magni, a lonely house on the rocky shore, a house Mary hated from the day they moved in. News of Allegra's death had just arrived, and it was important to keep Claire away from Byron: perhaps this explains the rush to move to such an unsuitable house. Mary was depressed and angry, and her marriage was in a bad state. Percy Shelley and Edward Williams spent the days sailing their boat on the bay; Shelley flirted with Jane Williams; Mary lost her baby to a miscarriage. On 1st July, Shelley and Williams set off to sail to Livorno, to meet Leigh Hunt on his arrival there from England. On 8th July, having settled the Hunts into their lodgings at Pisa, the two men set sail from Livorno on the return journey. Their boat was sunk in a storm, and they drowned.

During the four years Mary lived in Italy before Shelley's death, their lives were hardly ever in a state of emotional calm. Reading the biographers' accounts of those years, you hear of a brief three weeks, perhaps a month, of tranquillity – such as the Autumn of 1820 in a villa at Bagni di Pisa – but the few such brief islands of calm are always interrupted or destroyed either by Claire's demands and troubles, Shelley's vagaries and flirtations, sudden decisions to uproot and move, or by the deaths of children. At the same time, there were other worries. Godwin was always in debt, and sometimes in danger of debtor's prison; and he maintained his imperious demands upon the Shelley purse. The Shelleys had some money worries of their own. Scandalous reports concerning the baby Elena Adelaide circulated among the English expatriate community in 1820, and the Shelleys' old servant Paolo Foggi began to blackmail them. Maintaining our distance from all the detail of those years, we can suggest three emotional crises that attacked Mary's happiness. First, the death of baby Clara that she blamed on her husband's thoughtlessness. Following this event was a lengthy period of depression and comparative estrangement from Shelley. Then, the death of William the following Summer. It seems that something of Mary's youth inevitably died with her little son: that she could never again love as fully or feel free of worry. Even in later years as her second son Percy grew up, Mary could not bring herself to trust in the future as firmly as she had before William died. Finally, there was the fact that she could never be sure of Shelley's loyalty, as his enthusiasms often took the form of flirtations. Nobody is sure who was the mother of the baby in Naples in 1819; but it is at least likely that Shelley was the father. There is a strong presumption that he maintained a sexual relationship with Claire, on and off, throughout his life. He perhaps had affairs with one Emilia Viviani, in 1821; and with Jane Williams in 1822. Mary must often have felt, particularly during the final 18 months of their life together, that her marriage was effectively finished. In their final two months together, at the Casa Magni, Mary behaved angrily towards Shelley, who complained about her mistreatment of him to anyone who would listen. After Shelley's death, Mary suffered terribly from remorse because the last few months of their married life together were soured by her own foul temper.

Shelley's and Williams's bodies had been washed ashore, and the Italian authorities immediately buried them in quicklime as a precaution against infection. The Shelleys' friend Trelawny arranged with the authorities to dig up the bodies so that they could be cremated on the beach at Via Reggio, in a simple ceremony with Byron and Leigh Hunt also present. Mary was not there. Trelawny took Shelley's ashes to Rome and buried them in the Protestant cemetery where William had been buried three years previously. Shelley's heart (reputedly – although some think it was really his liver) survived the fire, and Mary begged this souvenir from Leigh Hunt, who eventually gave it to her.

The two widows Mary and Jane, with Claire and little Percy, left the Casa Magni as quickly as possible and went to Pisa. From there, Claire left to join her brother Charles in Vienna, and Mary stayed with the Hunts at Genoa for the winter, with Byron nearby. Throughout that desperately depressed winter, Mary waited on negotiations with her father-in-law Sir Timothy Shelley, hoping for an allowance towards the upbringing of his grandson Percy. The following August she returned to England, perhaps hoping that the little boy's presence would soften his grandfather's heart.

Mary Wollstonecraft Godwin Shelley was now 26 years old. Her youth had been lived at a high tempo, crammed with incident, passion and tragedy; crammed with movement, change and surprise. The remaining 28 years of her life were not by any means empty, but were lived at an easier pace, with incidents more widely spaced. Essentially, Mary made her home in London for most of the remainder of her life. Her time was spent bringing up her son; pursuing her own literary career; protecting the memory and editing the works of Percy Bysshe Shelley; and maintaining a social life.

Mary cared for her one surviving son, Percy Florence, as he grew up. In 1826, Charles Bysshe, Shelley's son by his first wife, died. Consequently, Percy inherited the Shelley title and estate when old Sir Timothy Shelley died, in 1844. In 1848 Percy married a young widow, Jane St. John, a woman who would have been Mary's own choice for him. Percy inherited none of his parents' genius, but became a goodhearted young man of steady character. Mary moved to Harrow during his childhood, so that she could afford to pay his fees at the school as a day boy; and she was always worried in case Sir Timothy should revoke the small allowance he made towards Percy's education. Nonetheless, Percy brought great consolation into Mary's life, particularly when he and two university friends invited her to accompany them on a Summer's trip to Lake Como, in 1840: she felt that such an invitation from three young men was a great compliment. In 1848 Percy was a parliamentary candidate in Horsham, but was not elected, and after this attempt at a public career he settled down to living in obscurity.

Mary struggled to earn a living with her pen, and continued to produce novels, travel writing, and numerous essays, stories and articles, up until the time when Percy inherited the Shelley estate. An account of Mary's works is given in the second section of this chapter. We need only record here that her income was rarely sufficient for her needs: money was a perennial worry, and easier circumstances only arrived in the 1840s, first with her editions of Shelley's works, and then with Percy's inheritance.

Sir Timothy Shelley had always been horrified by the scandals that surrounded the son he had virtually disowned; and his second daughter-in-law, herself sprung from dangerous radicals, and a brazen adulteress, was no less dangerous to his good name. He made it a condition of any help he gave towards Percy's upbringing, that the Shelley name should not be further mired in scandal by any action of Mary's. In 1824 Mary published Shelley's *Posthumous Poems*, but the book was immediately suppressed at Sir Timothy's insistence. It is against this background that we can understand Mary's attitude towards protecting her dead husband's memory. She saw herself both as the custodian of Shelley's reputation and as protecting her son's future. She hoped that Percy would be able to live respectably, and she dreamed that he might have a career in public life. Naturally, any fresh revelations about his father's scandalous ideas and more scandalous life would have extinguished Percy's prospects at a stroke. We can allow the view that Mary's parents, or Percy Bysshe Shelley himself, would never have compromised with the honesty of their beliefs; would never have hidden their opinions. According to this view, Mary was disloyal to the memory of her husband, who was politically far more outspoken and radical than she represented him; and according to this view, Mary was one of those Romantics – like Wordsworth – who were firebrands in youth, but sold out to the conservative establishment in later life.

Mary always intended to write a biography of Shelley herself, but when Sir Timothy's death eventually removed the main obstacle to this, she did not undertake it. In 1829 Trelawny had wanted to write Shelley's life, and appealed to Mary for information and help, which she declined. On that occasion she pleaded a mishmash of reasons including her desire to live privately, and supposed shyness. However, there is little doubt that Percy's allowance was prominent in her mind. In 1839, Mary accepted the generous offer of £600 to edit an edition of Shelley's *Poetical Works*. She was still forbidden to write his biography, but included biographical notes on the poems. Some of Shelley's friends were angry that she had censored *Queen Mab*, and omitted its dedication (to Harriet Shelley). She has also been criticised since, for suppressing atheistical material, which she did at the bookseller's request. Mary also edited and published Shelley's prose under the title *Essays, Letters from Abroad, Translations and Fragments*, in 1839. These two works were successful, and brought a measure of financial ease to Mary's life at the start of the 1840s.

With regard to Mary's social life, this continued to be an unsatisfying struggle with hopes and disappointments, until well into her final decade. Mary seems to have been both restrained in manner, and emotionally needy, with occasional outbreaks of gaiety coinciding with stress or unhappiness. This was an unfortunate combination of qualities, giving her a personality very difficult for others to read, and emotions an observer might not suspect, let alone understand. We should add to this assessment that Mary had a habit of investing emotion in others, often on the basis of an imagined return, and being cruelly hurt when her investment was betrayed. Mary fantasized a romance with Washington Irving, largely created by his friend John Howard Payne's infatuation with her. She clung to a passionate friendship with Jane Williams that was clearly one-sided, as she discovered when she heard that Jane was describing the Shelley marriage as on the rocks before his death, and blaming Mary. She thought that one Aubrey Beauclerk might love her, but he chose instead the much younger Rosa Robinson. Not only did this disappoint Mary's hopes of Beauclerk, it also made part of what she perceived as her betrayal by the Robinsons, on whom she had lavished her care and affection. Finally, there was the Gatteschi affair. He was an Italian exile Mary met in Paris, returning from a continental trip with Percy. He must have recognized that he could inflame this Englishwoman's passions with his brand of exciting tales and political idealism. Mary wrote passionate letters to Gatteschi after her return to England, incidentally revealing 'details with regard to my past history, which it wd. destroy me for ever if they ever saw light', as she wrote in a letter to Alexander Knox. Gatteschi threatened publication, and Mary was at her wits' end. Finally, her young friend Knox went to France, where he arranged for the police to seize Gatteschi's papers, using Mary's money to smooth the way. Her indiscreet letters were thus recovered and destroyed.

Another blackmail episode was not a result of Mary's indiscretion. A plausible and clever forger, calling himself Major Byron and claiming to be a legitimate son of the poet from a secret marriage, had obtained a few of Byron's letters, and some of Shelley's and Mary's. In 1846 he offered these for sale only a few at a time, and cleverly copied their handwriting, forging more letters. At first, Mary bought some of these letters, paying £30, and offered to pay a pound for any letter of Shelley's. When the blackmailer returned offering more goods, six months later, Mary refused to deal. A threatened publication in 1848 was averted by legal action, and Major Byron then sold some letters to a bookseller, who offered them to Mary. Eventually, she paid six guineas for five of Shelley's letters and the manuscript of a poem, at a sale in December 1848.

As an account of Mary Shelley's life after her return to England, this is sketchy at best, and a number of important incidents as well as significant people are not even mentioned. For example, Mary was constantly meeting or in correspondence with Claire, and always closely involved with the life of her father, despite her continued dislike of the second Mrs Godwin. In 1836 Mary suffered significant bereavements. First, Maria and John Gisborne died within a few months of each other. Once a pupil of Mary Wollstonecraft, Mrs Gisborne had been a dear friend, almost a mother-figure for Mary, both in Italy and since her return to England. Then, William Godwin died after a short illness. He was 80, and Mary and Mrs Godwin nursed him continuously throughout his final few days.

Mary was always eager to fight for and maintain a position in society, and tenacious of the people she met; and she certainly wished to overcome her own scandalous reputation. She met and cultivated a large number of people, only a very few of whom are mentioned in this account. As we have suggested, her emotions were quickly inflamed or rebuffed, by imagined or real encouragements and slights.

As late as 1850, sparks were flying from Claire, who was convinced that Mary had an affair with Alexander Knox, a man young enough to be her son. Claire made libellous accusations against Percy and Jane, as well. This was a final estrangement between Mary and the step-sister who had haunted her life. Increasingly ill, Mary spent the winter of 1849–50 in the south of France, with her son and daughter-in-law. They returned to England in the Summer of 1850, and made arrangements to let the Shelley family home at Field Place. They purchased Boscombe Lodge, just outside Bournemouth, hoping that the sea air would be healthier for Jane, as well as Mary, than the damps of Field Place which made both women ill. However, Mary was not well enough to move and they remained in London during the Autumn of

1850. Towards the end of the year Mary became partially paralysed. On 23rd January 1851, she suffered a series of fits and went into a coma. This lasted for eight days, and she died on 1st February. A month later the town house was sold, and Sir Percy and Lady Jane Shelley moved to Boscombe Lodge.

Mary Shelley's Works

In her introduction to the 1831 edition of *Frankenstein*, the author tells us that 'As a child I scribbled; and my favourite pastime during the hours given me for recreation was to "write stories" ' (*F* 5). It has been assumed that Godwin's and Mary Wollstonecraft's daughter naturally became an author, but it is equally possible that such parents would be off-putting: how could Mary possibly compete? Mary tells us that she indulged 'waking dreams' and enjoyed 'the formation of castles in the air'. On the other hand, she also tells the downright lie that 'I lived principally in the country as a girl . . . my habitual residence was on the blank and dreary northern shores of the Tay, near Dundee' (*F* 5–6). In the light of this falsehood, how far can we trust the picture of imaginative childhood that Mary paints in her introduction? There is a record of William, aged eight, delivering a speech on 'The Influence of Government on the Character of the People', written by 13-year-old Mary; but this was a far cry from writing 'stories'.

We know for certain, however, that after eloping with Percy Shelley, Mary's literary activities were encouraged. They wrote the journal of their travels together, Shelley devised a fearsome programme of reading and study, which Mary followed – as well as learning Greek and Latin – and Mary was urged to write essays. Shelley also dictated the beginning of his novel to her, during their honeymoon. As we know, this build up of literary pressure culminated in the ghost-story-writing competition with Shelley, Byron and Polidori, which resulted in Mary writing *Frankenstein*, her first novel, between June 1816 and May 1817. She wrote six more novels during her life.

Following the death of her son William, in 1819, Mary wrote *Mathilda*, a novel concerning the incestuous passion of a father for the eponymous heroine, who is then courted by Woodville, a young poet.

This novel is clearly a vehicle for the expression of Mary's personal depression, the suicidal gloom she felt following the deaths of two children. Mary sent the manuscript to her father, who was shocked by some of the content, and refused to return it. *Mathilda* was not published during Mary's lifetime.

The fiction project Mary developed to follow *Frankenstein* was taking shape before she wrote *Mathilda*. It was an historical novel set in fourteenth-century Italy, based on the story of 'Castruccio, Prince of Lucca', which was Mary's initial title for the work. Having researched early renaissance Italian history and visited the area of the novel's setting, Mary began writing in 1820 and finished in November 1821, when she sent this manuscript also to her father. William Godwin changed the title to *Valperga: or, the Life and Adventures of Castruccio, Prince of Lucca*, and made other editorial changes which he hoped would improve the text. *Valperga* was published in February 1823, and reviewers were generally impressed. It is a very long and wordy novel, and has an 'at times surprising lack of integration',[4] both qualities that put off modern readers. The theme, of a man who chooses political ambition over domestic happiness and whose quest for power leads him to an empty nullity, has some similarities with *Frankenstein*, where the hero's neglect of Elizabeth Lavenza brings disaster as does Castruccio's rejection of Euthanasia, the oddly named heroine of *Valperga*.

In the winter of 1823–4 Mary began work on *The Last Man*, a futuristic novel set in the twenty-first century when Britain has become a Republic. The story is of a plague that destroys the world's population, and is told by Lionel Verney, who by chance survives longest and so becomes the 'Last Man'. However, the novel is dominated by the two figures who attempt to lead the diminishing population while the plague destroys mankind: these are Lord Raymond, an adventurer who is clearly a portrait of Byron, and Adrian, a gentler, more contemplative character based on Shelley. Mary finished work on the novel in 1825, and it was published in February 1826. The reviewers were not enthusiastic. For a long time, and still for many people, Mary Shelley has been regarded as a one-book writer. *Valperga* and *The Last Man* are the only two works other than *Frankenstein* that are generally known outside the world of specialist literature studies, and that are often available in print. *The Last Man* is Shelley's only novel where the original idea could compare with that of *Frankenstein*. Unfortunately, it is one of those futuristic works that seems to have become obsolete now that its future has arrived. For the author of *Frankenstein*, who so deftly hinted at her scientist's laboratory, equipment and techniques, it seems odd that *The Last Man* describes a future where no technological progress has taken place – not even railways have arrived in the imagined twenty-first century. Further, why did the author who evoked an arctic ocean, empty deserts, the 'mer de glace' and the mighty Alps set so much of an apocalyptic story in the Home Counties near Windsor? Nonetheless, there is some gathering of horror and pace as society disintegrates and the plague whittles the remaining population down to a few hundreds, then a few tens, then a few, and finally one. The novel's idea is bold, and its warning of a dangerous future can perhaps be compared to that of *Frankenstein*.

In 1828–9, Mary wrote another historical novel, *The Fortunes of Perkin Warbeck*. In her version, Warbeck is the legal heir to the throne; but it is his decision to continue pursuing his hopeless cause, thus sacrificing his chance of love, that interests Mary: the theme is reminiscent of that in *Valperga*. Mary's choice of subject may have been influenced by her fading confidence in herself – missing the encouragement of Shelley, perhaps she felt safer founding her story on painstaking historical research: she could lean on fact, secure against criticism. As it happened, *Perkin Warbeck* was not a success when it was published in 1830. Although it was given a friendly reception, Mary received hardly any money from the work, and her main satisfaction may have been that it earned praise from her father.

In 1833 Mary began another foray into full-length fiction, *Lodore*, which was completed at Harrow while Percy was at school there, and published in March 1835. Mary drew another word-portrait of Byron as Lodore, and the story and characters show several traits and situations that are arguably drawn from her own life (such as the love-in-poverty scenes of Edward and Ethel Villiers, reminiscent of Mary's and Shelley's experiences when they returned to England in 1814). *Lodore* was relatively successful, and provided Mary with some welcome financial rewards, at a time when she was struggling to support Percy's education.

Mary's final novel was *Falkner*, written during 1835 and 1836. The story centres on Elizabeth Raby, another heroine with a dead mother and a passionate relationship with her adoptive 'parent' Falkner, the man who brings her up as his child. Elizabeth's lover, Gerald Neville, is set upon uncovering the secret crime that has disgraced his dead mother's name. The climax comes about because the guilty party is Elizabeth's dear adoptive father. This novel was written in haste, largely during the year when William Godwin died; and apparently Mary was careless about checking her text. *Falkner* was published in 1837, but was unsuccessful. Mary seems to have been partly relieved, and quite soon announced that this novel would be her last.

Aside from her seven novels, Mary Shelley did a great deal of writing of other kinds. Her works include essays, stories and complete or incomplete dramas, as well as some poetry. As she earned much of her living from writing, between 1823 when she returned to England and 1844 when Percy inherited the Shelley estate, Mary had to take a number of 'hack' commissions as well as more respected work. So, she wrote numerous romantic stories for young women's annuals. These annuals targeted the fast-growing audience of middle-class girls who were whiling away their time before marriage. Such work was lucrative, and Mary produced many articles and stories for magazines and annuals, between 1824 and 1839.

Mary put a great deal more of her pride, interest and personal philosophy into biographies written for Lardner's *Cabinet Cyclopaedia*. She wrote a large number of these, beginning with lives of eminent Italian authors, in 1833, and followed by Spanish, Portuguese and French volumes in 1837 and 1839. Mary's contributions to the *Cyclopaedia* involved much research, and had to be both accurate and readable. It is clear that she also took the opportunity, while ostensibly writing about anybody from Petrarch to Voltaire, to express her own ideas, and describe her own feelings under a safely deceptive guise. It is also likely that Mary felt comfortable with biography: that this kind of writing, rather than fiction, was a form to which her abilities were ideally suited. Perhaps she preferred factual writing, as it left her less vulnerable to personal hurt from criticism.

After giving up fiction with *Lodore*, Mary Shelley was urged to undertake a life of Godwin. She embarked on this project, deciding to treat the subject in two books, the first being a life of Godwin and Mary Wollstonecraft, ending with her own birth and her mother's death, in 1797. The notes and fragments that survive show that Mary tried to re-write history, for example trying to hide her own illegitimacy by fudging the date of her parents' marriage. The life of Godwin was never completed, although Mary seems to have been still working on it in 1840. Instead, honouring and protecting the memory of her husband dominated Mary's literary activities. In 1838 Edward Moxon commissioned her to edit the *Poetical Works* of Percy Bysshe Shelley, and these were published in four volumes, with Mary's biographical notes attached to the poems, in 1839. Further volumes also edited by Mary, of Shelley's *Essays, Letters from Abroad, Translations and Fragments* appeared in December 1839, dated 1840. It is clear from her journal and letters that Mary found the task of editing her husband's works a painful duty, as it revived him and their relationship in her memory, and brought back vividly the remorse she felt about the way their life together had ended. Then, when the poems were published, she was accused of censorship, particularly for having cut the dedication and much of the substance from *Queen Mab*; and several of Shelley's friends accused her of distorting Shelley by portraying him as a dreamy anodyne figure rather than a political radical. Mary's edition of Shelley's works is still a controversial topic. It is generally accepted that she diluted Shelley for the world, and that her daughter-in-law fought long and hard to protect the effete image of a dreamy, otherworldly poet that Mary had created. Argument occurs between those who accept Mary's view – that she did the best she could in a narrow-minded age – and those who believe she betrayed him, his causes, and his friends out of a miserable devotion to her own respectability.

Our last port of call in this overview of Mary Shelley's literary output is travel writing. In 1817 and with Percy Shelley's help, Mary expanded the journal they had kept during their 'honeymoon' trip in 1814. Adding letters she had written to Fanny, letters Percy had written to Peacock, from abroad, and Shelley's poem 'Mont Blanc', Mary made up a volume called *History of a Six Weeks Tour*, which was published in November 1817. In 1844 she completed a book called *Rambles in Germany and Italy*, which was an account of her travels on the continent with her son Percy and his friends, in 1840 and

1842–3. This travel book took a firm anti-Austrian political stance on the subjection of Italy, possibly influenced by Mary's friendship with Gatteschi, which had yet to turn sour. Her writing was sensitive to beauties of art, architecture and landscape, and was very appreciatively reviewed.

It is difficult to sum up Mary Shelley's literary works, as she wrote a great deal and contributed to so many genres, including futuristic, historical and domestic novels, travel writing, biography and editorial writing; as well as arguably founding the genre of science fiction. The last part of the twentieth century has done a great deal to reclaim most of these works from obscurity, and critical interest in Mary Shelley continues to grow. However, there is still no doubt that *Frankenstein* is her pre-eminent novel: the most enduring and successful, because both original in concept and exciting in execution.

7

The Historical and Literary Context

Some Historical Remarks

What was the political climate of the *Frankenstein* decade? International relations were in chaos after the long efforts of the Napoleonic wars. The allies entered Paris and Napoleon was defeated at the beginning of April 1814; and that same summer Mary and Shelley and Claire Clairmont travelled through a disastrously war-ravaged France on their 'Six Weeks' Tour' of elopement. They were back in England before two months had passed, and remained there during Napoleon's reappearance the following year – the 'hundred days' leading to his final defeat at Waterloo in June 1815. Just 12 months after Waterloo, Mary was in the Maison Chapuis on the shores of Lake Geneva, beginning to write *Frankenstein*. The wars against Napoleonic and Revolutionary France were a huge international upheaval. They lasted, with only a short intermission, more than 20 years. It is not enough, however, for us to mention 1814 and 1815 – even if those military events allowed Percy, Mary and Claire to take their continental jaunt. What is most important for us as we try to understand the eighteen-teens is that this decade would lead up to a 40th year of waiting, for those radicals who wished to make Britain more equal and more free.

The cause of liberty grew stronger and louder and more difficult for established governments to suppress, throughout the second half of the eighteenth century. However, from an English perspective, ideals of liberty and equality were resoundingly asserted by the American colonists who declared independence in 1776 and effectively threw off the yoke of British rule by their victories at Chesapeake and Yorktown in 1781. The idealism that began to be unleashed might have found a route to parliamentary expression and timely reform. There were several reform-minded politicians at the time, such as John Wilkes, or the much more respectable Edmund Burke. What then happened, however, stopped the entire process of British social and political evolution, in its tracks. There was revolution in France, in 1789, and the establishment in England was terrified. Suddenly, people who spoke or wrote critically of the government and its institutions were imprisoned and, in some cases, tried for treason. In short, in the 1790s the government sat down hard upon any ideas of greater freedoms or reforms. Soon, the war become a reason to shut everybody up: it was unpatriotic to criticize. And the war dragged on, as we know, until 1815. Mary's father William Godwin, we remember, published his *Enquiry Concerning Political Justice* in 1793, not to mention Tom Paine's *Rights of Man* (1791) and Mary Wollstonecraft's *A Vindication of the Rights of Woman* (1792); and Godwin sat in the treason trials courageously supporting the accused, in 1794. Mary was approaching her 20th year, and writing *Frankenstein*, nearly 30 years later, and the radicals were still waiting for things to get better.

Meanwhile, the industrial revolution rolled onward, creating a growing population of urban workers in slum housing, exploited by long hours and pitiful wages while their employers became rich. Greater equality, freedom and justice in British society were long overdue: hence the luddite industrial troubles that plagued the decade. Seventeen luddites were tried and hanged at York after disturbances across the midlands and the North of England, in 1811–13; the Pentrich rising took place in 1817; and the Peterloo massacre occurred in 1819. Remember that workers' associations or 'unions' were illegal. Industrial troubles in those days were not strikes, but pitched battles between workers and troops. So, the anger and frustration of the radical thinkers, and the desperation and fury of the working class, had grown to a point near explosion, from being so long denied. That anger and frustration at a hypocritical establishment, and a reactionary government, can perhaps best be conveyed by the tone of Percy Shelley's 'Lines written during the Castlereagh administration', which he wrote in 1819:

> Corpses are cold in the tomb;
> Stones on the pavement are dumb;
> Abortions are dead in the womb,
> And their mothers look pale – like the death-white shore
> Of Albion, free no more.
>
> Her sons are as stones in the way–
> They are masses of senseless clay–
> They are trodden, and move not away,–
> The abortion with which SHE travaileth
> Is Liberty, smitten to death.
>
> Then trample and dance, thou Oppressor!
> For thy victim is no redresser;
> Thou art sole lord and possessor
> Of her corpses, and clods, and abortions – they pave
> Thy path to the grave.
>
> Hearest thou the festival din
> Of Death, and Destruction, and Sin,
> And Wealth crying 'Havoc!' within?
> 'Tis the bacchanal triumph that makes Truth dumb,
> Thine Epithalamium.
>
> Ay, marry thy ghastly wife!
> Let Fear and Disquiet and Strife
> Spread thy couch in the chamber of Life!
> Marry Ruin, thou Tyrant! and Hell be thy guide
> To the bed of the bride!

As Godwin's and Wollstonecraft's daughter and Shelley's consort and then wife, Mary was surrounded by the political angers, frustrations, debates and outrages of the time. In *Frankenstein*, we have suggested, she created the daemon as a vehicle to symbolize the excluded, exploited and dispossessed; and we can hear some of the outraged tone of Shelley's poem, perhaps, in his speech which ends: 'Even now my blood boils at the recollection of this injustice' (*F* 224).

So we may conclude, the single most important observation to be made about the decade during which *Frankenstein* was written, particularly for those in Mary's and Shelley's milieu, is that the country was still waiting. Mary's novel must have originated, at least partly, as a warning to the complacent and the reactionaries, that the country could not go on waiting much longer.

The Literary Context

Frankenstein is a highly individual and original piece of writing. This section attempts to discuss where, if anywhere, Mary Shelley's novel fits into the development of English Literature.

The Birth of *Frankenstein*

Frankenstein had an exceptionally literary birth: its inception was instigated by conversations between two of the greatest Romantic poets, and the challenge to write a ghost story, issued by one of them. Furthermore, Mary Shelley's story was accompanied into existence by John William Polidori's *The Vampyre: A Tale* (1819), and by the unfinished story Byron eventually published at the end of his *Mazeppa, A Poem* as 'A Fragment' (1819). Byron was induced to publish his own fragment, because many attributed Polidori's story to him. The poet's incomplete story is just that, incomplete: despite the death of the mysterious Darvell, who 'was a prey to some cureless disquiet; but whether it arose from ambition, love, remorse, grief, from one or all of these, or merely from a morbid temperament akin to disease, I could not discover' (*F* 238), we cannot tell how the story would have developed.

Polidori's *The Vampyre: A Tale* was completed, and is supposed to be the first vampire story in English. It is only a short story, but became extremely popular and is credited with inspiring the genre of vampire fiction. In particular, Polidori's little story is seen as the source for *Varney the Vampire*'s appearances in the 'Penny Dreadfuls' (popular horror magazines) of 1845–7; Sheridan Le Fanu's *Carmilla* (1871), the story of a lesbian vampire; and the classic standard of the genre, Bram Stoker's *Dracula* (1897). *The Vampyre: A Tale* is the story of a Lord Ruthven, a man who has a curious effect upon women, and who appears to delight in others' disasters. While travelling on the continent with the author, Ruthven is shot and dies, but his body disappears. Later, the author meets Ruthven, brought back to life, and is horrified that his own sister becomes the resuscitated vampire's next victim. This story shows some similarities with Byron's fragment, and we can take it that Polidori used that opening as a model. However, *The Vampyre* displays none of the characteristics Mary Shelley noted of Polidori's effort in the competition – there is nothing in it about a skull-headed lady, a keyhole, or the tomb of the Capulets (see *F* 7). Polidori's vampire story may, then, have been a delayed outcome of the famous competition: if Mary is to be believed, his first effort was ridiculed, and abandoned.

The noticeable feature of both Byron's and Polidori's efforts is that they took the challenge literally. As it is recorded in the 'Extract of a Letter from Geneva', which Polidori published with his story, the challenge was 'that each of the company present should write a tale depending upon some supernatural agency'. Clearly the promise the author gives to the dying Darvell, in Byron's fragment, will lead to supernatural consequences; and Polidori's 'undead' vampire is obviously supernatural. Mary Shelley, however, disobeyed the rules. She ignored the supernatural, and aimed to inspire fear. Upon waking from her famous dream, she declared, 'I have found it! What terrified me will terrify others!' (*F* 9). She did not write the 'ghost story' she reports Byron demanding: *Frankenstein* is not a 'ghost story'. However, by breaking the rules Mary Shelley created an original work, and founded the genre of science fiction.

Gothic Fiction

Frankenstein is not a ghost story, then. What antecedents did *Frankenstein* draw upon? What was the literary context within which

Mary Shelley began to write? The obvious place for us to start answering this question is with the genre called 'Gothic fiction'.

Many people point to Horace Walpole's *The Castle of Otranto* (1764) as the first truly Gothic novel, and date the genre as developing from there. However, new forms, genres and styles do not usually appear suddenly in one work, but evolve in a much more complex manner. So, for example, we could say that the economic and social circumstances suitable to Gothic fiction had to be present first, in the form of a growing market for sensational stories. Then, we could add that Walpole wrote his book at a time when there was already an increased interest in antiquity, and in images based on medieval times, which was beginning to show itself in architecture and landscape gardening as well as, for example, in Chatterton's pseudo-medieval poetry. Furthermore, the qualities of reason, moderation and proportion that were revered by neo-classical culture and were the hallmarks of the Enlightenment were beginning to beget a backlash. So, controlling your personal desires for the rational good of the community bred a contrary desire to indulge them. Admiration of the moderate and reasonable bred a contrary desire to celebrate the wild, the extreme and the unreasonable. In short, about half-way through the eighteenth century, there began a changing of direction – a change that, in the broadest sense, would gradually usher in the Romantic period in literature. One of the symptoms of this change was Gothic fiction.

We should also note that Gothic novels did not take off immediately upon the publication of *Otranto*: another 25 years passed before the real heyday of the Gothic. Some argue that the ideal conditions for Gothic fiction only arrived with the shock of the French Revolution in 1789. According to this view, Gothic romances provided sensationalism and escapism in fiction, at a time when there was a desire to escape from the disturbing thoughts provoked by events in France.

Gothic novels were generally set in ruined medieval castles, monasteries or churches; and their plots included tyrants, villains, bandits, madness, persecuted maidens, ghosts and other supernatural phenomena, dungeons, secret passages, locked doors, family curses, darkness, mystery, wicked cardinals, lustful priests, tortures and suchlike. Many of these novels exploited protestant prejudices about Catholicism, particularly focusing on corruption, or the tortures of the Inquisition in Spain and Italy. After Walpole's *The Castle of Otranto*, William Thomas Beckford published *Vathek, an Arabian Tale* in 1786, but the genre reached its height only in the 1790s. The acknowledged doyenne of Gothic novels was Mrs Ann Radcliffe, who wrote *A Sicilian Romance* (1790), *The Mysteries of Udolpho* (1794) and *The Italian* (1797), among other titles, and achieved enormous popular success. Matthew Gregory Lewis included sexually shocking material in his *The Monk* (1796), although the driving force of his novel is the agonizing characterization of Ambrosio, a pious monk tortured by temptations, guilt and sin. As we have mentioned, Lewis visited Byron at the Villa Diodati, and met Mary Shelley during the summer of 1816. Another two years were to pass, after the famous Diodati summer, before two parodies of the 'Gothic' form were published: both Jane Austen's *Northanger Abbey* and Shelley's close friend Thomas Love Peacock's *Nightmare Abbey* came out in 1818.

The term 'Gothic' has since been more loosely used. It is now often applied to a much wider range of the trappings of horror stories, and has lost its connection with medieval settings and ruined architecture, as well as its predilection for the more lurid tales of medieval Catholicism's excesses. The term has almost become synonymous with 'melodramatic', and can now connote almost any form of horror tale. I would argue that *Frankenstein* belongs to this wider definition of 'Gothic'; but that it is definably distinct from the gothic tradition as it existed for Mary Shelley, that is, the tradition of the 1790s. The settings in *Frankenstein*, for example, are not Gothic. There is no suggestion that the Frankenstein family houses, either in Geneva or on Belle Rive, are anything other than wide, light and comfortable, or that their fixtures are not modern and convenient. In Ingolstadt, Frankenstein has a laboratory at the top of a house; and on Orkney, in one room of a two-room dwelling. We must remember that many of the gothic trappings we may associate with the story have been given to us by the film industry. In the novel, there is no mediaeval architecture, and there are no ruins.

The elements of the plot also differ from the Gothic: Mary Shelley insists that the daemon was created by science, and through no supernatural agency. His strength is due to the way Frankenstein built him, not to any supernatural power. Furthermore, there is a distinction between terror and horror; and while the majority of Gothic novels mainly inspire the former, *Frankenstein* focuses more upon the latter. We feel terror when we fear the future: it is provoked by anticipation, by suspense. Many critics have remarked that Mary Shelley's use of suspense is rather clumsy, and tends to provoke impatience rather than terror. The flabby narrative of Victor's illness, and the elaborate interpolated story of Justine's trial, followed by excerpts from Mary's travel journal as Victor climbs to the 'mer de glace', for example: much of that part of the novel seems to be there simply to delay our second meeting with the daemon. Then, the entire episode in Ireland seems to have been stretched out only to prevent Victor's wedding-night from arriving too quickly. Horror, on the other hand, is provoked when we feel a revulsion from what is described. In *Frankenstein*, Victor's researches in graveyards and slaughterhouses, and Shelley's economic yet extraordinarily vivid depictions of the daemon's ugliness, fit into this category. So, rather than a terrifying tale of the supernatural, *Frankenstein* is a horrifying tale of the scientifically possible.

One of the biggest surprises in *Frankenstein* is the response Mary Shelley evokes in us, for the daemon. His voice and his emotional appeal burst upon the novel with extraordinary power; but we do not fear him. Rather, we pity him and vividly imagine his friendless state. In this respect, the daemon is not like a 'Gothic' villain, who was, typically, a depraved and cruel tyrant for whom the reader feels nothing but fear.

There are, of course, some obvious elements shared between *Frankenstein* and the gothic tradition. For example, the use of darkness and lightning, when Victor glimpses the daemon at the scene of William's murder, could have been drawn directly from one of Mrs Radcliffe's works; and it is arguable that the bleak and isolated settings in the Alps, and on the northern ocean, have a Gothic pedigree. We also remember that the story of *Frankenstein*'s origin, as told to us in the author's 1831 'Introduction', foregrounds Gothic stories as the entire inspiration, occasion and aim of Mary Shelley's writing. Byron's challenge may as well have been re-phrased as 'We will each write a Gothic story'; and Mary reports that she sought 'a story to rival those which had excited us to this task' (*F* 7); which were, of course, 'some volumes of ghost stories', gothic tales of the supernatural.

Shelley's 'Preface' attributes to the author an entirely different motive, the 'exhibition of the amiableness of domestic affection' (*F* 12); and we have already noted that Mary broke the rules by inventing science fiction rather than a story of the supernatural.

In summary, it is clear that the upsurge of Gothic fiction in the preceding 20-odd years had an influence upon *Frankenstein*. On the other hand, it is also clear that Gothic antecedents do not account for very much in Mary Shelley's novel. Indeed, we could argue that *Frankenstein* is critical of the Gothic, saying to its readers: there is plenty to be frightened of in the real world – there is no need for ghosts and spirits and the silly paraphernalia of the gothic. Whether *Frankenstein*'s author intended such a critique is debatable. That the influence of *Frankenstein* helped contribute to an expansion of the Gothic is not. Some subsequent works that are allied to a Gothic tradition clearly benefited from the way in which *Frankenstein* widened the field of horror writing, and from the particular psychology of the daemon. We can mention, for example, Emily Brontë's *Wuthering Heights* (1847); Edgar Allan Poe's *The Fall of the House of Usher* (1839) and Stevenson's *The Strange Case of Dr Jekyll and Mr Hyde* (1886).

It has been argued that *Frankenstein* owes a great deal to William Godwin's most successful novel, *Caleb Williams* (1794), a work Mary knew intimately and greatly admired. This is the story of a servant, Williams, who discovers a terrible secret about his master, Falkland. Williams runs away, Falkland pursues him, and Godwin exploits the story of this chase to highlight the power a rich squire like Falkland has over an ordinary man like Williams. Such a story, of two opposed characters locked together by a guilty secret into a pursuit neither can escape, is strongly suggestive of the pursuit theme between the daemon and Frankenstein. The mutual invasion of each other's minds, first by Williams's pursuit of the truth about Falkland ('I will watch him without remission. I will trace all the mazes of his thought'),[1] then by Falkland's pursuit of Williams, becomes so close that the only escape seems to be in death: 'why should I sustain the contest any longer? I can at least elude my persecutors in death. I can bury myself and the traces of my existence together in friendly oblivion; and thus bequeath eternal doubt, and ever new alarm, to those who have no peace but in pursuing me!'[2] The intimacy of the relationship between Godwin's two opponents, and their bi-directional invasion of each other's minds and morals, as well as the extended theme of pursuit, show a number of similarities to the fated opposition between Frankenstein and the daemon.

If *Frankenstein* owes a debt to Gothic fiction – which we have said it does – then it is also defiantly an original re-definition of that genre. Indeed, we will argue that *Frankenstein* founds the new genre of science fiction, and transforms elements of the Gothic in the process. Similarly, if Mary Shelley was influenced by her father's novel *Caleb Williams*, her pursuit theme, with its four cross-over points and reversals, and with the father/child relationship added, takes hunter and hunted into new regions. In short, the more we consider immediate antecedents as sources for *Frankenstein*, the more we are struck by the originality of Mary Shelley's novel. It is not that we cannot build up long lists of probable sources for this or that detail – we can.[3] It is rather that the drawing together of these elements into an unprecedented whole, the *Frankenstein* idea and story, created something entirely new, something that does not resemble any of its ancestors or relations.

Paradise Lost, and the Faustus Story

Looking further back, we can suggest that *Frankenstein* should be read in the context of two influential stories: John Milton's *Paradise Lost*, and the story of Dr Faustus. In Chapter 4 we discussed the references Frankenstein and the daemon make to the story Milton tells in *Paradise Lost*, showing how both characters identify with Satan and with Adam at different times; and how Eve's creation and first day of life are incorporated into the story. *Paradise Lost* is also specifically cited in the text, as one of the three books which formed the daemon's education. Now, we should look at Mary Shelley's use of *Paradise Lost* in the context of Romantic revisions of Milton's epic.

When Mary Shelley wrote *Frankenstein*, the Romantic movement was re-interpreting *Paradise Lost* in a subversive way. William Blake expressed the new opinion most succinctly when he wrote that Milton was 'a true Poet, and of the Devil's party without knowing it',[4] and in his prophetic poem *Milton* (circa 1810) has Milton descending from

Heaven and entering Blake's foot, bringing a new level of vision and prophecy. Percy Bysshe Shelley, in *In Defence of Poetry* (1819), also treats Satan as Milton's hero: 'Milton's Devil as a moral being is as far superior to his God, as one who perseveres in some purpose which he has conceived to be excellent in spite of adversity and torture, is to one who in the cold security of undoubted triumph inflicts the most horrible revenge upon his enemy'.[5]

In her novel, Mary Shelley adds to the interpretation of the fallen angel as hero. Her daemon's vengeful actions are determined by external powers he is unable to resist. This argument is supported by the daemon's powerful description of his own remorse. Where Milton's God suggests that man was created 'sufficient to have stood, yet free to fall',[6] Mary Shelley's daemon tells us that there was no freedom. Percy pointed out that God has the 'security' of 'undoubted triumph' because his victory over Satan is assured. The daemon tells us that the victory of nurture over his nature is equally assured. He has no choice and no chance because misery and rejection are more powerful than his will. In relation to *Paradise Lost*, then, *Frankenstein* clearly contributes to the subversive re-interpretation of Milton's Christian epic, that was taking place during the Romantic period. Mary Shelley's determinist daemon attacks the concept of freewill, and seems to be preparing for the later nineteenth-century philosophies of Marx, Darwin and Freud.

We have mentioned the Faustus story; but Faustus himself is only one example of a kind of protagonist found in many stories: the over-reaching magician or alchemist, who seeks forbidden knowledge and power. The popular endurance of the Faustus story is shown by the fact that Christopher Marlowe's *The Tragical History of Doctor Faustus* was staged in 1604, while the first part of Goethe's *Faust* appeared in 1808.[7] Prior to Marlowe's play, which was based on a German source, 'Devil's Pact' dramas had been periodically performed from as early as the fourth century. We discussed Mary Shelley's incorporation of the Prometheus myth into *Frankenstein* in Chapter 4. We commented that her novel is a 'modern' version of Prometheus, because it brings the myth of the over-reacher, the thief of fire, into a modern age in which science wields dangerous power. We can make the same comment on the tradition of homiletic fables about magicians and alchemists. Mad magicians and greedy alchemists traditionally stole unnatural powers, and sought to distort nature (e.g. by transforming base metals into gold). These are fables warning against hubris and pride, as is Mary Shelley's version. The difference is that Victor Frankenstein uses science, not magic; and in this way *Frankenstein* becomes the 'modern' *Faustus*. After *Frankenstein*, the ethical ambivalence of scientific power, descendant of Faustus's ethically ambivalent desire for knowledge, has become the model theme for almost all science fiction.

Having discussed the possible precursors of *Frankenstein*, we can suggest a general conclusion: that there were numerous sources of particular elements in Mary Shelley's novel, and we can recognize numerous influences upon her ideas; but none of these accounts for more than a small part of the entirely original concoction that became *Frankenstein*. The parts may be recognizable from elsewhere, but the whole was completely original, was Mary Shelley's own. One obvious consequence of this is a contrast between sources and influence of *Frankenstein*. Where we are necessarily hesitant in answering the question: *where did Frankenstein come from?* We can be forthright and confident describing the influence the book has exerted. We have already considered *Frankenstein*'s development into a modern myth, and its transformations at the hands of modern media, in Chapter 4. In the remainder of this chapter, we will look at three specifically literary ways in which Mary Shelley's 'hideous progeny' has exercised an influence.

The Influence of *Frankenstein*

First, as we have already remarked, *Frankenstein* founded the genre that is called science fiction. In using pseudo-science to give her character's achievements verisimilitude, we have argued that Mary Shelley merely adapted what had previously depended upon magic or superstition – a fable such as the Faustus story, or even the Prometheus myth. In using science, then, Shelley merely modernized these archetypal stories. However, in doing so she also gave new significance to issues that were being lost beneath the sensationalist trappings of the Gothic. We can understand this point if we look at the moral issues on which the Faustus story focuses. Doctor Faustus is a brilliant man who is not wicked, but he does have an inordinate desire for knowledge. At the outset, the world admires Faustus for his brilliance and erudition. The tragedy of his story occurs because knowledge is both wonderful and dangerous; because even admirable qualities such as education and understanding can be misused by temptation and pride, and so lead to disaster. In *Frankenstein*, scientific knowledge plays the same role as knowledge for Faustus. Victor's achievements in science are admirable: his research earns the plaudits of his teachers and fellow-students at Ingolstadt. However, scientific knowledge is ethically ambivalent. In one sense it may be admirable, but it is also dangerous; and the power it confers can be misused, leading to disaster.

By modernizing the old Promethean and Faustian stories, then, Mary Shelley founded science fiction in their image. This revived the serious ethical challenge posed by the original myths, setting it within the context of scientific progress, where its dilemmas remain as unanswerable as ever. Do we want the powers science and technology put into our hands? Yes, we do. Are we confident that we can use these powers for the good of the world? No, we are not. In fact, as we approach the second decade of the twenty-first century, we know that scientific progress has already placed the world in danger.

In Chapter 4 we pointed out several science-fiction works which show the influence of *Frankenstein*. In particular we mentioned Robert Louis Stevenson's *The Strange Case of Dr Jekyll and Mr. Hyde*, and H. G. Wells's *The Island of Dr. Moreau*, because of the dual personality in Stevenson's work, and the creation of neo-human monsters, in Wells's novel. However, in the broader sense of science fiction as a medium for investigating serious ethical dilemmas, we should also mention Wells's many other 'scientific romances' such as *The Time Machine* (1895), or *The War of the Worlds* (1898); Sir Arthur Conan Doyle's *The Lost World* (1912); and numerous twentieth-century works such as John Wyndham's *The Day of the Triffids* (1951) and *The Chrysalids* (1955), both of which explore the consequences of scientific irresponsibility, and Isaac Asimov's *Robot* series, on the theme of artificial life. This selection is quite arbitrary: there are many more titles we could mention in the same connection. However, these are enough to show that the science fiction genre continues to challenge the ethics of scientific power.

The second literary consequence of *Frankenstein* we wish to discuss is more difficult to define, and stems from the issues raised by the significance of the daemon. We found the daemon to symbolize a social danger and social fear: either he suggests the revolutionary mob or he stands for the exploited working class, the mass that may violently turn upon its upper-class creators. In brief, then, Mary Shelley uses her narrative to present the daemon as a metaphor for a possible future. *Frankenstein* is not, of course, futuristic in the sense that *The Last Man* certainly is. However, in its issuing of a moral warning, its social and political concern, and its use of a fantastical tale as a metaphor for society's future, *Frankenstein* provides a model for writers of futuristic dystopias. We will briefly consider three well-known examples.

H. G. Wells's *The Time Machine* takes his Time-traveller into the future, eventually to an evening of the world when humanity is extinct. His other journeys show development of society into two distinct species: a helpless, fragile race called the Eloï, who are descendants of the upper classes; and a subterranean race of grub-like cannibal hominids called the Morlocks, descendants of the working class. The Time-traveller does not return from his final voyage, implying that his knowledge of the future has led him to despair. Wells's picture of the future is, effectively, a metaphor for the society he saw in his own time. As with Frankenstein and his daemon, the ills of society are embodied as fatal division between classes, and the book does not contain any redemptive power capable of saving the situation.

Aldous Huxley's *Brave New World* (1932) is set in the twenty-sixth century. Babies are no longer produced by sexual reproduction. Instead, they are grown in jars in a laboratory, their gestation treated as a factory production line, and they are 'decanted' rather than born. In Huxley's vision of the future those in charge are benevolent: society is designed to keep everybody happy. So, for example, there are rigid 'classes', biologically conditioned to suit certain occupations: the problem of a rebellious working class is solved because 'Epsilon' people are semi-morons, just capable of menial work, but not capable of discontent. Sex is purely recreational and promiscuous, and the economy is devoted to leisure, entertainment and consumption. Again, Huxley's picture of the future is a metaphor for what he observed in the world around him: he took the idea of controlled mass-production, and applied it to people. Interestingly, circumventing the normal process of reproduction, which occurs in *Frankenstein*, returns in the form of Huxley's so-called 'Hatchery' – the production line for babies. In this, both Shelley and Huxley have shown a prophetic gift: it is only recently that genetic engineering has become capable of cloning and artificial reproduction techniques.

George Orwell's *Nineteen Eighty-four* (1949) is a futuristic novel about a totalitarian society where people have no privacy and no freedom of speech, being watched by the secret police on telescreens, at every hour of day and night. The hero, Winston Smith, who makes a hopeless attempt at dissent, is eventually brainwashed. He becomes a docile citizen who supports the government, showing that even people's thoughts can ultimately be controlled, thanks to brainwashing and the 'Thought Police'. To us, at the start of the twenty-first century, both Huxley's and Orwell's futuristic metaphors are chilling: the technological know-how for both their visions of society has almost arrived, and significant parts of their imagined futures already exist. For example, out-of-town shopping malls and entertainment complexes, or amusement parks, were effectively predicted in *Brave New World*; and that society's voyeuristic interest in John Savage reminds us of Big Brother (incidentally, named after the political leader in *Nineteen Eighty-four*). Meanwhile, in most cities of the developed world, you are on camera whenever you are not in your own home; your exact position can be pinpointed if you carry a phone; and your life and habits are closely monitored – even to the extent of carrying microchips around in your clothes!

This discussion could continue, but already suffices to show that futuristic and science-fiction authors repeatedly concern themselves with the themes raised in *Frankenstein*; and that these themes continue to be matters of serious concern. These are, of course, the themes of human hubris or 'over-reaching', which seeks the power to interfere with and control nature; and the future of a society seen as already fatally fractured in each author's day. Our contention is that *Frankenstein* contributed towards founding the vein of literary productions we have just described. It did so by suggesting that a combination of science and fantasy can create a penetrating metaphor for the moral quagmires and potential dangers of the present. Indeed, perhaps the first author to recognize the potential for futuristic dystopias that was implicitly opened by *Frankenstein* was Mary Shelley herself, when she wrote *The Last Man*.

Our third and final contention about the literary influence of *Frankenstein* concerns the novel's philosophical outlook. During our study, we have frequently mentioned determinism. The strongest outlook expressed in the text – the daemon's philosophical stance – is rigidly determinist; and its opposite, the idealism expressed by Victor when he asserts that 'vast mountains of ice' will 'vanish before the resolutions of man' (*F* 216), is normally presented in a context that undermines the assertion. We have also found that Shelley is critical of Frankenstein's patrician snobbery, the failure of judicial authority and the obsolescence of patriarchal authority: in short, that the text provides a rigorous analysis of class that previews Marx. In the practical rigour with which it portrays individuals as helpless children of their social background, and does not confer upon them the power to escape their class destiny, *Frankenstein* looks forward to some of the great novels of the mid- and later nineteenth-century. The conflict between remorse and revenge that rages in the daemon is comparable to some later novelists' depictions of an individual engaged in a tragic struggle between the determined and the ideal, or, the real and the desired. In this context, we could see the daemon-like figure of Heathcliff from Emily Brontë's *Wuthering Heights* (1847), struggling with his inability to believe that Cathy is dead, as a successor to Shelley's daemon. The Brontës are frequently discussed as practitioners in an enlarged Gothic tradition, so that the comparison of the daemon to Heathcliff does not surprise. However, our argument can be taken further. So, we could compare the daemon's struggles against his vengeful passion, to Jude's tragic struggle to rise out of his determined place, and live up to ideals too demanding for any nature, in Thomas Hardy's *Jude the Obscure* (1895); or to Lydgate's struggle to maintain his medical ambitions, in George Eliot's *Middlemarch* (1874).

This contention may, at first, seem far-fetched: and it would be absurd to suggest anything as naïve as a direct line of influence between *Frankenstein* and either Hardy or Eliot. On the surface, indeed, *Frankenstein* would seem to be one of the last fantastical tales before a tide of Victorian Domestic fiction arose: after *Frankenstein*, it seems, there was *Wuthering Heights* and then little more fantasy for a long time. On the other hand, our comparison of the determined predicament of the individual, between *Frankenstein* and these later works, is valid. At the least, this suggestion shows that the philosophical outlook with which Shelley imbued her novel looks forward towards the developing concerns of the nineteenth-century, rather than drawing its attitude from contemporary Romantic thought, or from the preceding Enlightenment period.

In this chapter we have not discussed the question of *Frankenstein* as a woman's text, or as having an influence on the development of feminism or feminist fiction. In our studies in Part 1, we discussed the novel's critique of masculine idealism, male hubris, romantic ambition, male scientific endeavour – call it what you will – at some length, showing that *Frankenstein* displays a trenchant and critical awareness of male gendered attitudes. On the other hand, the women in *Frankenstein* hardly exist in more substantial form than the most cardboard stereotypes of submissive gentleness. The only exception is Elizabeth's apparently brief venture into disillusionment.[8] It is arguable that the female characters' very vapidity and helplessness is a comment on gender: that their appearance in the novel as more-or-less passive victims, deliberately displays the marginal status of women at the time. However, the question of *Frankenstein*'s legacy as a feminist text is a particularly vexed issue, bringing up as it does a number of the suggested but competing psychological interpretations, not only of Victor but also of Mary Shelley herself, that are canvassed by the critics. We will not attempt this topic now, but will rather present some of the professional critics' opinions, in the next chapter, 'A Sample of Critical Views'.

8

A Sample of Critical Views

The Critical Reception

As *Frankenstein* was first published anonymously and dedicated to William Godwin, the novel was politically defined for most readers before they opened the covers: this was a production of one of Godwin's disciples, and many thought it the work of Percy Bysshe Shelley. We must remember the political climate when *Frankenstein* was published. Only the previous year, there was the Pentrich rising; five years before, 17 Luddites had been executed after a mass trial, at York, while working-class disturbances spread right across the country during the teens decade. The Government of the time was one of the most reactionary of the nineteenth century, and set its face firmly against the rising clamour for reform, a radical and reforming movement that had already been strong in the 1790s. Stringent and oppressive measures restricting freedom of speech had been brought in after the French Revolution, and maintained while Britain was at war with Napoleon's France. Godwin's *Political Justice*, and his courageous publications and appearances supporting the accused in the treason trials of 1794, had made him famous as a rallying-point for radicals and reformers. Therefore, in a period when politics was at its bitterest and most polarized, to dedicate a novel to Godwin was a radical political act.

Frankenstein's reviewers therefore tended to divide along their political battle-lines, and the right-wing press was outraged by the novel's hideous and impious fable. Of course, conservative outrage is often the best publicity a literary work can have, and shocked reviews probably did *Frankenstein* a service. Certainly it became notorious, and consequently more widely known, circulated and discussed than its printing of a mere 500 copies would indicate. The good and bad reviews are easily illustrated. The *Quarterly Review* said that *Frankenstein* consisted of 'horrible and disgusting absurdity'; but Sir Walter Scott, in *Blackwood's Magazine*, praised the author who 'seems to us to disclose uncommon powers of poetic imagination' and expressed 'a high idea of the author's original genius and happy power of expression'.

Much has been made of Mary Shelley's comment in a letter to Hunt, on her return to England in 1823, that: 'lo and behold! I found myself famous' as the author of *Frankenstein*, and it has been assumed that the novel was an immediate best-seller. For the reasons we have mentioned above, *Frankenstein* did quickly gain a reputation; but this can give a misleading impression about the book's sales. William St Clair's study of the publishing history shows that *Frankenstein* existed in fewer than a thousand copies, and was more-or-less unavailable between about the 1850s and 1880s: it had to wait almost until the turn of the century, 50 years after Mary Shelley's death, to become a best-seller. St Clair points out that 'During most of the nineteenth century, it was not the book but stage adaptations of the story which kept *Frankenstein* alive in the culture.'[1] As a result, the moral became distorted and the fable simplified, so that the word Frankenstein in Victorian times came to convey a conservative message: 'Do not free the slaves, do not reform parliament, do not give votes to the working class, do not give independence to the Irish. If you do, you will create a Frankenstein monster that will turn and destroy you.' As a result, St Clair argues, the political impact of *Frankenstein* – at least throughout the nineteenth century – became 'the direct opposite of what the author and her collaborator hoped for and intended'.[2]

The *Frankenstein* story has remained in popular consciousness in the twentieth century, thanks to numerous film versions and derivatives. However, it is only in the last few decades that the original book has attracted the academic critical attention it now enjoys. It could almost be said that the original book, so long half-forgotten in the shadow of images of Boris Karloff, and nineteenth-century stage melodramas, had to be re-instated. We do not have the space to represent anything like the full range of approaches different critics have brought to bear upon *Frankenstein* during recent decades. Instead, we have chosen a sample of five critics whose arguments we summarize. We have selected these five only on the grounds that they display different views, each of which may be stimulating, provoking your agreement, disagreement and urging you towards further thought and further critical reading.

Muriel Spark

Muriel Spark published her part-biographical, part-literary *Child of Light: A Reassessment of Mary Wollstonecraft Shelley* in 1951, and a revised version with the title *Mary Shelley* was issued in 1987. Spark allows for the author's extreme youth at the outset, suggesting that 'perhaps the wonder of it exists, not despite Mary's youth but because of it. *Frankenstein* is Mary Shelley's best novel because at that age she was not yet well acquainted with her own mind'.[3] She then moves on to an interpretation of the novel, in which she finds the central theme to be that of pursuit. She points out the inter-relatedness of Frankenstein and his daemon, and sees their mutual pursuits of each other as forming a shape she describes as a 'figure-of-eight macaberesque': the hunter and hunted's paths cross, on the 'mer de glace', and again on Orkney. Finally, and following the murder of Elizabeth on her wedding-night, the movement is reversed. Spark sees this as Frankenstein increasing 'his speed of execution' while the daemon 'slows down', and from being the hunted, Frankenstein becomes the pursuer.

When discussing the significance of this pursuit theme, Spark suggests that the two figures are symbolic. The daemon stands for reason or intellect, since he has been created by 'an obsessional rational effort'; while Frankenstein – at least after the animation of the daemon – is 'a disintegrated being – an embodiment of emotion and also of imagination minus intellect' (Spark 165). If these two interpretations are accepted, it is the emotional and intellectual that are in conflict. Neatly, Spark applies this idea to the final part of Victor's story. When he pursues the daemon over the polar ice, Frankenstein is chasing 'his fleeing reason', and as he does so he steadily becomes insane. Spark suggests that the magistrate Victor consults before leaving his native Switzerland, is the only person who recognizes his incipient insanity.

Spark also suggests a further interpretative connection, this time with Mary Shelley's life. She asks whether the conflict between emotion and reason, detected in the two protagonists of *Frankenstein*, was also a ruling conflict in Mary Shelley's life at that time. This would have been because of her exceptionally rational and literary background, and even the exceptionally intellectual romance with Shelley in which she was engaged, on the one hand; and the contrary emotional awakening and emotional demands of motherhood, the love Mary Shelley was called upon to invest in her little boy William. Spark suggests that this conflict was problematic for Mary, and perhaps expresses itself when, for example, intellect (the daemon) kills William (emotion) in the story.

Spark admires the power of Mary Shelley's 'alternating play upon the sympathy of the reader' (Spark 173), whereby we respond to the daemon with compassion, then fear, then compassion again, with each of his appearances in the story. This structural success compensates for Shelley's 'comparatively utilitarian style' (Spark 171), for faults of improbable incident and the novel's main failing, which Spark thinks is 'in general characterisation' (Spark 173). Paradoxically, however, Spark also believes,

> its [*Frankenstein's*] greatest power to occur in the specific development and depiction of the two protagonists, Frankenstein and the Monster. These are characters, however, so essentially complementary to each other, so engrossed one with the other, and in so many ways facets of the same personality, that they defeat powerful characterisation, which demands positive interplay of different temperaments. (Spark 173–4)

Spark then spends some time on each protagonist. She points out that Frankenstein makes shallow judgements based on appearances, for example, in the case of Krempe and Waldman; and similar adolescent behaviour shows in his reaction to his father's opinion of Agrippa. Frankenstein's character changes, however: 'After the creation of the Monster, since Frankenstein loses to him an integral portion of his being, his character is a study, and a well-executed one, in the mounting obsession of a lost soul to find itself' (Spark 176). The daemon's character, on the other hand, shows 'the whole gamut of mankind's journey from savage to modern times' which 'is played throughout the years of his life' (176). The influence of outward appearances on human relationships is emphasized as the daemon discovers his ugliness and its effect upon others: this is a theme stressed by both characterizations. Summing up her analysis, Spark re-iterates her point about the daemon representing reason or intellect:

> One important factor in the unfolding of his character is his lack of emotion. What passes for emotion – his need for companionship, his feelings of revenge towards Frankenstein – are really intellectual passions arrived at through rational channels. He is asexual, and demands his bride as a companion, never as a lover or even merely as a mate: his emotions reside in the heart of Frankenstein, as does Frankenstein's intellect in him.   (Spark 178)

We may feel doubtful whether the daemon is without emotion and shows only 'intellectual passions'. We have noted that he is a far more persuasive narrator and consistent thinker than either Frankenstein or Walton, which may have given Spark the idea of 'intellect'. On the other hand, we have also found that he inspires our compassion, which neither of the other narrators does. Also, the interpretation seems to simplify an inter-relationship between Victor and his creature that is much more complex than the traditional intellect/emotion dualism. On the other hand, Spark does notice the challenge of the characterization, which we found so surprisingly both suggestive and inconclusive, in Chapter 2 of our study; and she does tackle the question of composite characterization, and suggest a way of relating this back to conflicts in Mary Shelley's life at the time of composition.

Sandra M. Gilbert and Susan Gubar

Gilbert and Gubar brought out their important *The Madwoman in the Attic: the Woman Writer and the Nineteenth-century Literary Imagination* in 1979. This work looks at major works of fiction by nineteenth-century women, developing the authors' feminist contention that each author had to face specific challenges and make significant choices in being female and writing within a patriarchal literary tradition. In the section of their book entitled 'How are we Fal'n? Milton's Daughters', Gilbert and Gubar include a chapter on *Frankenstein*.[4]

They begin by noting Virginia Woolf's comment that all female authors seeking to resurrect 'Shakespeare's sister' need to 'look past Milton's bogey' in order to see clearly. From further discussion, they clarify 'Milton's bogey' as the powerful, insidious and poetically majestic monument of misogyny that is *Paradise Lost*, its myths of Adam, Eve, Satan and Sin, and the power of the Miltonic Cosmogeny to represent the Establishment view of the Western nations. Gilbert and Gubar then suggest that Milton's daughters were faced with two options. First, they could submit to their father's will, and be proud to 'minister to' the great man by copying from his dictation, and being his domestic slaves. Or, alternatively, they could secretly study in order to become wise, and so in time hope to work with him as his equals. Gilbert and Gubar show how Dorothea Brooke/Casaubon, in George Eliot's *Middlemarch*, aspired to the latter course, hoping to educate herself to be her Miltonic elderly husband's wise equal. Each female writer, however, had to take one or other of the alternatives on offer to 'Milton's daughters':

> We shall argue here that the first alternative is the one Mary Shelley chooses in *Frankenstein*: to take the male culture myth of *Paradise Lost* at its full value – on its own terms, including all the analogies and parallels it implies – *and rewrite it so as to clarify its meaning*.   (G & G 220)

Gilbert and Gubar begin their analysis of *Frankenstein* by noting that there has been a recent upsurge of interest in connecting Mary Shelley's myth of monster-manufacture, with the events in her own life, specifically her sexual awakening with Shelley and her teenage experience of motherhood. In particular they refer to Ellen Moers, who argued that '*Frankenstein* is a birth myth, and one that was lodged in the novelist's imagination, I am convinced, by the fact that she was herself a mother'.[5] Moers argued that *Frankenstein* enacts the anxieties produced by Mary Shelley's life-experience because they were 'the anxieties of a woman who, as daughter, mistress, and mother, was a bearer of death'[6], and consequently suggests that the blood-curdling combination of fear and guilt, depression and anxiety which are common emotions following the birth of a baby (she seems to refer to what is commonly known as 'post-natal depression'), create a specific type of horror story she calls 'Female Gothic'.

Gilbert and Gubar welcome this new interpretation but point out that *Frankenstein* and its author are both extremely literary. Mary Shelley 'may be said to have "read" her family and to have been related to her reading, for books appear to have functioned as her surrogate parents' (G & G 223). However, in 1815–17, Mary read the works of Milton, reading *Paradise Lost* twice, and her sense of her literary identity developed in the terms set by Milton simultaneously with her emerging sense of herself as daughter, mistress, wife and mother:

> It is as a female fantasy of sex and reading, then, a gothic psychodrama reflecting Mary Shelley's own sense of what we might call bibliogenesis, that *Frankenstein* is a version of the misogynistic story implicit in *Paradise Lost*. (G & G 224)

Frankenstein's structure as three concentric narratives has an analytical flavour reminiscent of *Paradise Lost*, and the main characters' questions about identity and existence strike Gilbert and Gubar as questions about the fall and as in some sense female because they are implicitly Eve's questions.

Most of the characters in *Frankenstein* are orphaned; Victor, Elizabeth and Justine all declare themselves guilty of William's murder; and there is a vein of incest running through virtually all of the relationships present or mooted in the novel: Victor and Elizabeth, his 'more than sister'; Alphonse and his daughter-like Caroline; even Justine; and of course the daemon and the proposed female mate, made by the same father. Gilbert and Gubar suggest that this atmosphere of incest imitates Adam and Eve, motherless and sprung from the same creator, and that 'the incestuous relationships of Satan and Sin, and by implication Satan and Eve, are mirrored in the incest fantasies of *Frankenstein*, including the disguised but intensely sexual waking dream in which Victor Frankenstein in effect couples with his monster by applying "the instruments of life" to its body and inducing a shudder of response' (G & G 229). Having pointed out these similarities between the characters' circumstances in Shelley's novel and Milton's epic, Gilbert and Gubar acknowledge the difficulties of interpretation we have found in our own study:

> Here we are obliged to confront both the moral ambiguity and the symbolic slipperiness which are at the heart of all the characterizations in *Frankenstein*. In fact, it is probably these continual and complex reallocations of meaning, among characters whose histories echo and re-echo each other, that have been so bewildering to critics.   (G & G 229)

However, they identify the difficulty as primarily one of characters who all play the same roles, and they say that these roles are all the 'neo-biblical parts' in *Paradise Lost*: God, Satan, Adam, parts which Mary Shelley's characters play over and over again. The part of Eve is a striking omission from this 'woman's book' about Milton', until we realize that 'for Mary Shelley the part of Eve *is* all the parts' (G & G 230). The critics then go on to apply this observation to Victor Frankenstein. He enacts the roles of Adam and Satan, but his most 'self-defining act transforms him definitively into Eve':

> Victor Frankenstein has a baby. His 'pregnancy' and childbirth are obviously manifested by the existence of the paradoxically huge being who emerges from his 'workshop of filthy creation,' but even the descriptive language of his creation myth is suggestive: 'incredible labours,' 'emaciated with confinement,' 'a passing trance,' 'oppressed by a slow fever,' 'nervous to a painful degree,' . . . And, like Eve's fall into guilty knowledge and painful maternity, Victor's entrance into what Blake would call the realm of 'generation' is marked by a recognition of the necessary interdependence of those complementary opposites, sex and death.   (G & G 232)

So, Gilbert and Gubar argue, Victor never really resembled the masculine Satan of *Paradise Lost* Book 1: he was always more like the curiously effeminate, outcast Satan of Milton's later books, who gives birth to Sin. They then exploit this comparison by suggesting that Victor's 'monstrous offspring', who has been produced by studying the wrong books, puts Victor in the position of the female author. Victor's story is thus an expression of Mary's own anxiety about her creative activity, also expressed in her famous comment about *Frankenstein* being her 'hideous progeny'.

Gilbert and Gubar then argue that, even in Victor's 'edenic' childhood, he showed the traits of Eve rather than Adam. If Victor is Eve, then, what happens in the crucial section when he locks himself away and gives birth to his monster? The answer must be, that it is at that time that he (as Eve) learns 'not that she must fall but that, having been created female, she *is* fallen, femaleness and fallenness being essentially synonymous'. Frankenstein learns, most importantly, that he is the source of the evil he has unleashed upon the world, and he is the one whose incestuous kiss kills both 'sister' and 'mother'. 'Doomed and filthy, is he not, then, Eve instead of Adam?' (G & G 234).

Turning their attention next to the monster, Gilbert and Gubar suggest that he also enacts the various parts prepared for him in *Paradise Lost*, comparing himself at different times to Adam, Satan and even to God. However, they then argue that none of these identities provides a satisfactory fit for the monster; and they point out the similarities between him and Mary Shelley, in particular that he is born without a history – as women are because they are excluded from the kind of masculine history seen in Plutarch's *Lives*; and that his education has come from listening and books rather than directly from people:

> Yet not only the monster's uniquely ahistorical birth, his literary anxieties, and the sense his readings (like Mary's) foster that he must have been parented, if at all, by *books*; not only all these facts and traits but also his shuddering sense of deformity, his nauseating size, his namelessness, and his orphaned, motherless isolation link him with Eve and with Eve's double, Sin. (G & G 239)

Women have seen themselves as 'monstrous, vile, degraded creatures, second-comers, and emblems of filthy materiality' because they have been taught to see themselves this way. Significantly, Shelley's monster is 'as nameless as a woman is in patriarchal society, as nameless as unmarried, illegitimately pregnant Mary Wollstonecraft Godwin may have felt herself to be at the time she wrote *Frankenstein*' (G & G 241). The final part of Gilbert and Gubar's analysis returns to Mary Shelley's life at the time when she was writing *Frankenstein*, and proposes that 'clearly feelings of rage, terror, and sexual nausea, as well as idealizing sentiments, accrete for Mary and the monster around the maternal female image' (G & G 244). The monster's crimes can therefore be seen as an enactment of Mary Shelley's sublimated rage.

Gilbert and Gubar's analysis is difficult to assess as a whole: it rolls forward past patches where the reasoning seems very tenuous (such as the comparison with *Paradise Lost* just because *Frankenstein* has an analytical structure) and others where it is persuasive (such as the evocation of Victor's 'pregnancy'); and in the end, the main point seems to be that Victor is Eve because, like Milton's Eve, he is guilty; while the monster is Eve because [s]he is like Mary. However, as an attempt to consider *Frankenstein* as a woman's novel, and to make Mary Shelley's life, her psychology and her invention cohere, the analysis confronts some important challenges that have become central for succeeding critics. How, for example, can we reconcile the critique of masculinity in the novel, with the absence of criticism directed at feminine stereotypes? And, how did Mary Shelley's psyche produce this story? Our next critic is Anne K. Mellor, who published her *Mary Shelley: Her Life, Her Fiction, Her Monsters* in 1988. Our sample, however, is drawn from a more recent essay.

Anne K. Mellor

Mellor begins with a discussion of the time-honoured question: 'why did the 18-year-old Mary Shelley give birth to this particular idea'?[7] Mary Shelley had given birth twice and no doubt expected to be pregnant again soon. Mellor agrees with Ellen Moers that *Frankenstein* is partly about 'the natural fears of a very young woman embarking on the processes of pregnancy, giving birth, and mothering' (Mellor 10); and a central theme of the novel is Victor's utter failure as a parent. Shelley was also anxious about her own birth-as-author. This did not derive 'from what Sandra Gilbert and Susan Gubar have famously called a female "anxiety of authorship", the fear of speaking in public in a literary culture that systematically denigrated women's writing' (Mellor 11). Rather, Mary Shelley experienced the opposite: she was

anxious because she was encouraged to become an author, and worried
about whether she would have any ideas. The idea that *Frankenstein*
is at least partly a story about writing *Frankenstein* is supported by
the dates: Walton's series of letters cover exactly nine months; and
Frankenstein dies on the same day as Mary Wollstonecraft, the author's
mother. The letters therefore cover the period from the author's
conception to her mother's death.

Mellor then discusses repressed sexuality, pointing out that this is a
hallmark of Gothic fiction. *Frankenstein* lacks a female protagonist and
Catholic villain, but does have 'the denial of all overt sexuality' and an
incest theme. There are passionate homosocial relationships (between
Walton and Frankenstein; between Frankenstein and Clerval) as well
as Frankenstein's attempt to reproduce without a female. It may be that
Mary Shelley is offering a 'bleak parody of Romantic love' in which she
criticizes Percy Shelley's idea that it originates when the lover imagines
'an idealized form of himself' (Mellor 13). It may also be that the novel
criticizes Frankenstein's – and by extension other men's – fear of female
desire. This theory is supported by the scene in which Victor destroys
the half-completed female. The narrative frames of the novel enable
the author develop her critique:

> By using three male narrators, Mary Shelley explores in minute detail
> the outsized, inhuman Romantic ambitions shared by Frankenstein
> and Walton, and scrutinizes their effects on the creature at the novel's
> core.   (Mellor 14)

Mellor then discusses the changes Percy Shelley made to the text, and
suggests that he did not always understand his wife's intentions. In particular, she takes issue with his alteration of the final sentence, which
she believes is more reassuring for the reader, than Mary's original version. The other textual issue Mellor discusses is the difference between
the 1818 text and that of 1831. She notes several changes, particularly
that fate or 'destiny' is much more present in the later version, and that
this removes some of the responsibility from Frankenstein, and makes
him almost a tragic hero rather than a guilty over-reacher. Then, the
re-writing also gives a harsher vision of the bourgeois family 'as the
site where women are oppressed, silenced, even sacrificed, and racial
prejudices are formed' (Mellor 17). These changes, the critic suggests,

are a consequence of Mary Shelley's bereavements and grief, and the betrayals she had suffered at the hands of some of her friends, in the period leading up to 1831.

Frankenstein provides what Mellor calls 'a feminist critique of science' (Mellor 17). She explains that the novel is based on the work of three scientists: Humphry Davy, Erasmus Darwin and Luigi Galvani. Shelley derived her portrait of Professor Waldman, Frankenstein's mentor, from the works of Humphry Davy. Davy believed that the modern chemist attempts 'to modify and change the beings surrounding him . . . and . . . interrogate nature with power', being 'active' not 'passive' (Davy, quoted by Mellor 18), and Mellor points out several further echoes between Davy's writings and the rhetoric of both Waldman and Frankenstein himself. Then, from Erasmus Darwin Mary Shelley derived a more positive idea of science:

> . . . that a good scientist attempts, not to alter the workings of nature, but rather to observe her processes closely in order to understand her. Bearing in mind Darwin's theory that dual-sex propagation is more highly evolved than asexual reproduction, we see the pitfalls of Frankenstein's science. (Mellor 18)

Mellor therefore suggests that Frankenstein is actually working in reverse of evolutionary progress, and that his attempt to create a species immediately violates the slow natural pace of evolution as described in Darwin's writings. Frankenstein's experiment is derived from the celebrated work of Luigi Galvani and his disciples, who attempted to reanimate lifeless matter by using electricity.

With these references, then, Mary Shelley develops her critique of Frankenstein's science. The critique is feminist because it notes the gendered concepts and language of the scientists (Davy, Francis Bacon, and Waldman and Frankenstein) who seek to hunt, violate and enslave nature, asserting their power over 'her'. Modern masculine scientific pursuit is also criticized for defying the earlier Renaissance concept of nature 'with whom humans were to live in a cooperative, mutually beneficial communion' (Mellor 19). As we know, Victor's experiment fails. Not only does the creature turn on him, nature itself fights back. Mellor believes that nature pointedly pursues Victor with the very electricity this Prometheus has stolen, in the form of the lightning playing around Mont Blanc and on Belle Rive, and the many storms and rain. Mary Shelley specifically genders this power as female.

Mellor then discusses the philosophical questions raised by *Frankenstein* and in particular by the creature. These are ontological (what is nature? Both the external world and human nature?) and epistemological (how do we know what we know?). The crucial assertion of the creature is that he was born innately good, as Rousseau and Condorcet asserted. Frankenstein believes him to be evil. This argument then also involves the second question, for Frankenstein judges the creature on his appearance, in keeping with contemporary phrenological theories. The novel's play upon knowledge derived from seeing, such as the scene where the creature first sees his own reflection; and upon knowledge achieved through hearing (both old blind De Lacey and we as readers can judge the creature from hearing only), explores the validity of perception, and how we can know what we believe we know. *Frankenstein* is:

> ... anticipating the insights of Jacques Derrida and Michel Foucault: human knowledge is the product of invented or linguistically constructed forms or grammars which societies have imposed over time on an unknowable ... ontological being. (Mellor 22)

The creature, with the ambivalent, unresolved reaction to him of Walton in the final scene, and his disappearance into 'darkness & distance', remains unknowable: his nature and his meaning remain unfixed. However, Mary Shelley is less interested in epistemology than in the moral consequences of labelling the unknown: in *Frankenstein*, people typically construct the unknown as evil and threatening, and give form to this construction in their language, thus participating in 'the cultural production of racist stereotypes' (Mellor 22).

The inter-relatedness and virtual identity of Victor Frankenstein and his creature is emphasized by the repeated allusions to Milton, where both characters enact Adam, Satan and even Godlike roles, and is demonstrated by their becoming one consciousness of remorse, revenge and despair and expressing the same ideas as each other in the final scenes. This underlines the point that, in 'reading the creature as a monster, then we write the creature as a monster and become ourselves the authors of evil' (Mellor 23). In conclusion, then, Mary Shelley's novel underlines a moral:

> When we write the unfamiliar as monstrous, we literally create the evil, the injustice, the racism, sexism, and class prejudice, that we arbitrarily imagine. Throughout the first edition of her novel, Shelley implicitly endorses a redemptive alternative to Frankenstein's egotistical attempt to penetrate and manipulate nature. This is an ethic of care that would sympathise with and protect all living beings, that would live in beneficial cooperation with nature, and that would bring about social reform not through violent French-style revolution but rather through peaceful, gradual evolution. (Mellor 23–4)

Mary Lowe-Evans

Our next critic, Mary Lowe-Evans, published her *Frankenstein: Mary Shelley's Wedding Guest* in 1993. In this short book she focuses on what she calls the 'marriage complex',[8] by which she means the fascination that existed among early nineteenth-century English men and women, with the future of marriage as an institution. Lowe-Evans argues that Mary Shelley was more than usually concerned with these debates due to her parentage and her own elopement and adultery. Lowe-Evans points out that during the early nineteenth century, a new form of stereotyping was appropriating and distorting earlier radical ideas:

> [the doctrine]. . .that Mary Wollstonecraft had hoped would liberate women was being reinterpreted to keep them in their domestic place. That place was a sphere of influence complementary to but decidedly separate from the public arena that men 'naturally' inhabited. Margaret Saville's position in *Frankenstein* demonstrates the pervasiveness of this latter-day distortion of Mary Wollstonecraft's philosophy, a distortion that Wollstonecraft herself may have invited in assertions like: 'Make women rational creatures, and free citizens, and they will quickly become good wives and mothers'. (L-E 35)

Lowe-Evans points out the unnaturalness and failures of marriages both potential (including that between the daemon and his mate) and actual, in the novel, and relates these problems closely to the concept of 'separate spheres' according to which men move in a public 'sphere' or arena, while woman's place is in a private or domestic 'sphere'. Another way of putting this is to talk of 'inside' and 'outside' spheres. Elizabeth's submissive passivity, and her remaining within her 'separate sphere' of domestic nurturing, ignorant of and unquestioning of Victor's activities in his male 'sphere' of public life and action, contributes to causing the catastrophe. Justine Moritz and Caroline Beaufort, equally representatives of the 'separate spheres' theory, also contribute to the impending disaster.

Lowe-Evans considers Elizabeth particularly in relation to the self-effacing letter in which she offers to release Frankenstein from his engagement. Lowe-Evans finds it hard to believe that Elizabeth loves Victor so selflessly. Instead, she suggests that Elizabeth has succumbed to cultural pressures just as Justine did earlier, and become hyperbolically self-effacing, 'free of desire and self-interest to such a degree that she lacks healthy passions' (L-E 62). Mary Shelley expects us to notice the satirical overstatement of Elizabeth's female perfections: like Blake in *The Marriage of Heaven and Hell*, which she had read, perhaps Mary Shelley is here reversing conventional definitions of good and evil when 'she employs her creature to "murder" Elizabeth, "execute" Justine, and "hound" Victor Frankenstein to death' (L-E 63). Perhaps, then, in a revulsion away from the proprieties of conventional middle-class female behaviour, and a criticism of the doctrine of separate spheres, Mary Shelley regards her female characters as partly guilty of their own destruction, and punishes them 'for adhering too closely to a model of propriety' (L-E 63).

With regard to Mrs Saville, Lowe-Evans feels that too little attention has been paid to her significance. She notes that Walton acknowledges his sister's 'gentle and feminine fosterage' which 'has so refined the groundwork of my character' (*F* 20): that is, that Walton benefited from a feminine educative and domestic influence; however, since he travelled away and out into the masculine public 'sphere', and his sister Margaret remains hidden away in her proper domestic place, Walton has fallen under the seductive influence of Frankenstein. Lowe-Evans shows how Walton's initial squeamishness about the 'brutality' normal on board ship, and his 'considerateness whenever the safety of others' is concerned, turn to accusations of 'cowardice' and 'injustice' when he is forced to turn back. Frankenstein's speech to the crew is 'a series of powerful, "heroic", but nonetheless empty clichés' (L-E 39). Eventually,

> It is apparent in this closing letter that only a very thin thread connects Walton to Margaret's world. Her early fosterage has barely rescued him from the seductions of Victor Frankenstein's sphere of influence.
>
> Mary Shelley has thus carefully designed these framing letters between Robert Walton and Margaret Saville, the 'civil servant' of the novel and her own surrogate, to establish the complicated ethical problems inherent in a society that advocated separate spheres of influence for men and women. (L-E 40)

With regard to the creature, Lowe-Evans notices that this figure is partly inspired by Mary Shelley's own feelings, particularly those of guilt. However, she also sees the creature as representative of Percy Shelley, whose effeminate looks led to his persecution at public school, whose opinions led to his expulsion from Oxford, and who was considered by conservatives to be 'psychologically if not physically deformed'. The creature, then, represents a 'nearly perfect balance of Mary and Percy Shelley at the most unspoiled and honest level of their beings' and is an answer to 'the marriage conundrum' on which Lowe-Evans focuses: '... you might say the creature *is* a marriage – but too perfect a union of masculine and feminine qualities to be allowed into the mainstream of a civilisation that still required that male and female operate in separate spheres' (L-E 82).

Joseph Kestner

Joseph Kestner's essay 'Narcissism as Symptom and Structure: The Case of Mary Shelley's *Frankenstein*' was first published in 1981, and appears in *New Casebooks: Frankenstein: Mary Shelley*.[9] Kestner takes a number of clinical psychoanalytical texts as his guides, and applies their descriptions of narcissism to the three characters Walton, Frankenstein and the creature, as well as to the three-narrator framed structure of the novel. Kestner's main authorities on narcissism are Richard Sennett, Gérard Genette and Sigmund Freud.

According to Sennett there are two kinds of narcissist: one shows symptoms like 'a demon breaking through the surface of polite order'. The other reports a general malaise: a feeling of blankness, an inability to become aroused. The manifest content will be reported as 'I cannot feel'. However, the latent content is that the Other – person or people – fails to arouse the narcissist. Consequently, those who try to respond to the narcissist are never the 'right ones', and are felt to be violating him. In this sense that there is more than one type of individual involved, Mary Shelley's *Frankenstein* is an exploration of pathological narcissism.

A narcissist, Frankenstein creates a reflection of himself who becomes the inadequate Other. Genette points out that the narcissist flees from one object who has become inadequate, on to the next person who is idealized until they begin to care, whereupon the narcissist flies from them, in turn. Because the narcissist sees his image in water, that image is unstable and constantly disappearing. So, the corollary of finding the reflection is flight:

> Victor Frankenstein's longing for the Other, then the fleeing from the Other, then the Other's pursuit of Victor, all constitute signal instances of the corollary of the narcissist's reflection, flight. As much as Mary Shelley's novel concerns 'The Modern Prometheus', it is much more involved with 'The Modern Narcissus'. (Kestner 70)

Kestner then considers how narcissism can be represented within a literary structure. He points out that looking at a reflection is to look at the surface of water, and it is either transparent, in which case the depth appears, or opaque, in which case the reflection covers an 'abîme' – an unseen depth. Putting one story inside another, which Kestner calls the *mise en abyme*, is therefore the form of narrative that can explore narcissism. *Frankenstein*, as he points out, has three narratives: that of the creature is placed within that of Frankenstein which is placed within that of Walton. Quoting Genette that 'Narcissus contemplates in the water another Narcissus who is more Narcissus than himself and this other is himself an abyss [*abîme*]', Kestner suggests that this 'triple embedding' helps us to understand the similarities between the three protagonists Walton, Frankenstein and the creature.

Furthermore, Freud asserted that the sacred number 3 stands for the male genitals, in 'Symbolism in Dreams', and Kestner suggests that Mary Shelley's use of three narratives hints at the latent homosexuality and egoism of the three characters.

The start of Walton's narrative is analysed to show his clear narcissistic symptoms, as his aim, 'the pole/penis' reveals that his object is not the good of mankind but 'self-love' (Kestner 72). When he finds his narcissistic Other in the form of Frankenstein, the homosexuality latent in Walton's narcissism is shown by his use of the phrase 'the brother of my heart', for Freud observed that homosexuals 'proceed from a narcissistic basis, and look for a young man who resembles themselves'. Naturally, while Walton is fixated on his new-found 'Self/Other', Mary Shelley provides the structural equivalent by placing Frankenstein's story as a *mise en abyme* enclosed within Walton's.

When we come to Frankenstein's account of his youth and experiments, Kestner refers to Freud's essay 'On Narcissism': the grandiose ego and incipient megalomania, the 'magical' method of dealing with the external world, and the attempt to choose a libidinal object where 'the subject's own ego is replaced by another one that is as similar as possible': all of these elements in Frankenstein's story confirm his narcissism. Victor's dream following the creation of the creature is a further exploration of his narcissism:

> the combined reflection and the desire to flee, the simultaneous idealisation and debasement of the Other, the longing followed by rejection, the self-exaltation leading to self-disgust, the self-projection leading to self-rejection. (Kestner 74)

The dream suggests that, as Frankenstein is now, as it were, the mother of his own image, he repudiates other women for the sake of the mother. However, the fact that in his dream his mother is dead suggests that Victor's narcissism has now developed further: his later choice of love-objects takes himself, not his mother, as his model. Frankenstein comments that he 'bore a hell within me', and Kestner agrees, 'the Creature was within Frankenstein (*I am an other*)' (Kestner 75). So, structurally, the creature's story is enclosed within Frankenstein's in Mary Shelley's narcissistic structural arrangement.

Kestner considers the two scenes, first when Frankenstein destroys the almost-completed female, then the wedding-night murder of Elizabeth. With regard to the first of these, Victor's supposed 'conscience' which urges him to destroy the female is a false excuse: he destroys her because of his latent homosexuality and his longing only for a 'Self/Other' of the same sex. With regard to Elizabeth's death, Kestner says, 'Like Echo in the Greek myth, Elizabeth is destroyed by her Narcissus. The whole truth of this episode is that, fearing sexual contact, Frankenstein wanted the woman dead, desiring only to love himself, latently homosexual' (Kestner 77). The narcissistic Other intervenes to prevent the normal separation of 'ego-libido' and 'object-libido' and Frankenstein's sexuality is 'a narcissistic auto-erotism'. As the narcissistic Other, he grins at himself from the window, or is himself grinning.

Kestner suggests that when Frankenstein takes the 'pen/penis' to correct Walton's notes, they share 'a narcissistic and onanistic gesture'. Kestner finally suggests that the two kinds of narcissist – the demon and the one presenting as 'I cannot feel' who he now calls the solipsist type – are both, by means of the structural *mise en abyme* of three concentric narrators, enclosed within Walton: 'The solipsism of Frankenstein and the demonism of the Creature, uniting in Walton through the *mise en abyme* / foetus narrative, reveal the nature of Walton's narcissistic "libidinal investment of the self"' (Kestner 77).

Concluding Discussion

We would have liked to include more of the different critical views on *Frankenstein* that are out there, than the five represented in this chapter. In particular, we would suggest that those interested in further critical reading might start with Peter Brooks, Margaret Homans (both represented in the *New Casebook*[10]) and Fred Botting.[11]

It will always be possible to argue that one or another of the selected critics would have been better replaced by another, not selected – or vice versa. However, the five whose ideas we have summarized have at least fulfilled the avowed purpose of this chapter: to show that a wide variety of critical interpretations of the text are possible and arguable, and that a wide variety of approaches and opinions exist.

We have met Frankenstein and the daemon as emotion and intellect, as Eve and Eve, or Frankenstein as masculine, or both as homosexual narcissists; we have heard that the novel's central theme is pursuit, or marriage, or narcissism, or the anxieties of a woman writer in a patriarchal literary context, or the origins of prejudice where, on writing prejudice, you become the evil you inscribe, or the possibility of living in harmony with the natural world. We have heard that Mary Shelley's biography contributed sublimated rage and other anxieties about birth; or the anxieties of a woman beginning to write in a Miltonic literary tradition; or, the feeling of namelessness due to her guilty adultery, that led her to create the daemon; or, a critical understanding of her husband's Romantic idealism; or, an awareness of the political dangers of an excluded class; or, anxieties over creativity because she was encouraged to write – and the list goes on. It seems that each of the major characters can enact Mary Shelley, or Percy (indeed we have heard that the daemon is, really, a perfect balance or 'marriage' of the two), and all of them can enact various figures from *Paradise Lost*. Meanwhile, various gender-characteristics are attributed to them, sometimes at different times in the story.

In fact, our selection of five critics has shown that almost anything goes in *Frankenstein* criticism. At the same time, we can recognize that there are the usual standard approaches which – in this chapter – include feminist readings, psychoanalytical readings, and biographical/historicist approaches. A final and humble reminder of just how doubtful the interpretation of *Frankenstein* is will be a sensible way to conclude this sample of views. Sandra Gilbert and Susan Gubar noted:

> Here we are obliged to confront both the moral ambiguity and the symbolic slipperiness which are at the heart of all the characterizations in *Frankenstein*. In fact, it is probably these continual and complex reallocations of meaning, among characters whose histories echo and re-echo each other, that have been so bewildering to critics. (G & G 229)

Gilbert and Gubar, with their theory that both Frankenstein and his daemon are, essentially, female Eves, have clearly not allowed what they call the 'symbolic slipperiness' of the text to inhibit their analysis. However, we may remember that we have found this quality throughout our study of *Frankenstein* in Part 1. Again and again, we have commented that the text is extraordinarily rich in suggestions, and resistant to definitive answers. The phrases 'symbolic slipperiness' and 'continual and complex reallocations of meaning' successfully evoke the suggestive and resistant quality we have found.

This quality may account for some of the wilder variations, and so help us to understand how such a variety of different critical views can exist, concerning *Frankenstein*. It may also helps to account for what could be called the 'impurity' of most *Frankenstein* criticism. All five of the critics represented in this chapter have been engaged in 'reading in' ideas: bringing them from Mary Shelley's biography and putting them into the novel. Perhaps this is because of the directness of the author's own question – 'How I, then a young girl, came to think of and to dilate upon so very hideous an idea?' (*F* 5) – a question all of our critics have striven, to a greater or lesser extent, to answer; perhaps also, it is a natural consequence of both the celebrity and the luridness of Mary Shelley's early life-history, which cries out to be a significant factor for her novel.

We remember what Gilbert and Gubar call *Frankenstein*'s 'symbolic slipperiness', however; and celebrate a novel that touches a neo-mythical power, and is at the same time never easy to explain or interpret.

Notes

Introduction

1. Mary Shelley, *Frankenstein: or, The Modern Prometheus*, Ed. Maurice Hindle, Penguin Books, London, 2003, pp. 7–8. In future references this edition will be designated by the abbreviation '*F*', followed by the page number, in brackets in the text, thus (*F* 7–8).
2. Margaret Homans, 'Bearing Demons: Frankenstein's Circumvention of the Maternal', *New Casebooks: Frankenstein: Mary Shelley*, Ed. Fred Botting, London & Basingstoke, 1995, p. 152.
3. *Ibid.*, p. 160.
4. Joseph Kestner, 'Narcissism as Symptom and Structure: the Case of Mary Shelley's *Frankenstein*', *New Casebooks: Frankenstein: Mary Shelley*, Ed. Fred Botting, London & Basingstoke, 1995, p. 77. Kestner's argument is summarized in Chapter 8, 'A Sample of Critical Views'.

The Narrative Frame

1. From 'Ode: Intimations of Immortality from Recollections of Early Childhood', 1807, ll. 63–7.
2. 'Narratives of Seduction and the Seductions of Narrative: The Frame Structure of *Frankenstein*', in *New Casebooks: Frankenstein: Mary Shelley*, ed. Fred Botting, London and Basingstoke, 1995, p. 172.
3. *Ibid.*, p. 172.

Characterization

1. *Paradise Lost*, Book IV, ll. 478–9.
2. In Chapter 8, 'A Sample of Critical Views', the theories of Muriel Spark (that Victor and the daemon represent emotion and intellect, respectively) and Joseph Kestner (that the daemon is Victor's narcissistic/homosexual love-object) are summarised.
3. 'Not this time, Victor!', from *Mary Shelley in Her Times*, ed. Betty T. Bennett and Stuart Curran, Baltimore and London, 2000, p. 3.
4. In Chapter 8, 'A Sample of Critical Views', we will find Sandra Gilbert and Susan Gubar's suggestion that the monster's crimes express Mary Shelley's 'sublimated rage' against Miltonic patriarchy, for example. Another theory is that the daemon represents Frankenstein's repressed rage against his bourgeois family (see Kate Ellis: 'Monsters in the Garden: Mary Shelley and the Bourgeois Family', in *The Endurance of Frankenstein: Essays on Mary Shelley's Novel*, edited by George Levine and U. C. Knoepflmacher, Berkeley, Los Angeles and London, 1979, pp. 123–142).

Nature, Society and Science

1. Daniel Defoe, *Robinson Crusoe*, Penguin Popular Classics, 1994. See, for example, Friday's pertinent question 'If God much strong, much might as the Devil, why God no kill the Devil?', pp. 214–5.
2. Jonathan Swift, *Gulliver's Travels*. For example, in Chapter 32 Gulliver attempts to explain war and law to his Houyhnhm master, who complains that Gulliver's 'discourse had increased his abhorrence of the whole [i.e. human] species, so he found it gave him a disturbance in his mind to which he was wholly a stranger before'.
3. For a collection of such references, particularly from Burke, see 'The Politics of Monstrosity', by Chris Baldick, in *New Casebooks: Frankenstein: Mary Shelley*, ed. Fred Botting, Basingstoke and London, 1995, pp. 54–60.
4. For example, Victor has a 'fervent longing' on p. 41.
5. From Anne K. Mellor, 'A Feminist Critique of Science', in *New Casebooks: Frankenstein: Mary Shelley*, ed. Fred Botting, London and Basingstoke 1995, p. 120. Mellor judges that 'Mary Shelley directly pitted Victor Frankenstein, that modern Prometheus, against those gradual evolutionary processes of nature so well described by Darwin. Rather than letting organic life-forms evolve slowly over thousands of years according to

natural processes of sexual selection, Victor Frankenstein wants to originate a new life-form quickly ...' (p. 119). This may be the case, but our point is that a science of the kind which leaves nature to its own devices, is not depicted in the novel's text.
6. William Wordsworth, *The Prelude*, Book I, lines 395–399.

Symbol and Myth

1. For example, Muriel Spark's idea that the daemon represents 'intellect' to Frankenstein's 'emotion' (see Chapter 8, 'A Sample of Critical Views') is only one of many theories that strikes us as being relevant, but only partly relevant to the text.
2. Plato, *Protagoras* 320c – 322a, trans. Jowett.
3. Wikipedia, *Prometheus*, 'Promethean myth in modern culture'.
4. For example, in the *Rig Veda*, the hero Mātariśvan recovered fire, which had been hidden from mankind.
5. In Chapter 8, we summarise the critical views of Joseph Kestner, who interprets Frankenstein as a narcissist, in his 'Narcissism as Symptom and Structure: The Case of Mary Shelley's *Frankenstein*', in *New Casebooks: Frankenstein: Mary Shelley*, ed. Fred Botting, Basingstoke and London, 1995, pp. 68–80.
6. *Paradise Lost*, Book III, l. 99.
7. William Blake, *The Marriage of Heaven and Hell*, 1793.
8. 'Production and Reproduction: The Case of *Frankenstein*', from *New Casebooks: Frankenstein*, ed. Fred Botting, Basingstoke and London, 1995, pp. 21–47.
9. *Dr Jekyll and Mr Hyde*, by Robert Louis Stevenson, 1886.
10. *The Island of Dr Moreau*, by H. G. Wells, 1896.
11. *Dr Strangelove, or: How I Learned to Stop Worrying and Love the Bomb*, dir. Stanley Kubrick, 1964.
12. Wikipedia: The Free Encyclopedia, http://en.wikipedia.org/wiki/Hulk_ (comics).
13. For a notable example of this concept, see Captain Kirk's peroration at the funeral of Spock, a Vulcan alien, in which he says that 'of all the souls I have encountered in my travels, his was the most ... human.' From *Star Trek II: The Wrath of Khan*, Paramount Pictures, 1982.
14. 'Study of Thomas Hardy', in D H Lawrence, *Selected Literary Criticism*, ed. Beal, Anthony, London, 1956, p. 176.

Themes, and Conclusions to Part 1

1. See, for example, Wordsworth's *Ode: Intimations of Immortality from Recollections of Early Childhood*; or Blake's 'The Lamb', from *Songs of Innocence*, and 'The Garden of Love' from *Songs of Experience*.

Mary Shelley's Life and Works

1. Such as, for example, the similarity of the dream to another dream, about rubbing her dead baby and so bringing her back to life (see e.g. Miranda Seymour, *Mary Shelley*, New York, 2000, p. 130, for an account of this dream).
2. Seymour, *op.cit.*, pp. 161–3.
3. Jane Dunn, *Moon in Eclipse: A Life of Mary Shelley*, London, 1978, pp. 131–2.
4. Jane Dunn, *Moon in Eclipse: A Life of Mary Shelley*, London, 1978, p. 236.

The Historical and Literary Context

1. William Godwin, *Things as They Are, or the Adventures of Caleb Williams*, 1794, Chapter 5.
2. *Ibid.*, Chapter 10.
3. Simple examples are Sir Humphrey Davy's lectures, and their contribution to the character Professor Waldman; or Mary Shelley's travel journal and the description of Victor's journey to the 'mer de glace'.
4. William Blake, 'The Voice of the Devil', *The Marriage of Heaven and Hell*, 1793.
5. Percy Bysshe Shelley, 'The Poetry of Dante and Milton', *In Defence of Poetry: an Essay*, 1819.
6. John Milton, *Paradise Lost*, Book III, l.99.
7. We may also remember that Goethe's *The Sorrows of Werther* was one of the daemon's three books (*F* 130).
8. See *F* 95–6, and the discussion at pp. 76–7 above.

A Sample of Critical Views

1. William St Clair, 'The Impact of *Frankenstein*', in *Mary Shelley in Her Times*, ed. Betty T. Bennett and Stuart Curran, Baltimore and London, 2000, p. 51.

2. *Ibid.*, pp. 55 and 56, respectively.
3. Spark, Muriel, *Mary Shelley*, New York and Toronto, 1987, p. 154. Subsequent references to this work will appear in brackets in the text thus: (Spark 154).
4. Sandra M. Gilbert and Susan Gubar, *The Madwoman in the Attic: The Woman Writer and the Nineteenth-Century Literary Imagination*, New Haven and London 1979, Chapter 7: 'Horror's Twin: Mary Shelley's Monstrous Eve', pp. 213–47. Future references to this work will appear in the text in brackets, thus: (G & G 213).
5. Ellen Moers, 'Female Gothic', in *The Endurance of* Frankenstein: *Essays on Mary Shelley's Novel*, eds. George Levine and U. C. Knoepflmacher, Berkeley, Los Angeles and London, 1979, p. 79.
6. *Ibid.*, p. 86.
7. Mellor, Anne K., 'Making a 'monster': an Introduction to *Frankenstein*', *The Cambridge Companion to Mary Shelley*, ed. Esther Schor, Cambridge, 2003, p. 9. Subsequent references to this work will appear in brackets in the text thus: (Mellor 9).
8. Lowe-Evans, Mary, *Frankenstein: Mary Shelley's Wedding Guest*, New York and Toronto, 1993, p. ix. Subsequent references to this work will appear in brackets in the text thus: (L-E ix).
9. Kestner, Joseph, 'Narcissism as Symptom and Structure: The Case of Mary Shelley's *Frankenstein*', *New Casebooks: Frankenstein: Mary Shelley*, ed. Fred Botting, Basingstoke and London, 1995, pp. 68–80. Subsequent references to this work will appear in brackets in the text thus: (Kestner 68).
10. *New Casebooks: Frankenstein: Mary Shelley*, ed. Fred Botting, Basingstoke and London, 1995.
11. Botting, Fred, *Making Monstrous: Frankenstein, Criticism, Theory*, Manchester, 1991.

Further Reading

Your first job is to study the text. There is no substitute for the work of detailed analysis: that is how you gain the close familiarity with the text, and the fully developed understanding of its content, which make the essays you write both personal and convincing. For this reason I recommend that you take it as a rule not to read any critical works about the text you are studying, until you have finished studying it for yourself.

Once you are familiar with the text, you may wish to read around and about it. This brief chapter is only intended to set you off: there are hundreds of relevant books and we can only mention a few. However, most good editions, and critical works, have suggestions for further reading, or a bibliography of their own. Once you have begun to read beyond your text, you can use these and a good library to follow up your particular interests. This chapter is divided into *Works by Mary Shelley*, *Reading around the text*, which lists a number of works which are contextually relevant either by date, content or genre, by other writers; *Biography*, which includes both memoirs by people who knew Mary Shelley, and some of the many accounts of her life; and *Criticism*, which gives a selection of suggested titles that will introduce you to the varieties of opinion among professional critics.

Works by Mary Shelley

Mary Shelley wrote seven novels. In this book we have focused on *Frankenstein, or, the Modern Prometheus* (1818 and 1831). The next novel to read, in order to build your knowledge of Mary Shelley's works is

The Last Man (1826, currently available in Oxford World's Classics). This is regarded as Shelley's second most interesting work after *Frankenstein*; and it is arguably connected to the better-known title, as we have suggested, because *Frankenstein*'s originality may well have opened up the idea of a futuristic dystopia. Following this, your reading of Mary Shelley's novels may depend upon your interests. If, like many people and professional critics, you are fascinated by her character and life, you may be drawn towards *Mathilda*, which has been published by Penguin Books in 1992, in a volume together with Mary Wollstonecraft's *Mary* and *Maria*. *Mathilda* was written 1819–20, first published 1959, and is now available in the Penguin already mentioned; from Alan Rodgers Books; or the text can be downloaded from Project Gutenberg. Also, you may look at *Lodore* (1835, currently out of print, but available second-hand). Both of these novels are interesting for their autobiographical content. If you are more interested in Mary Shelley's theme of love versus political ambition, you may look at her two historical novels. These are *Valperga; or, The Life and Adventures of Castruccio, Prince of Lucca* (1823, currently available in Oxford World's Classics) and *The Fortunes of Perkin Warbeck, A Romance* (1830, currently available from Kessinger Publishing). Finally, the most satisfying and independent characterization of a woman in Mary Shelley's fiction is that of Elizabeth Raby in her final novel, *Falkner, A Novel* (1837, currently available from Wildside Press).

Mary Shelley's other writings include her *Collected Tales and Stories*, edited by Charles E. Robinson (Baltimore, 1976) and *Mary Shelley's Literary Lives and Other Writings*, edited by Tilar J. Mazzeo (London, 2002), both of which collections give a flavour of how she earned her living by writing, between her husband's death in 1822 and her son's inheritance in 1844. The *Literary Lives* in particular contain interesting interjections of personal opinion and philosophy. The scholarly interest of recent times has resulted in reliable and thorough editions of Mary Shelley's journals and letters, also. Both of these have been issued during the 1980s by the Johns Hopkins University Press (Baltimore). *The Journals of Mary Wollstonecraft Shelley, 1814–44* have been edited by Paula R. Feldman and Diana Scott-Kilvert; and *The Letters of Mary Wollstonecraft Shelley* have been edited by Betty T. Bennett. With regard to her travel writing, Mary Shelley's account of her elopement 'honeymoon', *The History of a Six Weeks' Tour Through a Part of France, Switzerland, Germany, and Holland* (1817) can be read at www.english.upenn.edu., and *Rambles in Germany and Italy in 1840, 1842 and 1843* can be read on books.google.co.uk, or ordered from google books.

Reading around the Text

Because of its originality, it is hard to find novels analogous to *Frankenstein*;
but for a sense of literary context it is useful to look at some 'Gothic' fiction.
Try Ann Radcliffe's *The Mysteries of Udolpho* (1794) and Horace Walpole's *The
Castle of Otranto* (1764), to obtain a flavour of Gothic in its classic Radcliffe
flowering, and as it began. Then read Matthew Gregory Lewis's *The Monk*
(1796), one of the most powerful and shocking examples of English Gothic;
and perhaps look at Charles Robert Maturin's *Melmoth the Wanderer* (1820),
a late contribution to the genre. Two of the most entertaining novels we can
suggest are the satires on Gothic: Jane Austen's *Northanger Abbey* (1818) and
Thomas Love Peacock's *Nightmare Abbey* (1818), both appeared in the same
year as *Frankenstein*.

An important possible source text for *Frankenstein* is William Godwin's
Things as They Are, or the Adventures of Caleb Williams (1794), which is
also often listed as a 'Gothic' novel. The single most important neo-gothic
successor to *Frankenstein* in the nineteenth century is *Wuthering Heights*, by
Emily Brontë (1847). Next to Emily's novel may be put her sister Charlotte's
Jane Eyre (also 1847), followed perhaps by Wilkie Collins's two thrillers *The
Woman in White* (1860) and *The Moonstone* (1868). These works display
some Gothic trappings and elements of horror, but in general they follow
the example set by *Frankenstein* in keeping clear of, or at least remaining
ambivalent about, the supernatural. For later examples of the Gothic-with-
supernatural, try *Carmilla* by Joseph Sheridan Le Fanu (1872), *Dracula* by
Bram Stoker (1897), and for a successful modern ghost story, Susan Hill's
The Woman in Black (1983).

We have mentioned that *Frankenstein* effectively founded its own genre,
Science Fiction; and we have mentioned in passing a number of examples.
There are, of course, thousands of titles which belong in the Sci-Fi genre, and
which exhibit the *Frankenstein* trademark theme of ethically ambivalent scientific power. In this short Further Reading section, we will limit ourselves to
mentioning one or two of the most relevant classics together with some combinations of science-fiction and futuristic imaginings. The dual-figure motif
of Frankenstein and daemon becomes central in Robert Louis Stevenson's
classic *The Strange Case of Dr Jekyll and Mr Hyde* (1886); and another laboratory where creatures are tortured in order to create human life artificially
features in H. G. Wells's *The Island of Dr Moreau* (1896). John Wyndham's
science-fiction novels are good examples of serious 'science-gone-wrong'
fables: try *The Chrysalids* (1955), which is set in a post-nuclear-holocaust
world. In Chapter 7 we discussed three classic futuristic dystopias with

political themes, as successors to a *Frankenstein* tradition. They are *The Time Machine*, by H. G. Wells (1895); *Brave New World*, by Aldous Huxley (1932) and *Nineteen Eighty-Four*, by George Orwell (1949).

In this Chapter we are limiting ourselves to the printed word, and so we will only mention in passing that there are, of course, many plays and films based on *Frankenstein*, as well as strip cartoons such as the Marvel Comics mentioned in Chapter 4. A very full list of modern *Frankenstein* derivatives in various media, can be found on the Wikipedia website, on a page entitled 'Frankenstein in Popular Culture'.

Finally, in reading around *Frankenstein*, it will be worth your while to look at some of the source texts known to have been in Mary Shelley's mind. Look at *Paradise Lost*, by John Milton (1674), at least sufficiently to become familiar with its subject-matter and style, so that you can judge the references to this poem made by Frankenstein, his daemon and Mary Shelley. See (preferably) or read *The Tragical History of the Life and Death of Doctor Faustus*, by Christopher Marlowe (1589); and read Samuel Taylor Coleridge's poem, *The Ancient Mariner* (1798).

Biography

There is a great deal of published material about Mary Shelley's life. The first biography to make use of the author's journal was R. Glynn Grylls's *Mary Shelley: A Biography* (London, New York and Toronto, 1938). However, I shall suggest two more recent, full-length biographies. First, Jane Dunn's *Moon in Eclipse: A Life of Mary Shelley* (London, 1978). Jane Dunn writes lucidly and makes an intelligible and sympathetic character of her subject, although her coverage of the years after Percy Bysshe Shelley's death (1822–51) is much less detailed than the rest. Next, there is *Mary Shelley*, by Miranda Seymour (New York, 2000). Miranda Seymour's account has benefited from the availability of more material in the form of letters and parts of journals, by Mary Shelley and other people who were part of her circle at the time, that have surfaced due to the increased scholarly interest from the 1950s on. The result is a much more detailed biography, although as a consequence of this level of detail, Mary Shelley's character and private emotions are sometimes more difficult to elucidate. Both of these biographies attempt to use deductive reasoning to penetrate the mysterious events of Mary Shelley's life – notably the relationship between Percy Bysshe Shelley and Claire Clairmont, and the truth about the baby born in Naples. Neither biographer is entirely successful or convincing at these moments.

These are full-length biographies; but the reader interested in Mary Shelley's life and works will find a rich variety of material in the form of works which combine biography and literary criticism, starting with Muriel Spark's *Child of Light: A Reassessment of Mary Wollstonecraft Shelley* (1951, but revised and re-issued as *Mary Shelley*, in 1987). Spark's book is a biography, with additional chapters giving a critical discussion of *Frankenstein* and *The Last Man*. We have summarized her critical response to *Frankenstein* in Chapter 8. Anne K. Mellor's *Mary Shelley: Her Life, Her Fiction, Her Monsters* (New York, 1988) develops a feminist approach to Mary Shelley. We also looked at Mellors' critical views in Chapter 8, although not focusing on this work. Emily W. Sunstein wrote *Mary Shelley: Romance and Reality* (Baltimore, 1989) as her contribution to a reassessment during the 1980s; particularly refuting the accusation that Mary Shelley became an establishment conservative after her husband's death, and arguing that she remained politically and socially liberal and concerned. For a clearly written account of the author's life and succinct, well-argued assessments of her writing, go to John Williams's *Mary Shelley: A Literary Life* (Basingstoke, New York and London, 2000).

There are also descriptions of Mary Shelley and accounts of parts of her life, in biographies of others in her circle. Most notably, of course, are the many biographies of Percy Bysshe Shelley (such as this year's *Percy Bysshe Shelley: A Biography*, by James Bieri, Baltimore, 2008) and of Lord Byron (such as Fiona MacCarthy's *Byron: Life and Legend*, London, 2002) to be found; but there are also William St Clair's *The Godwins and the Shelleys: The Biography of a Family* (New York, 1989) as well as biographies of some of the less celebrated figures. It can be revealing to focus on a contrary view of Mary Shelley, perhaps by looking at Robert Gittings and Jo Manton's *Claire Clairmont and the Shelleys* (Oxford, 1992). For a contemporary memoir with a strong personal viewpoint, you cannot do better than look at Edward John Trelawny's *Records of Shelley, Byron, and the Author* (1858).

Criticism

The critical works sampled in Chapter 8 are Muriel Spark, *Mary Shelley* (New York and Toronto, 1987); Chapter 7, 'Horror's Twin: Mary Shelley's Monstrous Eve', pp. 213–247 from Sandra M. Gilbert and Susan Gubar, *The Madwoman in the Attic: The Woman Writer and the Nineteenth-century Literary Imagination* (New Haven and London, 1979); Anne K. Mellor, 'Making a "monster": an Introduction to *Frankenstein*', pp. 9–25 in *The Cambridge Companion to Mary Shelley*, ed. Esther Schor (Cambridge, 2003);

Mary Lowe-Evans, *Frankenstein: Mary Shelley's Wedding Guest* (New York and Toronto, 1993); and Joseph Kestner, 'Narcissism as Symptom and Structure: The Case of Mary Shelley's *Frankenstein*', pp. 68–80 in *New Casebooks: Frankenstein: Mary Shelley*, ed. Fred Botting (Basingstoke and London, 1995).

Anthologies of critical essays and articles are a good way to sample the critics. You can then go on to read the full-length books written by those critics whose ideas and approaches you find stimulating. The New Casebooks series (general editors John Peck and Martin Coyle) published by Macmillan collects a variety of critical articles together, and provides an introduction which discusses the critical history of the text. The volume on *Frankenstein* is edited by Fred Botting, and contains the article by Joseph Kestner we sampled in Chapter 8, as well as essays by Margaret Homans, Beth Newman, Peter Brooks, and Paul O'Flinn's discussion of two film versions. *Mary Shelley in Her Times*, ed. Betty T. Bennett and Stuart Curran (Baltimore and London, 2000) collects works of scholarship particularly focusing on historical context, and not confined to *Frankenstein*, such as William St Clair's revealing study of *Frankenstein*'s publishing history. *Mary Shelley's Fictions: From* Frankenstein *to* Falkner, ed. Michael Eberle-Sinatra (Basingstoke, London and New York, 2000), contains a few articles on *Frankenstein* but also covers the other fiction. Similarly, *The Cambridge Companion to Mary Shelley*, ed. Esther Schor (Cambridge, 2003), includes some articles about *Frankenstein* and a number which focus on Shelley's other writings. The article by Anne K. Mellor we sampled in Chapter 8 is found in this anthology. A number of major contributions to *Frankenstein* interpretation, including the influential 'Female Gothic' of Ellen Moers, appear in *The Endurance of* Frankenstein: *Essays on Mary Shelley's Novel*, edited by George Levine and U. C. Knoepflmacher (Berkeley, Los Angeles and London, 1979).

The following full-length critical works may also be of interest and should be stimulating whether you agree or disagree with the writer's analysis. Christopher Small's *Ariel Like a Harpy: Shelley, Mary, and Frankenstein* (London, 1954 and Pittsburgh, 1973) is a semi-biographical charting of myths, symbols and influences, particularly between Percy Shelley and Mary. Jane Blumberg's *Mary Shelley's Early Novels: 'This Child of Imagination and Misery'* (Basingstoke and London, 1993) is a study that aims to establish Mary's 'disloyalty' to the idealistic radicalism of Percy Bysshe Shelley and his circle, because she came to reject many of her husband's tenets. *Making Monstrous: Frankenstein, Criticism, Theory*, by Fred Botting (Manchester, 1991) calls itself 'post-structuralist' but is really more eclectic, and an interesting view. William Veeder's *Mary Shelley and Frankenstein: The Fate of Androgyny*

(Chicago, 1986) argues that Mary Shelley saw an androgynous approach to life as necessary to human survival; but she despaired of it ever occurring.

There are also significant numbers of books and articles which discuss the influence of *Frankenstein* on various media in the present day. We have mentioned, in passing, Paul O'Flinn's article in the *New Casebook*. However, should you wish to follow up such an interest, try *Frankenstein: Creation and Monstrosity*, edited by Stephen Baum (London, 1994), an anthology of studies mainly concerned with the later cultural history of the *Frankenstein* myth; or Chris Baldick's *In Frankenstein's Shadow: Myth, Monstrosity, and Nineteenth-Century Writing* (Oxford, 1987).

Some of the most influential criticisms of *Frankenstein* have appeared within critical works with a wider scope than the one author or text (like the work of Sandra M. Gilbert and Susan Gubar sampled in Chapter 8), or as articles in anthologies or periodicals. In this connection, it is worthwhile to use the subject-index in a library, and references and bibliographies which appear in the critical works you try first, both of which will point you towards many valuable contributions to the critical debate that you would not otherwise find. For example, if you look under Gothic and Fantasy, rather than *Frankenstein* or Mary Shelley, you will find Clive Bloom's *Gothic Horror: A Guide for Students and Readers* (Basingstoke, 2007), which collects a number of documents, extracts and essays, many of them relevant to *Frankenstein*; Angela Wright's *Gothic Fiction* (Basingstoke, 2007) and Rosemary Jackson's *Fantasy: The Literature of Subversion* (London and New York, 1981). Or, if you look under nineteenth-century women's writing, you would come upon Margaret Homans's *Bearing the Word: Language and Female Experience in Nineteenth-century Women's Writing* (Chicago, 1986), within which is an influential analysis of *Frankenstein*. When you are in a library, use the catalogue system resourcefully. There are numerous books which appear to be on different subjects – Romantic studies, the Literature of Revolution and so on. A large number of these may contain chapters or essays about *Frankenstein* which bring an illuminating angle to bear upon this unique text.

Index

Abbot and Costello Meet Frankenstein (film),
    Universal (1948), 164
Addams Family, the (television), 164
America, War of Independence of, 204
Analysis, methods of, 44–5, 85–7, 125–6
    diction analysed, 13–15, 23–4, 31, 86
    imagery analysed, 24–5, 86
    notes to help thinking, 104–5
    reason and emotion in characters, 85
    repetition, 14–15, 22–3, 51–3
    sentences analysed, 12, 21–2, 30–1, 77–8
    summarising paragraphs, demonstrated,
        10–12, 20–1, 29, 49–51
    using leading questions, 125–6
Asimov, Isaac, *I, Robot* (1950) and the *Robot*
    series of novels, 167, 215
Austen, Jane, *Northanger Abbey* (1818),
    209, 248

Baldick, Chris, 'The Politics of Monstrosity',
    105n3
    *In Frankenstein's Shadow: Myth, Monstrosity
        and Nineteenth-Century Writing*
        (1987), 252
Baum, Stephen (Ed.), *Frankenstein: Creation
    and Monstrosity* (1994), 252
Baxter, Christy, 185
Baxter, Isabella, 185
Baxter, William, 184
Beckford, William Thomas, *Vathek, an
    Arabian Tale* (1786), 209

Bennett, Betty T
    and Curran, Stuart (Eds.), *Mary Shelley in
        her Times* (2000), 251
    (Ed.) *The Letters of Mary Wollstonecraft
        Shelley*, 247
    'Not this time, Victor!', 72n3
Bieri, James, *Percy Bysshe Shelley: A Biography*
    (2008), 250
Blake, William
    The Marriage of Heaven and Hell (1793),
        159 and 159n7, 212, 234
    Milton (circa 1810), 212–13
Bloom, Clive, *Gothic Horror: A Guide for
    Students and Readers* (2007), 252
Blumberg, Jane, *Mary Shelley's Early Novels:
    'This Child of Imagination and Misery'*
    (1993), 251
Botting, Fred
    Ed., *New Casebooks: Frankenstein: Mary
        Shelley* (1995), 1n2, 2n4, 36n2,
        105n3, 122n5, 154n5, 164n8,
        235–8, 251
    *Making Monstrous: Frankenstein, Criticism,
        Theory* (1991), 238, 251
Branagh, Kenneth (dir.), *Mary Shelley's
    Frankenstein* (film, 1994), 164
Brontë, Charlotte, *Jane Eyre* (1847), 248
Brontë, Emily, *Wuthering Heights* (1847), 40,
    211, 218, 219, 248
    Heathcliff a successor to the daemon, 218

Brooks, Mel (dir.), *Young Frankenstein* (film, 1974), 164
Brooks, Peter, 'What is a Monster? (According to *Frankenstein*)', 238, 251
Byron, Clara Allegra (Claire Clairmont's daughter)
  birth, 189
  death, 190, 191
Byron, Lord George Gordon
  affair with Claire Clairmont, 188
  'A Fragment' (1819), 206
  and ghost-story competition, 188, 197, 206
  at Pisa, 1822, 191
  in Villa Diodati, 1816, 188
  writing *Manfred*, 188
'Byron, Major G.' (forger), 195–6

Canning, George, parliamentary speech (1824), 163
Characterization, 46–87
  composite (Frankenstein and Walton), 62–5, 82–3, 84
  failure of positive qualities (Elizabeth and Alphonse), 79
  inconclusive and suggestive (Frankenstein and Walton), 54–5, 61–5, 80–1
  people not naturalistic, 82, 84
  secondary characters, 69–79, 81–2
Chatterton, Thomas, 208
Clairmont, Charles (Mary Shelley's step-brother), 183
Clairmont, Jane (later Claire, Mary Shelley's step-sister), 183
  accompanies the elopement, 186
  attention-seeking, 186, 191
  birth of daughter, 189
  final quarrel with Mary, 196
Clairmont, Mary Jane, *see* Godwin, Mrs. Mary Jane (previously Clairmont, Mary Shelley's stepmother) ·
Clerval, Henry
  characterization, 69–72
Coleridge, Samuel Taylor, *The Ancient Mariner* (1798), 249
  recites to the child Mary Shelley, 184
Collins, Wilkie, *The Moonstone* (1868), *The Woman in White* (1860), 248

Curran, Stuart, *see* Bennett, Betty T.
Curse of Frankenstein, The (film), Hammer Films (1957), 163–4
Cushing, Peter, 163

Daemon, the, 7
  an archetypal figure, 68, 81
  characterization of, 65–9
  a combination of Mary and Percy Shelley, 235
  as 'dark' side of Frankenstein, 68–9, 134–6
  determinism of, 33–4, 81, 87, 178, 213, 218
  his narrative analysed, 27–36
  his political significance, 104–6, 177, 216
  innocence of society, 102–3
  and knowledge, 122, 176
  problematic appeal of, 35–6
  surprise of his style, 41
  as a symbol, 132–6
Darwin, Charles, 34, 213
Darwin, Erasmus, 231
Davy, Sir Humphrey, *A Discourse, Introductory to a Course of Lectures on Chemistry* (1802), 114–15, 118n3, 231
Defoe, Daniel, *Robinson Crusoe*
  Friday on Religion, 102 and 102n1
Determinism, 26, 33–4, 81, 87, 93–9, 178–9, 213, 218
Doyle, Sir Arthur Conan, *The Lost World* (1912), 215
Dunn, Jane, *Moon in Eclipse: A Life of Mary Shelley* (1978), 188n3, 198n4, 249

Eberle-Sinatra, Michael (Ed.), *Mary Shelley's Fictions: From* Frankenstein *to* Falkner (2000), 251
Eliot, George, *Middlemarch* (1874), 218, 225
Elizabeth Lavenza, *see* Lavenza, Elizabeth
Ellis, Kate, 'Monsters in the Garden: Mary Shelley and the Bourgeois Family', 83n4

Faustus, Doctor, 166, 212, 213–14
  mad alchemist figure, the, 166, 214–15
Feldman, Paula R. and Scott-Kilvert, Diana (Eds.), *The Journals of Mary Wollstonecraft Shelley 1814–44*, 247

Foggi, Paolo, 190
  blackmails Shelleys, 191
Frankenstein, 246
  1831 Preface, 1, 2, 188, 197, 207, 210
  composition of, 188, 197, 206–7
  and the critics, 1–2, 220–40
  dedicated to Godwin, 220
  a feminist text, 172–4, 219
  lacking in Gothic trappings, 209–10
  latent homosexuality in, 237
  modern myth of, 162–9, 252
  political message erased, 163–4
  as a political warning, 108–9, 206
  in popular culture, 1, 162–6
  proto-Marxist, 109, 176–8, 213
  psychoanalytical interpretations of, 1–2,
    61–2, 80–1, 83, 131, 152–4, 161,
    169, 224–9, 235–8
  published anonymously, 220
  resists interpretation, 124–5, 147–8,
    169–70, 171–2, 239–40
  rich in suggestions, 131, 147, 169–70,
    239–40
  sales of, 221
  the story altered, 162–4
  as a study of prejudice, 232–3
  two texts, 1818 and 1831, xi, 73–4, 118,
    130, 230
Frankenstein, Alphonse
  characterization of, 77–9
  embodies wisdom and authority, 78
  fate of his family, 109
  increasingly ineffectual, 78–9
Frankenstein, Caroline (née Beaufort), 73,
  152–3
Frankenstein (film), Universal (1931), 163
Frankenstein, Victor, 7
  abnormal psychology of, 61–2, 80–1, 131,
    152–5, 161, 174
  characterization of, 55–65
  fits of unpredictable action, 60–1
  his dream discussed, 129–31
  his narrative analysed, 17–27
  mad scientist, as, 165–6
  moral reflection, absence of, 57–8
  narcissistic, 154–5
  nature and nurture, indecisive on, 96–7

  our scepticism of, 25
  science of, hubristic, 116–17
  snobbery of, 25
  as a superior being, 99–100
Frankenstein, William
  appearance of innocence misleading, 177
  as a superior being, 100
  two accounts of his murder discussed, 37–8
French Revolution, the, 105–6, 204,
  208, 220
Freud, Sigmund, 34, 213, 235–8
  'On Narcissism', 237
  'Symbolism in Dreams', 237

Galvani, Luigi, *Commentary on the Effects of
  Electricity on Muscular Motion* (1791),
  118, 231
Gaskell, Elizabeth, *Mary Barton* (1848), 162,
  163
Gatteschi, Ferdinando Luigi, 195
Gender
  gender-stereotyping of women, 26, 42,
    75–7, 172–4, 219, 233–5
  male ambition and hubris, 16–17, 42,
    62–4, 116–17, 172–4
Genette, Gérard, 235, 236
Gilbert, Sandra and Gubar, Susan, *The
  Madwoman in the Attic: The Woman
  Writer and the Nineteenth-Century
  Literary Imagination* (1979), 83n4,
  224–9, 250
Gisborne, Maria and John, 196
Gittings, Robert and Manton, Jo, *Claire
  Clairmont and the Shelleys* (1992), 250
Godwin, Fanny (Mary's half-sister), 183
  suicide, 189
Godwin, Mrs. Mary Jane (previously
  Clairmont, Mary Shelley's stepmother),
  183
Godwin, Mrs. Mary Wollstonecraft, *see*
  Wollstonecraft, Mary
Godwin, William, 2
  anger at Mary's elopement, 187
  cold and rational character, 184
  death, 196
  demands for money, 187
  Father of Mary Shelley, 183

Godwin, William – *continued*
  his idealism satirized, 104
  money troubles, 185, 191
  move to Skinner Street, 184
  Political Justice (1793), 183, 187, 204, 220
  *Things as They Are, or the Adventures of
    Caleb Williams* (1794), 211–12, 248
  at treason trials (1794), 204, 220
Godwin, William (son of above), 183–4, 197
Goethe, Johann Wolfgang von, *Faust* (Part 1,
  1808), 213
Gothic, the, 139, 144, 207–12
Grylls, R. Glynn, *Mary Shelley: A Biography*
  (1938), 249

Hardy, Thomas, *Jude the Obscure* (1895), 218
Hill, Susan, *The Woman in Black* (1983), 248
Hogg, Thomas Jefferson, 187
Homans, Margaret, 'Bearing Demons:
  Frankenstein's Circumvention of the
  Maternal', 238, 251
  *Bearing the Word: Language and Female
    Experience in Nineteenth-Century
    Women's Writing* (1986), 252
Hunt, Leigh, 189, 191
Huxley, Aldous, *Brave New World* (1932),
  216–17, 249

Industrial revolution, the, 105–6, 204–5

Jackson, Rosemary, *Fantasy: The Literature of
  Subversion* (1981), 252
Job, the Book of (Old Testament), 160

Kestner, Joseph, 'Narcissism as Symptom and
  Structure: The Case of Mary Shelley's
  Frankenstein', 1–2, 69n2, 154n5,
  235–8, 251
Knowledge
  as a theme in *Frankenstein*, 121–2, 175–6
  the tree of, from Genesis, 176
Knox, Alexander, 195–6
  resolves the Gatteschi affair, 195
Kubrick, Stanley (dir.), *Dr Strangelove, or:
  How I Learned to Stop Worrying and Love
  the Bomb* (film, 1964), 166

Lavenza, Elizabeth
  aryan characteristics of, 73–4
  characterization of, 72–7
  exemplifies a failure of 'goodness', 79
  and femininity, 73–6, 86–7, 174, 234
  her functions in the novel, 75–7
  represents 'harmony', 174
  compared to Echo, 238
Lawrence, D. H., *A Study of Thomas Hardy*,
  168n14
Le Fanu, Sheridan, *Carmilla* (1871),
  207, 248
Levine, George and Knoepflmacher, U. C.
  (Eds.), *The Endurance of* Frankenstein:
  Essays on Mary Shelley's Novel (1979),
  83n4, 225n5, 251
Lewis, Matthew Gregory, *The Monk* (1796),
  209, 248
  visits Byron and Shelleys, 188, 209
Lowe-Evans, Mary, *Frankenstein: Mary
  Shelley's Wedding Guest* (1993), 233–5,
  251
Luddites, 105–6, 165, 204, 220

MacCarthy, Fiona, *Byron: Life and Legend*
  (2002), 250
Marlowe, Christopher, *The Tragical History of
  the Life and Death of Doctor Faustus*
  (1604), 213, 249
Marvel Comics, 249
  Lee, Stan, 167
  Superman, Batman, The Incredible Hulk,
    167, 168
Marx, Karl, 34, 103, 109, 213
Maturin, Charles Robert, *Melmoth the
  Wanderer* (1820), 248
Mazzeo, Tilar J. (Ed.), *Mary Shelley's Literary
  Lives and Other Writings* (2002), 247
Mellor, Anne K.
  'A Feminist Critique of Science', 122 and
    122n5
  'Making a Monster: an Introduction to
    Frankenstein', 229–33, 250
  *Mary Shelley: Her Life, Her Fiction, Her
    Monsters* (1988), 229, 250

Milton, John, *Paradise Lost*, 155–62, 212–13, 226–9, 239, 249
  the daemon compared to Adam and Satan, 155–7
  the daemon compared to Eve, 160–1, 228–9
  female daemon compared to Eve, 57
  Frankenstein compared to Eve, 227–8
  Frankenstein compared to God, and Satan, 157–8
  as 'Milton's Bogey', 225
  misogyny of, 173, 225
  re-interpreted by the Romantics, 159, 212–13
  Satan echoed by the daemon, 98, 155
Moers, Ellen, 'Female Gothic', 225–6 and 225n5, 226n6
Myth, 83, 147, 148–69
  founded upon archetypes, 151, 162
  modern myth of *Frankenstein*, 162–9, 252
  see also Milton, John, *Paradise Lost*; Narcissus; Oedipus; Prometheus

Napoleonic Wars, 186, 203–4, 220
Narcissus, 154–5, 161–2
  Frankenstein a study of narcissism, 235–8
Narrative frames, the, 7–45
  distancing effect of, 40–1
  misdirection of opening, 7–8, 10, 16
  as narcissistic structure, 235–8
  role of Mrs. Saville in, 15–16, 234–5
  and suspense, 41
  and unpredictability, 43
Narrators
  analysed, 8–36
  exploring the same themes, 39–40
  and impression of text's unity, 43
  self-revealing, 38–9
Nature
  as good, 99, 175
  and harmony, 93, 119, 124–5, 175
  as maternal, 90–1
  and nurture, 93–9, 178–9
  religion in, 90–2
  as a theme of *Frankenstein*, 34, 42–3, 75, 88–101, 119–20, 171, 174–5
  visibility, importance of, 92–3

Newman, Beth, 'Narratives of Seduction and the Seductions of Narrative: The Frame Structure of *Frankenstein*', 36–7, 251

Oedipus, 152–4
O'Flinn, Paul, 'Production and Reproduction: The Case of *Frankenstein*', 164, 251
Orwell, George, *Nineteen Eighty-four* (1949), 217, 249

Paine, Tom, *The Rights of Man* (1791), 204
Peacock, Thomas Love, 201
  Nightmare Abbey (1818), 209, 248
Plato, *Protagoras*, 148–9n2
Poe, Edgar Allan, *The Fall of the House of Usher* (1839), 211
Polidori, Dr John William, 197
  and ghost-story competition, 188, 197
  The Vampyre: A Tale (1819), 206–7
Prometheus
  myths of, 148–50
  relevance to *Frankenstein*, 150–2, 213

Quarterly Review, The, 221

Radcliffe, Mrs. Anne, 209, 210
  The Italian (1797), *The Mysteries of Udolpho* (1794), *A Sicilian Romance* (1790), 209, 248
'Rambo' (films) e.g. *First Blood* (1982), 167
Robinson, Charles E. (Ed.), *Collected Tales and Stories* by Mary Shelley (1976), 247
Robocop (film, 1987), 167, 168
Romanticism, 34, 178–9
  Mary Shelley critical of r. attitudes, 179
  social idealists satirized, 104

St. Clair, William, 'The Impact of *Frankenstein*', 221, 251
  The Godwins and the Shelleys: The Biography of a Family (1989), 250
Saville, Mrs. Margaret, 7
  as outermost 'frame', 15–16
  rescuing Walton, 233–5
Schor, Esther (Ed.), *The Cambridge Companion to Mary Shelley* (2003), 251

Science, 109–1, 120
  gendered approach to science, the, 112–15
  hubris criticized, 117
  and knowledge, discussed, 121–2
  masculine science, 72, 110–119,
    172–4, 219
  popular mistrust of, 165
  as theme, 171
Science Fiction, 109–10, 214–15, 248–9
  exploits a stranger's view of the world,
    102–3
  explores moral issues of science, 110,
    115, 165
Scott, Sir Walter, review of *Frankenstein*, 221
Sennett, Richard, 235, 236
Seymour, Miranda, *Mary Shelley* (2000),
    188n1, 249
Shelley, Clara (Mary's daughter)
  birth, 189
  death, 190
Shelley, Elena Adelaide (the baby at Naples)
  death, 190
Shelley, Harriet (Percy Bysshe's first wife), 185
  suicide, 189
Shelley, Jane (previously St. John), Mary's
    daughter-in-law, 193
  fight to protect P. B. Shelley's image, 201
Shelley, Mary Wollstonecraft (née Godwin)
  account of her childhood distorted, 197
  conflict with her step-mother, 184
  death, 196–7
  deteriorating marriage, 192
  distorted her husband's memory?, 194, 201
  edits *Essays, Letters from Abroad,*
    Translations and Fragments by Percy
    Bysshe Shelley (1840), 201
  edits *The Poetical Works of Percy Bysshe*
    Shelley (1839), 201
  elopement, 185–6, 203
  encouraged to write by Percy Bysshe, 197
  Falkner (1837), 200, 247
  final quarrel with Claire Clairmont, 196
  first daughter dies two weeks old, 187
  The Fortunes of Perkin Warbeck (1830),
    199, 247
  Frankenstein, writing, 188–9, 203

  her journals, 247, *see also under* Feldman,
    Paula R. and Scott-Kilvert, Diana
    (Eds.), *The Journals of Mary*
    Wollstonecraft Shelley 1814–44
  her letters, 247, *see also under* Bennett,
    Betty T.
  History of a Six Weeks Tour (1817), 201
  keeps her husband's heart, 192
  The Last Man (1826), 198–9, 246–7
  leaves for Italy 1818, 190
  life, 183–97
  a life of Godwin, plans for, 200–1
  listens to Coleridge recite *The Ancient*
    Mariner, 184
  Lodore (1835), 199, 247
  marries, 189
  Mathilda (1819), 197–8, 247
  meets Percy Bysshe Shelley, 185
  miscarriage and haemorrhage in 1822,
    190, 191
  Rambles in Germany and Italy (1844),
    201–2
  Ramsgate, visits, 184
  return to England, 1823, 193
  travels on continent with her son and
    friends, 193
  Valperga: or, the Life and Adventures of
    Castruccio, Prince of Lucca (1823),
    198, 247
  writes stories for annuals, 200, *see also*
    Robinson, Charles E. (Ed.), *Collected*
    Tales and Stories by Mary Shelley
    (1976)
  writing for Lardner's *Cabinet Cyclopaedia*,
    200, *see also* Mazzeo, Tilar J. (Ed.),
    Mary Shelley's Literary Lives and Other
    Writings (2002)
  see also Frankenstein
Shelley, Percy Bysshe, 2
  In Defence of Poetry: An Essay (1819), 213
  drowned, 191–2
  effeminate looks, 235
  elopement, 185–6
  Essays, Letters from Abroad, Translations and
    Fragments (1840), 201
  flirtations, 191, 192
  funeral ceremony, 192

his idealism satirized, 104
interested in electricity, 118
'Lines Written During the Castlereagh
    Administration' (1819), 205
The Poetical Works of Percy Bysshe Shelley
    (1839), 201
the Preface of 1818, 63, 110, 211
thought to have written *Frankenstein*, 220
Shelley, Percy Florence (Mary's son)
    birth, 190
    education and marriage, 193
    move to Bournemouth, 196–7
    stands for Parliament, 193
Shelley, Sir Timothy (father of Percy Bysshe),
    192
Shelley, William (Mary's son)
    birth, 187–8
    death, 190
'Six Million Dollar Man, The', 167
Small, Christopher, *Ariel Like a Harpy: Shelley,
    Mary, and Frankenstein* (1954), 251
Society, 101–9, 120
    the daemon's significance, 104–6
    in decline, 108–9
    industrial conflict, 105–6, 165, 204, 220
    legal authority, 106–9
    social class, 25, 34, 42, 73–4
    a socialist critique of, 103–4, 106
    as theme, 171, 176–8
    wickedness in, 102–3
Spark, Muriel, *Mary Shelley* (1987), 222–4,
    250
    Mary Shelley in conflict between reason
        and emotion, 223
    theory of Victor's and the daemon's duality,
        69n2, 136n1
Star Trek II: The Wrath of Khan (film),
    Paramount Pictures (1982), 168n13
Star Trek: The Next Generation (television and
    film), 167, 168
Stevenson, Robert Louis, *The Strange Case of
    Dr Jekyll and Mr Hyde* (1886), 166 and
    166n9, 168, 211, 215, 248
Stoker, Bram, *Dracula* (1897), 207, 248
Sunstein, Emily W., *Mary Shelley: Romance
    and Reality* (1989), 250

Swift, Jonathan, *Gulliver's Travels* (1726)
    the Houyhnhm response to law and war,
        102n2
Symbolism, 128–4
    the daemon as determinism, 133–4
    danger of over-interpretation, 128
    of the moon, discussed, 136–40
    political, 132
    of sight and hearing, 144–7
    of water, 140–2

Themes
    father-child relationships, 25–6, 31–3
    give moral fables, 119–20
    'harmony', 124–5, 171–2, 174
    more complex than simple fables, 120–5
    see also under Determinism; Gender;
        Nature; Science; Society
Trelawny, Edward John
    arranges Percy Bysshe Shelley's funeral, 192
    Records of Shelley, Byron and the Author
        (1858), 250
    writing a life of Shelley, 194

'Varney the Vampire', 207
Veeder, William, *Mary Shelley and
    Frankenstein: The Fate of Androgyny*
    (1986), 251–2
Verne, Jules, 109

Walpole, Horace, *The Castle of Otranto*
    (1764), 208, 248
Walton, Robert, 7
    characterization of, 46–55
    conflict not resolved, 53–5
    his narrative analysed, 8–17
    our scepticism of, 14–15
Wells, H. G., 109
    The Island of Dr Moreau (1896), 166 and
        166n10, 215, 248
    The Time Machine (1895), 215, 216, 249
    The War of the Worlds (1898), 215
Wikipedia (Internet encyclopaedia), 167n12,
    249
Williams, Edward, 191
    drowned, 191–2
Williams, Jane, 191, 195

Williams, John, *Mary Shelley: A Literary Life*
    (2000), 250
Wollstonecraft, Mary, 2
  death, 183
  grave of, 185
  mother of Mary Shelley, 183
  A Vindication of the Rights of Woman
    (1792), 183, 204
Woolf, Virginia, 225

Wordsworth, William
  '*Ode: Intimations of Immortality from
    Recollections of Early Childhood*', 34,
    175n1
  The Prelude (1805), 123–4 and 124n6
Wright, Angela, *Gothic Fiction* (2007), 252
Wyndham, John, *The Chrysalids* (1955),
    The Day of the Triffids (1951),
    215, 248